SIDE EFFECTS

SIDE EFFECTS

SIDE EFFECTS

Mexican Governance Under NAFTA's Labor and Environmental Agreements

Mark Aspinwall

Stanford University Press
Stanford, California

Stanford University Press
Stanford, California

Printed and bound by CPI Group (UK) Ltd, Croydon, CR0 4YY

Library of Congress Cataloging-in-Publication Data
Aspinwall, Mark, author.
  Side effects : Mexican governance under NAFTA's labor and environmental agreements / Mark Aspinwall.
     pages cm
  Includes bibliographical references and index.
  ISBN 978-0-8047-8229-6 (cloth : alk. paper) — ISBN 978-0-8047-8230-2 (pbk. : alk. paper)
  1. Administrative agencies—Mexico.   2. Environmental policy—Mexico. 3. Environmental law—Mexico.   4. Canada. Treaties, etc. 1993 Sept. 13.   5. Labor policy—Mexico.   6. Labor laws and legislation—Mexico.   7. Canada. Treaties, etc. 1993 Sept. 14.   8. Mexico—Politics and government—1988–2000.   9. Mexico—Politics and government—2000-   I. Title.
  JL1242.A79 2012
  354.30972—dc23
                                                                    2012022089

Typeset by Westchester Publishing Services in 10/14 Minion

For Leticia

Contents

Contents

Illustrations

Figures

Tables

Preface

IN SEPTEMBER 2008, THE MEXICAN CENTER FOR ENVIRONMENTAL LAW (CEMDA), a nongovernmental organization, celebrated its fifteenth anniversary in Mexico City with a gathering of several hundred activists, supporters, politicians, and civil servants. The keynote speaker was Juan Elvira, secretary of the environmental ministry, SEMARNAT. Elvira's presence was a sign of how far environmental politics had moved. Twelve years earlier, CEMDA had filed a landmark complaint about Mexico's failure to respect its own environmental law, which infuriated SEMARNAT. The ministry broke off all interaction with the fledgling NGO, calling it anti-Mexican. Now, twelve years later, CEMDA was a central pillar in Mexican environmental governance.

Non-co-opted labor leaders in Mexico can only dream of the success that environmentalists achieved by 2008. For them, it's hard to imagine that the secretary of the labor ministry would be an honored guest (or accept an invitation) to a gathering of independent labor activists. Whereas environmental authorities listened to—indeed, eventually welcomed—those who were seen initially as dissident and troublesome, the same collaborative scenario does not appear to be possible for labor. In labor, corrupted institutions leave many feeling that politics remains a question (to paraphrase Harold Lasswell) of who steals what, when, and how.

This is a story about governance in Mexico. On January 1, 1994, two spotlights were switched on simultaneously, one shining on Mexico's environmental authorities, the other on its labor authorities. The spotlights (which also shone on Canada and the United States) came from the labor and environmental accords that accompanied the NAFTA treaty. These so-called side agreements—with their requirements to respect the rule of law—provide a natural experiment because in important ways they are very similar. They offer a valuable opportunity to compare their respective effects on two different sectors, each with its own constellation of domestic agencies and interests. This comparison takes us beyond traditional international relations studies of governance and into the very heart of domestic agencies. Most studies treat the state as a unit, buffeted by demands from global organizations and networks of activists. Here we get a far clearer understanding of what works and what doesn't in terms of how external incentives can lead to improvements in governance.

Across the world, developing countries are finding that the transnational regimes they join—whatever their original purpose—ratchet up the pressure on their systems of regulation, governance, and norms. Trade and investment agreements affect regulatory standards (such as environmental, safety, labor, and consumer), modes of governance (accountability, transparency, participation, rule of law), and behavioral norms (over individual and group rights, for example). But external-origin pressures are not always transmitted formally through international organizations, transnational integration agreements, or partner states. They can be felt informally, too, through transnational advocacy networks and ad hoc bilateral or multilateral pressure.

How exactly are these pressures received by the agencies of the target country? Why do some agencies in a given state accept that the old ways of doing things need to change before other agencies in the same state? I began this project by focusing on rule of law because the NAFTA side agreements stipulate that member states enforce their own laws and because that was the original rationale of the accords. But I quickly found that the picture was more complicated, and, like many books, the end was different from what I imagined at the outset. The picture was complicated because compliance and law enforcement showed both good news and (plenty of) bad news. In many cases, compliance remained poor, corruption was rampant, and officials prioritized development over rule of law. But it was also complicated because rule of law turned out to be as much about *attitudes* as results. Attitudes had begun to shift in the federal environmental agencies, but much less so in the labor agencies.

And it was not simply rule of law but also policies, institutions, procedures, and practices where results mattered. Something new was happening. Spurred on in large part by the NAFTA side agreements, Mexico was strengthening impact assessment and permitting processes, and it was improving workers' rights. New laws were brought into effect. Disruptive, non-co-opted interests were consulted. Public meetings created new opportunities for citizen participation. In some cases, institutions themselves were changing. Communication with agency officials in the United States (and, to a lesser extent, Canada) shot up. Officials were trained in new procedures. In short, capacity and oversight were strengthened. True, in many cases these changes were limited and strategically designed to satisfy external "auditors." And not all change was NAFTA-inspired. The courts and independent domestic agencies played a role of their own. But a real process of change had begun—a regional agreement designed to liberalize trade now had another effect, this time on governance.

The highlight of the story is the strengthening of civil society. Starting from a strong preference for co-opted, compliant interests, federal environmental agencies now welcome dissident voices. They hire professionals from NGOs to fill civil service positions, and they draw civil society groups into wider discussions about environmental governance. For their part, environmental NGOs have learned how to be players in the system: they make fewer unrealistic requests, and they do not take to the streets when they don't get everything they want. They have advanced degrees in law, sciences, and administration. They have become professionals.

Capacity was built among labor interests, too, because independent (non-co-opted) unions, research organizations, lawyers, and NGOs created links with like-minded groups in the United States and Canada, filed complaints together under the labor side agreement, and forged new understandings, new expertise, and new opportunities. But labor agencies and traditional union confederations continue to resist incursion from independent unions and activists. Labor suffers from a *triángulo de hierro* of rent-seeking interests and bureaucrats. Many have little knowledge of labor law, less interest in due process, and fat bank accounts. Not surprisingly, the course of justice is regularly perverted.

So this project was a process of discovery. I found that certain features of the NAFTA institutions and particular characteristics of domestic politics were more conducive to improvements in governance. The Commission for Environmental Cooperation, the trinational environmental institution created by NAFTA, was relatively independent of member state control, had the power to inspect and report, and included civil society groups directly within its institutional structure in an advisory capacity. This institution was better equipped to exert pro–rule of law and good governance pressures on Mexico. Likewise, where domestic agency and NGO officials were trained to high professional standards, governance was better. Domestic NGOs were critical to improving governance because they communicate directly between the trilateral institutions and the domestic agencies, raise red flags when things go wrong, and participate in decision making and agenda setting at both levels. They were the capillaries of good governance.

In making these discoveries, I am indebted to a host of individuals and organizations. Several dozen interviewees generously gave their time. They came from the trilateral regional institutions (the Commission for Environmental Cooperation and the Commission for Labor Cooperation), the bilateral Border Environment Cooperation Commission, Mexican and American federal agencies, Mexican state agencies, and civil society groups in the environmental and labor sectors in both Mexico and the United States. Most spoke openly, and no problem or shortcoming or institutional failing was too ugly to be discussed with great candor. To my good fortune, several of them agreed to be interviewed repeatedly—none more than Gustavo Alanís, president of CEMDA.

I am very grateful to have been awarded a Visiting Scholar position at the *Instituto Tecnológico Autónomo de México* (ITAM) for Fall 2008. From the conversations with Jim Robinson and Erika Ruiz to the research assistance of Ursula Ramírez to the general hospitality and cheerful question answering of Andrea Herrera, ITAM provided support in many ways. I tip my hat to a group of real professionals. My colleagues at the University of Edinburgh heard various versions of this research over the years and made very valuable comments. I would single out especially Iain Hardie, David Howarth, and Moritz Liebe for a careful reading of—and probing comments on—key arguments in the book.

Sometimes small is better, and small but effective grants from the Royal Society of Edinburgh, the Carnegie Endowment, and the University of Edinburgh made the fieldwork possible. My thanks to them. Other times, big is better, and one of the biggest names in the business must be Stanford University Press. I feel very fortunate indeed to be counted among their authors. The manuscript was reviewed thoroughly and positively by two readers, and their comments have strengthened my arguments considerably. Stacy Wagner and Jessica Walsh from Stanford have been extremely supportive and positive, have drawn the best from the manuscript, and pushed me to make it better. My heartfelt thanks go out to them.

Finally, the most important discoveries come from within, and so my thanks and love go to four very special people: to my son and daughters, Harry, Bonnie, and Lila, and to my wife, Leticia, who opened the door to an incredible country.

Abbreviations

ANAD	National Association of Democratic Lawyers
BECC	Border Environment Cooperation Commission
CAB	Conciliation and Arbitration Board
CEC	Commission for Environmental Cooperation
CEMDA	Mexican Center for Environmental Law
CLC	Commission for Labor Cooperation
Conanp	National Commission for Protected Natural Areas
Conafor	National Forestry Commission
CROC	Revolutionary Confederation of Workers and Peasants
CROM	Regional Confederation of Mexican Workers
CTM	Confederation of Mexican Workers
IFAI	Freedom of Information Institute
ILO	International Labor Organization
INE	National Ecology Institute
JPAC	Joint Public Advisory Committee
NAAEC	North American Agreement on Environmental Cooperation
NAALC	North American Agreement on Labor Cooperation
NADB	North American Development Bank
NAO	National Administrative Office

OECD	Organization for Economic Cooperation and Development
PAN	National Action Party
PRD	Democratic Revolution Party
PRI	Institutional Revolution Party
PROFEPA	Office of the Environmental Attorney General
RMALC	Mexican Network Against Free Trade
SEMARNAP	Secretariat of the Environment (until 2000)
SEMARNAT	Secretariat of the Environment (after 2000)
STIMAHCS	Metalworkers Union
STPS	Secretariat of Labor

SIDE EFFECTS

SIDE EFFECTS

1   A Tale of Two Side Agreements

O N OCTOBER 4, 1992, PRESIDENTIAL CANDIDATE BILL CLINTON gave a speech at North Carolina State University in which he took a position in favor of the recently negotiated North American Free Trade Agreement (NAFTA).[1] Yet he faced a dilemma. On the one hand, he called for Americans to embrace the global economy and wider economic integration. Indeed, much of his campaign strategy was focused on the economy—even as he spoke, a now-famous sign hung on the wall in his Little Rock campaign headquarters that read (in part): "It's the economy, stupid." The election was fought in the context of recession, and economic policy was Clinton's main weapon.

But on the other hand, Clinton also made direct reference to environmental and labor standards being violated in Mexico and to the fact that the agreement negotiated by President George H. W. Bush did nothing to address these problems. He vowed to create supplementary institutions to guarantee enforcement of standards, as well as encourage capacity to be developed through cooperative activities between the partners. Once elected, Clinton followed through on his promise and established two "side agreements," the North American Agreement on Environmental Cooperation (NAAEC) and the North American Agreement on Labor Cooperation (NAALC). They were signed in September 1993, despite the irritation of the Canadian and Mexican governments, who thought they had secured a deal and who were not happy about bearing the cost of Clinton's campaign promises.

This book looks at what happened next. It examines the impact of NAFTA's side agreements on Mexican governance and the conditions under which a pro–rule of law norm has been absorbed by environmental and labor authorities. The side agreements require member states to uphold and enforce their labor and environmental laws. It was widely acknowledged (though never codified in the side agreements) that it was Mexico in particular that had a problem with law enforcement and might enjoy an unfair trade advantage by failing to enforce its own laws and regulatory standards. Under the new side agreements, Mexico could no longer turn a blind eye to the flouting of its own rules.

We begin with a puzzle. External scrutiny (through the NAFTA side agreements) and domestic oversight (through strengthened courts and freedom of information) brought equivalent pressures to both the environmental and labor sectors. But pro–rule of law norms have been internalized to a greater extent in Mexican environmental agencies than in the labor agencies. Given that they were subjected to the same pressures, why did they not adapt at the same rate?

Most analysts of rule of law take the state as the unit of analysis, meaning that change happens to the state as a whole, rather than to certain parts of the state, such as sectoral ministries. No intrastate variation in rule of law is accounted for. For example, international relations (IR) theorists claim that variations in external "mechanisms of socialization" (such as persuasion and shaming) are responsible for variations in the rate at which domestic actors absorb ideas about rights and governance (Checkel 2001, 2005; Johnston 2001). Economists theorize that only states with long-term systems of equality and absence of abuse of authority will sustain rule of law (Weingast 2009).

Similarities between the environmental and labor cases allow a number of potentially important variables to be controlled, and we thus have an excellent natural experiment, enabling us to draw far more fine-grained conclusions about what causes changes to attitudes about rule of law in developing states and how regional agreements can play a part. It is important that we not lose the opportunity to compare these cases. Broader multistate studies of norm change (Risse and Sikkink 1999) and empirical analyses of rule of law (World Justice Project 2011; Kaufmann et al. 2009; United States Institute of Peace 2011) that use the state as the unit of analysis cannot provide this level of nuance.

I have two overarching aims in this book. The first aim is to examine the capacity-building and institutional development effects of the NAFTA side agreements. There is no comprehensive treatment of capacity-building and institutional development, even though it is an important aim. In fact, most accounts conclude that the institutions created by NAFTA to oversee enforcement of environmental and labor rules have failed to live up to expectations (Hufbauer and Schott 2005). From a policy perspective, understanding how the design of regional institutions affects institutional development and capacity building is important, given the growth of regional trade agreements and the inclusion of emerging and developing countries within them.[2]

The second aim is theoretical. I seek to contribute to a more general understanding of how differences in institutional design (of the side agreements) and differences in domestic capacity (between the labor and environment sectors) influenced norm socialization. I argue that the relevant design and capacity factors are, first, the independence of the side agreement institutions from national control and the extent to which they permit citizen access and, second, the levels of professionalization and technical capacity of domestic bureaucrats and civil society actors. Professionalization is affected by the level of mobility of actors across professional boundaries (especially from civil society to ministerial positions), the permeability of domestic institutions, leadership within bureaucracies, and the level of politicization of civil service positions.

The most important policy lessons from this study are that regional agreements seeking to improve norms of good governance in developing states need to incorporate (1) citizen complaint mechanisms, (2) opportunities for independent regional authorities to create public factual records that highlight transgressions, (3) means by which civil society can influence the work agenda of the regional institution, and (4) capacity-building resources for domestic authorities and civil society groups.

Domestic authorities should encourage (1) parallel institutions at the national level, such as transparency authorities and independent judiciaries, that reinforce external normative pressures; (2) education and training programs for civil society actors and bureaucrats; (3) opportunities for inward mobility into bureaucracies for trained nongovernmental organization (NGO) personnel; and (4) more secure (depoliticized) career paths for senior civil servants to retain technical capacity within government. Relatively low-cost extrastate institutions with oversight powers, the ability to communicate directly with domestic NGOs, and independent reporting powers can be surprisingly effective in leveraging normative pressures on governments.

The study reveals that although there has been governance change in both areas, environmental governance has improved more. Rule of law norms are more widely accepted, and technical capacity among civil society and government officials has been strengthened. Mexico has made use of the environmental side agreement to improve federal institutions, upgrade the quality of environmental information, encourage civil society, and develop the border. Mexican environmental bureaucrats now think differently about their own environmental rules. In the labor sector, powerful, government-connected union confederations have for decades controlled unionization and helped repress workers' rights, restricting the normative socialization effect of the labor side agreement. Although some independent unions, labor NGOs, lawyers, and activists have tried to use the NAFTA labor accord to bring rule of law to Mexican labor practice, the path dependency of long-standing corruption and closed opportunity structure prevents a relatively weak external force from exerting enough pressure to bring about adaptation.

These issues are critically important for development and democratization. Transnational markets bring increasing pressures to standardize norms and rules (Bruszt and McDermott forthcoming). Trade agreements formalize compliance pressures. New trade agreements have been concluded (both by the United States and by other developed states) that contain extratrade provisions on environmental, labor, and other regulatory standards. Such pressures are felt acutely by developing states, whose capacity to comply can be severely restricted. Coming to grips with how best to strengthen local capacity and promote pronorm behavior is essential to the task of development and democratization.

Capacity building, institutional development, and norms of good governance matter not simply because they help level the playing field in trade, but because they strengthen domestic politics. In other studies, strong, capable bureaucracies have been shown to improve economic outcomes (Goldsmith 1999; Evans and Rauch 1999). They help a state resist corruption or arbitrary exercise of power on behalf of powerful interests, and they also outlive shifting political priorities. When public policy changes, budgets are cut, or leaders forced out of office, bureaucracies that know how to apply rules fairly and make decisions based on accepted procedures will be healthier. Politicians will be less capable of forcing them to apply rules unequally or arbitrarily. Pro–rule of law attitudes imply that those responsible for enforcing rules take them as given and necessary. They enforce rules even when no one is looking—that is, when those responsible for scrutinizing public behavior are not watching. Conversely, weak rule of law undermines investment and growth, exacerbates poverty and security problems, and erodes public participation and trust. Rule of law is critical to economic success, social cohesion, and legitimacy (World Justice Project 2011; Americas Society and Council of the Americas 2007).

This book goes beyond a simple accounting exercise of resources devoted to enforcing the law and looks instead at whether and how a culture of rule of law has taken hold. Mexico clearly has a long way to go. Despite some improvements to the institutions of the state, a culture supportive of the rule of law has yet to be created. Without inclusivity, participation, transparency, consensus, and a sense of common ownership, the rule of law cannot root itself (United States Institute of Peace 2011; Finn 2004; Stromseth 2008, 2009). A culture of public trust and confidence in formal institutions is necessary.

Sadly, Mexico continues to suffer from widespread criminality and weaknesses in the justice system, where police, prosecutors, judges, lawyers, and the military can be unprofessional, poorly trained, and underpaid (Cornelius and Shirk 2007). In fact, the militarization of crime fighting may actually weaken other institutions, such as the police. One recent study showed that weak property rights and uncertainty about arbitrary confiscation lead to lower investment in productive activities by individuals and that Mexico needs independent, efficient, and trained judiciaries and bureaucracies; oversight mechanisms such as an ombudsman; and competitive elections by which political leaders are held accountable (Haber et al. 2008).

Regionalism and Domestic Political Change

Both external influences and domestic factors have an impact on how states make the transition from authoritarianism to democracy. Preexisting external links (such as ties to the West) can affect how regimes manage the transition (Levitsky and Way 2010). The role of external advocates and international organizations can also be influential (Keck and Sikkink 1998; Checkel 2005). Likewise, long-standing domestic practices are sometimes slow to change, even under pressure from outside. Rigid, politicized relationships based on particularistic advantage often obstruct reform and opening.

Regional agreements are important external sources of pressure. They can help foster domestic changes. They are crucial tools for development.[3] However, our knowledge of how regionalism promotes development is limited, especially outside the European Union (EU). The EU has helped its lagging member states and regions converge with the economic levels of its wealthy member states, and it distributes funding for these purposes through its structural funds. This contrasts with NAFTA, where guaranteeing market access is assumed to provide a sufficient engine of economic growth and development. There is no large-scale transfer of resources and no requirement to adopt an *acquis communautaire* or ensure democratic or human rights standards. The EU is a "welfare region," and NAFTA is a "market region" (to borrow from the lexicon of comparative political economy), and so the means by which they encourage development of their poorer member states differs. Unfortunately, however, we know very little about how the market region achieves its development aims, leaving us with no basis for comparison to other regions.

Because much of the U.S. opposition was based on the idea that free trade would cause race-to-the-bottom externalities, NAFTA is the first agreement to link trade opening with environmental and labor issues. Opponents assumed that heavily polluting industries would be encouraged to migrate to Mexico, which did not have the resources to enforce its own regulations or the willingness to raise standards (COHA 2007). Competition from China would undermine willingness to enact and enforce strict environmental controls. The negative effects of NAFTA were thought to be exacerbated by an investor rights provision, prohibiting subnational authorities in any member state from creating new barriers to investment, whether environmental or otherwise.

A counterargument claimed that free trade would lead to environmental benefits because productivity growth in sectors facing import competition creates efficiency gains and resource savings, a reduction in subsidies and other wasteful practices, and transfer of pollution prevention technologies (Galindo 2000: 186; Deere and Esty 2002: 3–4). According to one study, the most heavily polluting sectors were also the most protected, and opening up sectors to competition was likely to reduce pollution (Galindo, 2000: 186). Likewise, economic growth can lead to more resources being devoted to environmental protection.

However, empirical studies of the effect of NAFTA on Mexico's environment have yielded mixed results (cf. Gallagher 2004; Husted and Logsdon 1997). The studies use different methodologies, applied to different kinds of environmental questions, leading to widely varying results (Deere and Esty 2002: 12). Husted and Logsdon (1997) examined three periods immediately surrounding the entry into force of NAFTA (before 1990, 1990 to 1993, and after 1993) to determine whether environmental policies and regulatory standards were increased, whether enforcement was strengthened, whether behavioral standards among firms changed, and whether there were significant changes to environmental outcomes. Over this period, they found institutional strengthening and increased budgets in Mexico.

Still, Gallagher found that environmental outcomes worsened measurably after NAFTA came into effect, mainly because neither the Mexican nor the U.S. government committed resources to tackle environmental problems (Gallagher 2004: 2). Compliance and enforcement remained a problem, and after 1993 (when NAFTA entered into effect) real spending and plant-level environmental inspections both fell significantly (Gallagher 2004: 9). Compared with other Organization for Economic Cooperation and Development (OECD) countries, Mexico spends one third as much on the environment, controlling for gross domestic product (GDP) (Gallagher 2004: 71). Other assessments focus only on government compliance and fulfillment of treaty obligations (Deere and Esty 2002: 11). For example, Delgado and colleagues (2006) review Mexican environmental law and levels of pollution, as well as information on institutional responsibilities in the Secretariat for the Environment and Natural Resources (SEMARNAT). But they do not ask what the effect of the NAAEC has been on Mexico's capacity to solve environmental problems or on attitudes among civil servants.

Likewise, on the labor side there are mixed views. Opponents claim that free trade agreements depress wages and standards in developed countries. Although economists paint a mixed picture, the popular imagination is fed by the idea that labor-intensive or low-value production would migrate from the United States and Canada to Mexico, which has little incentive to raise standards or engage in reforms likely to increase costs of production (Gallagher and Wise 2009). Studies confirmed the suspicion that inequality increased in Mexico following NAFTA. Manufacturing plants offered temporary work with few protections, and the agriculture sector suffered high levels of import competition from heavily subsidized U.S. exporters (AFL-CIO 2008: 137ff.; Polaski, 2003).

Furthermore, many consider the NAALC agreement to be virtually worthless because it has not resulted in material improvements to the lives of Mexican workers or corrected abuses on the ground (Alcalde 2006; Bouzas 2006; Bensusán 1999, 2006b). Others point to the limited but detectable changes in practice in the federal labor ministry (STPS) and among some companies on an ad hoc basis, the (slightly) improved dialogue between the government and independent unions, the capacity-building programs undertaken between STPS and the U.S. Department of Labor, and especially the improved relationship between independent Mexican unions and organized labor in the United States and Canada (Nolan 2009; Compa 2001; Teague 2002).

Like NAFTA, the EU exerts adjustment pressure on member states. Its members are required to comply with the *acquis communautaire*, the accumulated body of EU law, as well as be functioning democracies (among other things). But the EU's institutions are much more powerful and have a longer history. Adjustment pressures in the EU emanate from EU-level legislation backed up by supranational courts. Although scholars have spent some years studying adjustment processes in the EU, they are only just beginning to apply the same energy to other regions.[4] Because NAFTA lacks legislative instruments, its requirements were negotiated at the outset. It is an intergovernmental agreement and provides far more scope for national autonomy. Its purpose (in the side agreements) is simply to ensure that domestically determined labor and environmental laws are enforced, though there are also provisions for transfer of best practice and capacity building. That makes NAFTA a less likely motor of domestic change than the EU.

Yet despite wide differences, the logic of action at work in NAFTA is the same as in the EU—credible regional integration agreements between states bring about pressures for adjustment at the domestic level (Bruszt and McDermott forthcoming). In both, developing states are under pressure to conform to norms originating in a more developed and powerful center. The pressures vary, and regional agreements may simply be one among many motors of change.[5] In the EU, scholars have shown that although the pressure for domestic adjustment comes from the regional organization, domestic institutions and interests vary in their acceptance of (and ability and inclination to push for) adaptation at the domestic level, depending on the sector and the power of organized interests (Börzel and Risse 2003).[6] Domestic institutions and policies can be resistant to transformative pressures: "European signals are interpreted and modified through domestic traditions, institutions, identities, and resources in ways that limit the degree of convergence and harmonization" (Olsen 2002: 936; see also Schmidt 2002; Green Cowles et al. 2001 6–9; Knill 2001).

Although NAFTA has no provisions like the EU's Copenhagen criteria or explicit requirements to adjust institutions or policies, like the EU, it does provide an external source of legitimacy for domestic leaders seeking to reform and modernize. In fact, NAFTA is interpreted as part of a broad Mexican reform strategy that began with the failure of the import substitution model in the wake of the 1982 debt crisis. In other words, NAFTA may be understood as an effect rather than a cause (Dominguez 2004: 380). Nonetheless, it has constrained the policy options of successor governments in Mexico (Denise Dresser, cited in Fox, 2004: 258). To the extent that it brought subsequent unexpected and unwelcome changes in its aftermath, it is worth examining closely. To better understand the effects of regional commitments (as well as understand what works), we need to isolate the NAFTA effect and determine how relevant and important it is to domestic change.

Definitions
Let's clarify some of the concepts used in this study. I use the term *regional organizations* to refer to trade agreements (such as NAFTA), as well as more comprehensive organizations (such as the EU). I use the term *regional institution* (RI), to refer to the formal trilateral side agreement arrangements put in place to monitor compliance. *Capacity building* connotes a range of skills in both bureaucracies and civil society, including higher levels of information processing, acceptance of recognized techniques for solving problems, and better communication, and it can result in a closer worldview among bureaucrats and NGO groups.[7] *Professionalization* (another important concept in this study) can result from capacity building. It refers both to technical proficiency (knowing the rules and how legal procedures operate) and also to the ability and willingness of individuals to apply rules equally and nonarbitrarily.

Attitude change means agencies have internalized (or socialized) a pro–rule of law norm. Actors are drawn in to the "norms and rules of a given community" (Checkel 2005: 804).[8] Applied to the norm of rule of law, it means that officials believe in nonarbitrary application of the law. Due process is respected, appeals are available, and legal procedures are followed. Pro–rule of law socialization does not mean that law enforcement is perfect, but attitude change is an early sign that authorities are moving toward good governance. As we will see in the next two chapters, where problems were uncovered through complaints and investigations, environmental agencies typically offered explanations and plans for improvement, signs that it was beginning to take seriously its commitment to respect the rule of law (Risse and Sikkink 1999). Labor agencies denied the existence of problems and accused investigators of interference in national sovereignty.

What do we mean by *rule of law*? Rule of law—a slippery concept—has been defined as public accountability, legal clarity, fairness in terms of creating and enforcing laws, and open and fair administration of justice (World Justice Project 2011). Research sponsored by the World Bank names rule of law as one among six indicators of governance (separating it from factors such as corruption, which in other studies form part of a definition of rule of law); the others are voice and accountability, political stability and absence of violence, government effectiveness, regulatory quality, and control of corruption (Kaufmann et al. 2009). A legal perspective holds that rule of law signifies "a commitment to the process of public justification"—holding public authorities to account (Finn 2004: 13). For the purposes of this study, my concern is with attitudes toward enforcement of existing domestic law. A pro–rule of law attitude respects existing legal norms and standards, despite political pressures to allow the law to be flouted or procedural steps to be avoided.

Certain conditions that I will outline make it more likely that rule of law norms will supplant countervailing norms, principally sovereignty and development. A prosovereignty norm can work against adoption of the rule of law when the latter is perceived as an imposition from external forces. A prodevelopment norm can also inhibit adoption of the rule of law because tourist, manufacturing, and other projects may be undertaken even if they incur significant environmental damage or result in infringements to legal protections for workers. Ignoring legal protections for workers and environmental regulation reduces costs and promotes business activity and employment. Therefore, a rule of law logic in the environmental sector implies that existing legal safeguards are respected in terms of full environmental impact assessments and clear reporting and respect of the results. In the labor sector, a rule of law logic means legal requirements on labor rights are respected, such as permitting independent unions to form and bargain collectively. A development logic implies maximizing growth through development, thereby providing jobs; environmental regulation and labor rights might be ignored, but that is considered less damaging than insufficient development.[9]

A Framework for Understanding Attitude Change to Rule of Law

States are bombarded by information every day, including scientific and technical studies and best-practice techniques. They go through social processes by which this information is handed over—either in depoliticized, technical settings or in more public arenas, where their behavior may be compared with a normative ideal and evaluated accordingly. The process may be low-key and technical, or it may be high profile and politicized. The agents providing the pressure may be networks of activists, international organizations, states, or some combination. But when these external pressures reach the coalface of the state, different things happen. They do not have uniform results across all agencies of a state. Instead, there are variations, not simply in the kinds of pressures a state faces from outside, which IR scholars study, but also in the state's capacity to adjust. Pro–rule of law socialization happens at different rates.

Thus, our understanding from the IR field of how external actors encourage norm socialization is incomplete. We need to look at variation in the capacities of domestic institutions and individuals, too. Both labor and environmental civil servants have a high level of direct, technocratic contact with their ministerial counterparts in the other NAFTA member states, via e-mail and telephone. They receive numerous technical studies and participate in countless meetings. They have been subject to periodic public reports that highlight policy and enforcement shortcomings. Both sectors faced preexisting pressures for reform, not just within Mexico but also from outside organizations.[10]

Neither labor nor environmental bureaucrats in Mexico lacked information—they knew perfectly well what was expected of them and how they fell short of internationally accepted standards. There is little need for persuasion in the sense of convincing because everyone knew what it means to respect the rule of law and what the advantages of doing so are. But all too often their behavior did not reflect that knowledge. In fact, we know very little about why this was the case and how civil servants change their minds about norms. Scholars do not elaborate on what constitutes a convincing argument— how do we know when actors have been convinced by hearing something from others (Johnston 2001: 493)?

When confronted with challenges from the RIs, both environmental and labor agencies reacted strategically. They responded to pressures by delaying or avoiding responsibility and by denying wrongdoing.[11] But environmental agencies eventually went through a process of normative adaptation, in which actors "actively and reflectively internalize new understandings of appropriateness" (Checkel 2005: 812). They are further along the path toward rule-consistent behavior (Risse and Sikkink 1999). Environmental agencies are more likely to engage in discussions, try to right wrongs, compensate, apologize, and carry out activities appropriate to a regime that is respectful of the norms it claims to uphold. They act to correct inappropriate behavior. Words begin to match deeds.

Why then do we find more attitude change in environmental agencies than in labor agencies? The answer lies in variations in institutional design and capacity. They affect assimilation of norms because they render mechanisms of socialization (i.e., persuasion and shaming) more or less effective. There are two key variations. The first is the *design of the side agreement institution*: (1) its relative independence from member state control and (2) the access and standing given to NGOs and other civil society groups. The second is *professionalization and capacity building of domestic elites*—both in agencies and in civil society. Professionalization is, in turn, affected by institutional openness to outside influences and by the level of mobility of civil servants and NGO activists between positions.

To get a better grip on this issue, I set out how design and capacity differences are expected to operate, drawing on scholarly work from a range of disciplines to show how my framework is a logical extension from existing findings. The single most important lesson for designers of RIs is that norm transfer succeeds when RIs involve civil society groups, when those groups have a technical proficiency that enables them to participate as equals in technical discussions, when domestic civil servants are professional, and when RIs are relatively independent of member state control. To put it bluntly, what matters is not power or money, but inclusion, professionalization, and independence.

Independence of Regional Institutions

Independence increases the ability of the RI to pressure governments for three reasons. The first is that it is more able to set an agenda of inspections, reporting, and oversight independent of what member state principals support. The second reason is that its activity is by definition more neutral of national control, which reduces the impact of national conflict. All member states second civil servants to work in the RI. Like domestic systems of justice, which are thought to be fairer and more legitimate when the makeup of society is fully represented in the institutions, RIs denationalize compliance oversight when they include representatives of all parties. The third reason is that they reduce variations in oversight due to waxing and waning political support stemming from changes in the ideological composition of governments. Governments less supportive of inspections are unable to block them if the inspection authorities are independent.

Thus, independent RIs provide continuity in agenda setting, work plans, strategies, and other tasks that are not tied to political cycles, such as elections, or dependent on good will. They depoliticize norm diffusion because they are better able to resist nationalist power politics and ideological changes in member state governments, both of which can undermine continuity in investigations. Legalized RIs, such as transnational courts and tribunals, reduce the power of states vis-à-vis transnational NGOs (Goldstein et al. 2000). They allow nonstate actors greater scope to set the agenda independently of member state control (Keohane et al. 2000: 458). The processes of legalization of norms and professionalization of standards make arbitrary decision making less likely. Judicial independence means that authorities must justify the exercise of power "against published, uniform, and stable norms" (Finn 2004: 15). Reasoning that is open and consistent (using precedent) and based on known legal principles is the basis for judicial contribution to the rule of law. Through dialogue, states self-entrap, justifying their transgressions and eventually getting caught in a web in which they commit themselves to the norms they are violating (Risse and Sikkink 1999: 28).

Regional institutions also provide information. Fact-finding and reporting powers are important because they bring legal and technical arguments into the public domain. They enable rhetoric to be juxtaposed with actual practice. Couched in neutral, legal terms, these reports can nevertheless be quite damning. Informational power is not necessarily related to independence—RIs with relatively little autonomy from member state principals may still have fact-finding and reporting powers. However, the impact of fact-finding and reporting is likely to be greater if the RI has relative independence from member state principals because it is more likely to be treated as authoritative and untainted by power politics.

Thus, independent RIs increase the impact of pronorm messages because member states have less capacity to interfere in fact finding and reporting than in nonindependent international organizations. Continuity is more likely. Independent RIs establish and follow set criteria for investigations. Moreover, investigations are less prone to nationalistic sensitivities and ideologically driven variations in member state support. There is more consistency, certainty, and clarity about likely actions, and this provides NGOs with greater certainty in bringing cases. They reduce the sense of meddling or power politics (Pevehouse 2002: 523).

Access and Standing Before Regional Institutions

Domestic interests generate compliance pressures because there are winners and losers when a government complies with an international agreement (Dai 2005). Alliance with an international organization can be a significant resource for these interests, especially in authoritarian states. A classic study on transnational advocacy networks (TANs) showed how closed domestic political opportunity structures force rights groups to look for allies outside the domestic polity (Keck and Sikkink 1998; on the labor side agreement as a political opportunity structure, see Kay 2011). Domestic interests acquire leverage through coalition building abroad, uniting NGOs, foreign governments, and international organizations in a network of shared norms and ideas. By making information publicly available, TANs can hold governments to account.

When RIs are political opportunity structures, they can have an important rebound effect, amplifying the message that TANs seek to convey (Keohane et al. 2000; Kay 2005; Graubart 2005). But the effectiveness of RIs depends on their features. Some provide activists with opportunities to set agendas, scrutinize member states, and lodge complaints. They provide institutionalized participation by civil society activists. They represent a forum for activists' complaints to be heard, which raises their importance within the home country because the acceptance of a complaint means that their grievance is taken seriously by experts outside. There is a crucial difference between the environmental and labor side agreements. The former provides NGOs with permanent standing on committees or working groups. Permanent standing locks groups into the process. It increases their commitment to the institution and to its work on oversight, investigation, and capacity building. They are less likely to abandon it if they are unhappy with a finding or judgment—their commitment carries them through disappointment. Though they may complain about lack of progress, their involvement makes it harder for member states to backtrack on commitments because of scrutiny from activists. It reinforces their ability to make the case to states that their behavior needs to be changed.

Thus, *access* denotes the formal means to make complaints in the RI, and *standing* refers to permanent institutional participation within committees or other structures. Granting access and standing for civil society incentivizes them to mobilize and legitimizes their claims (Keohane et al. 2000: 481). It enables NGOs to contribute to agenda setting and problem solving and to communicate with the permanent secretariat and with member state principals over institutional priorities. Nongovernmental organizations serve in specified, ongoing capacities within the RI; they influence the work agenda, and they are taken seriously by agents of the RI. They build their own legal and technical expertise through this process: they learn to use the legal process, work with other NGOs to file complaints, compile information, and request investigations. They are more capable of communicating on scientific and rational grounds, increasing the likelihood that they will have an impact on domestic civil servants back home.

Access and standing before the RI also increase their legitimacy and credibility in the national political arena. Because they are taken seriously by an RI and their arguments are heard outside the domestic arena, it is therefore more difficult to marginalize them in domestic debates. Credibility enhances the effectiveness of a message (Zimbardo and Ebbesen 1969: 48–49). Credibility is also affected positively when NGO employees are given positions of authority of some duration within the RI. Transnational rights are thus legitimized (Kay 2005), and this legitimacy in turn affects compliance (Cialdini and Trost 1998: 170). The boost in credibility and legitimacy for NGOs is especially visible in developing and transition states (Reimann 2006: 62). Nongovernmental organization access to international organizations has "often reshaped the domestic political context for NGOs and aided their growth by expanding the [political opportunity structure] at the national level" (Reimann 2006: 58).

Professionalization and Capacity Building

Even with independent RIs supporting the legitimacy and credibility of domestic activists, we can't be sure these activists will have an impact back home without knowing more about the characteristics of domestic actors. It is hard to imagine that socialization would affect a ministry en bloc, much less a country, without there being some kind of intervening socialization process of the individuals who are responsible for making decisions. Yet we know little about how this process occurs. As I mentioned earlier, states have been seen as "generalized wholes" subject to macro changes and influences (Johnston 2005: 1014). We need to know more about the micro level to determine from the individual level of analysis who is being socialized and how and what is required before a tipping point is reached, such that a ministry or other organization can be said to have a new normative standard.[12]

A rich and lengthy literature on technocrats (in Mexico and elsewhere) helps us get started with this issue. The influence of technocrats on Mexican politics began as early as the Porfiriato of the late nineteenth and early twentieth centuries, and a tradition of studying their impact reaches back at least to the 1960s (Vernon 1964; Dominguez, 1996). Who are the technocrats, and what motivated them? Under Carlos Salinas, they tended to be foreign educated, conversant in neoliberal economics, and capable of understanding the language of the markets (Centeno 1997). Studies up to the 1990s found changing characteristics among elites, with younger generations more involved in planning and finance, more likely to be educated abroad, and more likely to have studied economics and administration rather than humanities (Centeno and Maxfield 1992; also Camp 2002).

Although the rise of technocrats is explained by the need to respond to economic crisis, the technocrats were also politicized through their connections to party and president (Centeno and Maxfield 1992; Grindle 1977). In fact, not only were technocrats often appointed on political grounds, such as patronage, but also they captured politicians and became politicized themselves. The distinction between technocrat and politician was less than it seemed in theory. Periodic bursts of technocracy did not guarantee proper governance, only that elites would have more control. Technocracy did not protect Mexico from rent seekers and rule breakers. Specialized training at graduate level did not necessarily lead to depoliticized positions or to employment activities devoid of political influence.

Studies of technocrats in Mexico lack three things: (1) they do not include studies of civil society groups, (2) they tend to look at technocratic roles in policy and planning rather than law enforcement or other aspects of governance, and (3) they do not consider the role of external actors in shaping the functions and behaviors of technocrats. Elite, trained civil servants administer and plan, but the quality of their governance (such as rule of law, public participation, and transparency) is affected by their professionalization. Education and training are part of professionalization, but, equally, understanding of and respect for the law are crucial because they reduce the likelihood that special interests will capture political elites and extract rents.

Findings across a range of disciplines, from social psychology to law to organizational sociology, point to the importance of professionalization. Professionalization can lead to behavioral change, including higher levels of awareness of moral obligation and of the consequences of antisocial behavior

(De Groot and Steg 2009). Assignment of responsibility can translate into pressures for change as particular practices are identified which efficiently solve norm failures. Efficiency gains make norms easier to absorb (Strang and Meyer 1993). Ideas of efficiency, justice, and progress help propel norm diffusion because they are linked to modernity. Similarity—or cultural understandings of social commonality—also leads to more rapid norm diffusion among individuals (Strang and Meyer 1993: 491). Internal settings within domestic agencies may facilitate understanding and persuasion. Where civil servants and civil society interests share a technocratic professionalism, the potential losses associated with normative change will be reduced (Farrell 2001: 72; Meyer and Rowan 1983).

Social psychology research also shows the importance of expertise to normative diffusion. Where arguments are technical and complex, and targets do not have expertise in the issue, they may use heuristic shortcuts to look for cues, such as consensus (if everyone else agrees, it's probably right) and expertise (expert sources can be trusted). When sources have credibility, persuasion is easier (Fiske 2004: 524–25; Latané, cited in Cialdini and Trost 1998). Therefore, where domestic NGOs have recognized technical expertise and a shared consensus, they are likely to find it easier to promote norms because the transaction costs of evaluating and accepting arguments is lower, making it easier to persuade targets in bureaucracies. Their ability to communicate and raise awareness as equals is heightened.

Actors who professionalize learn how to use legal instruments, like impact assessments and appeals procedures. They learn how to use information sources, such as the Internet and freedom of information rules. Cognitive lessons are transferred (Hall 1993), leading to consensual understandings among epistemic communities and networks.[13] When NGO officials speak the same scientific and legal language as the bureaucrats they seek to persuade, their influence increases. Training, standard setting, professional literature, and social networks help tune the expectations, objectives, and values of professionals (Farrell 2001: 72). Epistemic communities are created, sharing norms, causal beliefs, ideas of validity, and a common set of policy practices (Haas 1992). Where this takes place, technocrats gain influence relative to political leaders (Legro 1997: 37).

But professionalization increases legitimacy as well as influence. Officials who are trained in legal methods are empowered because they are able to argue through legal reasoning, defined by the late legal scholar Thomas Franck as "the legitimacy-based demands of consistency, coherence, and adherence" (cited in Keohane et al. 2000: 478). Legalized processes draw the offending country to explain its behavior and grant legitimacy to petitioners. Acceptance of a petition sends a signal that the petition has merit and initiates a discussion over legal principles. The accused member state must justify its practices before an international tribunal. It can also serve as a benchmark for future review.

> Law's legitimizing power derives from legal discourse and process. Legal discourse is communicating according to principled ideas. Participants justify their behavior and propose resolutions based on accepted notions of appropriate behavior rather than on self-interest or functional needs. Participants frame their arguments through referencing terms of the treaty, invoking legal authorities, and reasoning by careful analogy to other principles and fact patterns. Legal process consists of the forum and procedures for mediating the legal discourse. In the international realm, legal process is likely to take place in an administrative or quasijudicial setting. The process includes reviewing competing legal arguments, gathering evidence, conducting investigations, and issuing findings or recommendations. The effect of legal process is to draw attention to the normative disputes and build authority for normative-based resolutions. (Graubart 2005: 104)

Exposure to new ideas and perspectives stemming from traditions not associated with the older nationalistic and prodevelopment perspectives results in attitudes more conducive to rule of law. As civil society personnel go through education and training programs, they become more proficient in science or law, and they themselves train other civil society personnel. They are able to communicate more effectively with federal and international technocrats than either street activists or older, untrained partisan elites.

An example of what can go wrong when professionalization does not infuse agencies will be evident when we reach the discussion on Mexican labor politics later in this book. Here, powerful labor confederations, corrupt government officials, and local businesses impose arbitrary and unfair decisions within federal and state labor agencies whose role is ostensibly neutral. Their sharply biased and unprofessional conduct is so widely acknowledged among activists, lawyers, trade unions, academics, and others that it is impossible to find an alternative point of view.[14] Poor training, low levels of education, and lack of familiarity with the law are widespread problems. In the Confederation of Mexican Workers (CTM), the principal trade union confederation, which ultimately represents almost 90 percent of unionized Mexican workers, it was not until 2005 that a leader with as much as an undergraduate university degree was appointed. Corrupt, clientelistic relationships and arbitrary decisions have been the result.

Other Contributing Factors: Mobility, Leadership, Institutional Permeability, Federalism

Mobility of personnel contributes to capacity building and professionalization. Inward mobility of trained, professional NGO officials into bureaucracies facilitates norm socialization, because respect for the processes of decision making (the sanctity of law and of procedural validity) is enhanced by the integration of trained interests with trained bureaucrats. Like an inoculation, the rule of law norm can be injected into ministries by close contact with NGOs. They share values and expertise and are able to communicate best practice. It is hard to be certain of the direction of causality, but at the very least, having personnel who were formerly advocates working in agencies makes it harder for the government to backtrack on commitments and to ignore the rule of law in its decision making. Training and shuffling spread (or help lock in) norms of good governance. This does not mean that decisions made by public authorities will necessarily please NGOs who work with them. But it does make it more likely that rules for making decisions will be followed and that arbitrary or corrupt practices favoring narrow interests and captured bureaucrats will decline.

The notion that proximity leads to persuasion also has theoretical roots in social psychology and sociology (Cialdini and Trost 1998: 164; Strang and Meyer 1993; on IR applications, see Farrell 2001). Empirical research on military innovation suggests that those entrepreneurs who are closest to the leadership of the target group will be most effective (Farrell 2001: 83). Social networks are necessary for mechanisms of transplantation—political mobilization (through TANs) and social learning (through epistemic communities) (Farrell 2001: 80).

Meritocratic hiring processes ensure that capacity and expertise are continually upgraded. Latin American civil services have a reputation for persistent patronage in recruitment, despite reforms meant to privilege and prioritize merit. Patronage can lead to arbitrary application of the law, as those appointed serve the interests of political masters or powerful special interests over the wider public good. Moving toward merit-based systems of recruitment would enhance "stability, professionalism, and expertise in public offices" (Grindle 2010: 2; Evans and Rauch 1999). Merit systems are based on evaluations of education or other measures of merit, they enable career progression based on credentials and experience, and they imply a certain amount of secure tenure (Grindle 2010: 4). Conversely, the practice of dismissing upper-level civil servants following elections can lead to loss of trained personnel. Depoliticizing these positions and creating career paths for top civil servants would retain the benefits of capacity building in ministries.

Mobility, in turn, is facilitated by two further factors. One is leadership. To be effective, ministries must be listening to outside individuals and groups. Leaders can facilitate a dialogue, require that ministerial ears be open, invite outsiders to participate, raise awareness, and make discourse possible. In those organizations in which leaders decide to move toward respect for rule of law and appoint committed outsiders, reform is more likely to follow. We will see an example of this in a local labor agency in Chapter 3. The second factor is institutional. Socialization depends on the level of permeability of domestic institutions—where institutions are relatively new or expanding, they are more likely to be open to outside influence. Where they are established and stable, public officials are more likely to be captured by economic interests and more likely to remain resistant to new norms that disrupt established patterns of privilege.

Figure 1.1 shows the intersection between professionalization and institutional permeability. Where professionalization is high, officials have technical capabilities in terms of knowledge of laws and regulations, methods of application, redress, and other issues. Where mobility is high, there are likely to be greater opportunities to interact and communicate. High levels of professionalization combined with high levels of communication will lead to greater consensus over standards of due process, correct application of the law, and other aspects of enforcement.

Finally, the disjuncture between different levels of government is also a factor. Incumbents in local jurisdictions can isolate their localities from the influence of national politics through "boundary control" (Gibson 2005). Boundary control preserves local authoritarianism when those in power are able to isolate themselves from national authorities. For example, although Mexico constructed an international image of itself as a liberal state under the Fox administration, local Chihuahua state politicians continued an oppressive and authoritarian approach to opponents who had formed an activist network around the Ciudad Juarez murders (Aiken 2010). Federal officials

Professionalization

		High	Low
Permeability	**High**	• Common and widespread technical capabilities (such as knowledge of relevant laws and regulations, as well as methods of application, appeal, dispute resolution, etc.) • High level of communication between agency officials and civil society • High level of consensus between agency officials and civil society	• Variable or low technical capabilities • High level of communication between agency officials and civil society • May result in misunderstandings regarding standards of due process, enforcement, application of law; consensus uncertain
	Low	• Common and widespread technical capabilities • Low level of communication between agency officials and civil society • May result in misunderstandings regarding standards of due process, enforcement, application of law; consensus uncertain	• Variable or low technical capabilities • Low level of communication between agency officials and civil society • Consensus unlikely regarding standards of due process, enforcement, application of law

FIGURE 1.1 Characteristics of professionalization and permeability

found it difficult to reject pressures to engage openly with concerned citizens in Juarez, but they also shifted blame to the state government, saying it had constitutional responsibility for addressing the murders. Thus, where federal officials have responsibility for actions at the state level, and state authorities act in contravention of good governance norms, it can be more difficult to promote normative change. Where federal officials can distance themselves by (legitimately) claiming that state officials have responsibility in a certain area, normative change at the federal level will be easier.

Methodological Challenges

How do we predict when government officials will respond to external demands such as NAAEC and NAALC by accepting the message and internalizing new norms? When does a tipping point occur, such that we can speak of the ministry as having been socialized? These are difficult questions to answer, but they are important both for theory development and for helping us design RIs beneficial to developing states.

There are several methodological challenges to this study. The first is that we need to be sure the sectors are comparable. Given the deep historical differences between Mexican labor and environmental politics, can they be compared? I argue they can, for at least two reasons: first, in both labor and environmental agencies, Mexican officials originally rejected reform pressure. Scrutiny was resisted for sovereignty reasons (Mexico did not want interference from the U.S. or NAFTA agencies) and because the federal government wanted to retain discretionary powers to apply the law in an arbitrary manner, free from oversight by courts or domestic information agencies (mainly to encourage inward investment). Second, both sets of agencies shared an original (pre-NAFTA) preference for co-opted civil society groups over independent and critical groups. They sought to buy or intimidate nonsupportive groups, and they actively promoted groups that were supportive of the government.

Similarities such as these enable us to rule out several potential causal factors and be more precise in determining likely causality. Moreover, the timing and rationale of the two side agreements are also the same. Both came into effect with the NAFTA treaty itself and were negotiated at the insistence of the United States, which feared that poor environmental and labor conditions in Mexico would encourage investment to migrate there. Mexico at first reacted negatively to both side agreements. Each had as the central purpose the requirement that member states respect and enforce their existing laws, and each provided for sanctions in the event of noncompliance. The rule of law logic was vulnerable in both cases to another compelling logic—development—in which labor rights abuses or environmentally damaging projects were tolerated (despite violating legal requirements) because they encouraged investment and created employment.

Another challenge is to determine whether any change that is observed is attributable to the NAFTA institutions and not some other cause, such as responses to internal crises or external pressures from non-NAFTA sources. For example, as part of the democratic transition, a transparency law was enacted in 2002. In 2007, the Congress extended the law to all levels of government—federal, state, and municipal.[15] This law had an impact on government accountability. Knowing how far the impact extends (and being able to discern its impact from that of the NAFTA institutions) is critical. Finally, it is important that we be able to determine as accurately as possible when new beliefs and norms have been internalized, what mechanisms were responsible for that change, and what conditions were present that permitted it.

Thus, comparing the two side agreements is a means of overcoming methodological challenges because a number of potentially important variables are held constant. Mexico did not have an a priori preference for (or commitment to) either side agreement—it saw both as an interference in its national sovereignty and an arrogant last-minute imposition by the United States. Nor did it have a better legal framework in one over the other because labor law and environmental law in Mexico were both in place as NAFTA began.[16]

Designing a valid test from which causal inferences can be made is a challenge. With only two cases to go on, there is little in the way of variation on the dependent variable, and that makes it harder to draw definite conclusions. Fortunately, controlling many other potentially significant independent variables helps overcome this limitation. A further methodological challenge is that there are few opportunities to quantify data. Without a comprehensive survey of ministry officials (which is hard to imagine, especially in the labor ministry) of the sort conducted in the European Commission (Hooghe, 2005), we cannot be certain how their views are altered by NAFTA membership.

Thus, the most effective way to gain evidence that Mexican officials have internalized norms is through interviews, of which more than sixty were conducted with Mexican and American federal officials, Mexican state officials, officials of the side agreement institutions, NGOs, academics, and other civil society groups and individuals. Ministerial elites matter because it is they who write reports, travel to meetings, communicate with other ministries and the public, make policy choices that reveal values and norms, and provide an image of what the ministry stands for. States cannot become socialized without these men and women becoming socialized first.

Interviews were semistructured, and questions were organized around several themes: (1) institutional and legal changes in the period since the early 1990s; (2) changes in the interaction of public officials with domestic civil society and changes in the activities, characteristics, and capacity of the domestic groups themselves; (3) the source of pressures for domestic rule of law reform, whether domestic or external; (4) the nature of reform pressures—whether directed at institutions, procedures, norms, or other areas—and the extent to which adjustment had occurred; and (5) the nature of interaction with NAFTA institutions and partners (among both public officials and civil society groups).

In addition to the interviews, I also examined the results of cases brought under the NAAEC and NAALC, along with interactions between the Mexican government and these institutions (and civil society groups). Through process tracing, I "investigate and explain the decision process by which various initial conditions are translated into outcomes [compliance, in this case]" (Checkel 2001: 565; also Cortell and Davis 2005: 5; Gurowitz 1999). These methods are supplemented by careful readings of official government documents—many of them available only in Spanish—as well as secondary analyses from consultants and academics and counterfactual analyses. The results enable me to derive a nuanced and sophisticated set of conclusions based on fine-grained consideration of difficult-to-quantify variables and permit me to present an analysis, however tentative, of the likely causal effects of the NAFTA side agreement institutions. At the very least, I am able to generate testable hypotheses, and I am clear and honest about the confidence level I have in the results.

In designing the research this way, part of my reasoning was deductive—based on existing theoretical expectations—and part of it was inductive, based on empirical process tracing in the two cases. The fact that I have one case where norm socialization has been unsuccessful helps me overcome some of the bias in the existing literature in favor of effective norm socialization, at the expense of failed cases (Legro 1997). Likewise, this study controls for temporal variation by looking at a norm introduced in one place, at one time, in two sectors. It therefore contributes to the norms life cycle model by examining why the shift from norm introduction to adoption is more successful in some cases than others (Finnemore and Sikkink 1998).

Conclusion

There is every reason to expect socialization pressures to grow, forcing authoritarian or transition regimes to respond. Whether through external pressures (such as depoliticized technical reports or high-profile public factual records) or gradual domestic capacity building, there is no shortage of information available to governments (and more to the point, being *pressed upon* governments). Their track records are less secret than ever. Nongovernmental organizations have more and more opportunities to press claims before international organizations and friendly states. It is easier and cheaper to link with like-minded networks of activists and other norm promoters beyond their borders because the cost of travel has declined and information is more widely available. Therefore, knowing how norm transfer takes place is critical. Domestic ministry elites are more likely to accept norm change when the relevant RIs are independent of national control. Civil society groups benefit most when they are included in the deliberations of the RI. Professionalization of civil servants and civil society also leads to norm socialization.

At this point, we have established the research framework. We know what our dependent variable is: adoption of rule of law norms by ministerial actors. We know which actors should be internalizing them (domestic Mexican elites in the environmental and labor agencies). We know that the independent variables are NAFTA-origin pro–rule of law pressures, filtered through the intervening contextual variables discussed in this chapter. In the following chapter, I look at how Mexican environmental politics has been affected by the experience with NAAEC. I ask how capacity to govern the environment changed in Mexico and whether NAFTA was the cause of that. I also ask how successfully rule of law norms were absorbed in environmental agencies. The chapter looks at the role played by Mexican environmental NGOs and how they used provisions of NAFTA to bring cases of noncompliance to light. The following chapter applies the same methods of analysis to labor governance, where the findings are very different. In the final chapter, I pull together the theoretical understandings and the empirical studies to clarify the likely effect of the NAAEC and NAALC on Mexican politics, and especially on the socialization of norms (or lack thereof) by officials of the public agencies.

2 Políticas Claras

Governing Mexico's Environment

I

F THE WEALTH OF NATIONS WAS MEASURED IN TERMS OF BIODIVER-
sity, Mexico would be one of the richest countries on the planet. With
only 1.4 percent of the land surface, it contains 10–12 percent of the world's
species (SEMARNAT 2007: 17). Yet it faces enormous challenges in its stewardship of the environment. Writing at the time Mexico was negotiating entry
into the North American Free Trade Agreement (NAFTA), Stephen Mumme
eloquently summarized the issues:

> Evidence of Mexico's ecological crisis is everywhere. Fifty years of economic
> miracles and debacles have left its environment in a shambles. Whether one
> considers the net reduction of Mexican forests by 66 percent overall, with an
> annual rate of loss in excess of a million acres, attendant problems of soil ero-
> sion and desertification, the reduction of the Lacandón jungle by 70 percent in
> the past 40 years, the loss of thousands of species of fauna and flora, the con-
> tamination of over 60 percent of its streams and rivers, the degradation of its
> two most celebrated lakes at Chapala and Patzcuaro, the massive oil spills
> along the Gulf of Mexico coastline, damaging national fisheries and aquatic
> life, the inadequate sanitation or sewage facilities in half of Mexico's cities and
> towns, Mexico City's dubious status as the world's worst metropolitan air pol-
> luter, or the virtual absence of hazardous-waste disposal facilities against a
> backdrop of intensive toxic waste production, it is clear Mexico's environment
> is at the breaking point. (Mumme 1992: 123)[1]

Given the inauspicious beginning, why (and how) has Mexico used NAFTA's side agreement—the North American Agreement on Environmental Cooperation (NAAEC)—to create a cleaner and more open environmental politics, a *política clara?* While enormous problems remain, NAAEC began to provide the incentives and resources to turn around environmental governance. It provided an independent watchdog that nongovernmental organizations (NGOs) could turn to, resources for training and mobility, infrastructure funds, incentives promoting public participation, and a rationale for stronger domestic institutions.

The North American Agreement on Environmental Cooperation prompted capacity building in two ways. The first way was Mexico's own reaction to the establishment of NAAEC: it took steps to redress shortcomings, both in enforcement and in institutional weaknesses. The second was NAAEC's capacity-building programs, which were aimed at public officials and civil society groups. It created opportunities for NGOs to pursue cases against the government and to build links across the border. Capacity building is one of NAAEC's legacies: it brought improvements in the technical and professional capabilities of both bureaucrats and NGO officials. It both built capacity and changed minds. Governance was strengthened, even as ecological challenges mounted. Note that NGOs are a critical element of this story. As in Bolivia and Costa Rica, where struggles to establish biodiversity regimes were won (Steinberg 2001), domestic NGOs made a difference. Though international funding and scientific expertise helped, in the long run the political resources of domestic groups themselves were essential to improving Mexican environmental governance.

According to the Mexican agency in charge of environmental protection, the main challenges to terrestrial environmental protection and sustainable development are deforestation, degradation (through natural causes such as hurricanes and forest fires, as well as human activities), and fragmentation of natural habitats by human activity (SEMARNAT 2007: 21–22). In 2001, the Secretariat for the Environment and Natural Resources also commented on loss of forest cover; biodiversity challenges; soil erosion; loss of water resources; threat to the coastal zone; pollution to water, air, and soil resources; hazardous waste threats; and solid waste disposal problems (SEMARNAT 2001).

Mexico ranked forty-seventh of 149 countries measured on the Socioeconomic Data and Applications Center Environmental Performance Index in

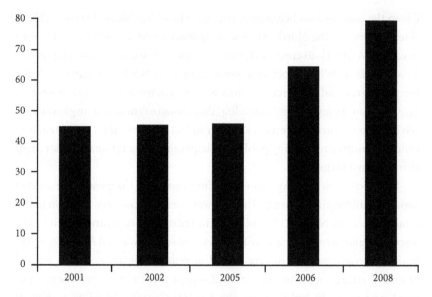

FIGURE 2.1 Mexican environmental sustainability and performance
(score out of 100)
SOURCE: Data from SEDAC; compiled by author

2008, with a score of 79.8 out of 100 (see Figure 2.1).[2] Although this is low by comparison with developed countries, Mexico's position has steadily improved since 2001, when this system of measurement began. A separate Environmental Sustainability Index developed by the Yale Center for Environmental Law and Policy in the early 2000s included a measure of social and institutional capacity, whereby "a country is environmentally sustainable to the extent that it has in place institutions and underlying social patterns of skills, attitudes, and networks that foster effective responses to environmental challenges." The index no longer has this separate social and institutional capacity indicator, but when it did, it showed that Mexico faced serious capacity challenges.

Environmental governance is affected by economic crises and preexisting social inequalities. Fragile economic conditions after the debt crisis in 1982 limited attention to environmental problems. Class and regional inequalities dominated discussion of developmental problems in that the social, sectoral, and regional consequences of transition and development were considered far more important than environmental protection (see Liverman 2002; also

Nuccio et al. 2002).[3] Natural resources are distributed unequally. Lack of infrastructure, political and economic incentives favoring exploitation of resources, urbanization, and other issues have contributed to poor environmental conditions (Liverman 2002; Husted and Logsdon 1997). These present profound challenges not simply for a clean environment but for social justice and equality, too.

Public oversight of Mexico's rich natural resources extends well back into the early twentieth century.[4] The approach was fragmented in the sense that institutions and laws were designed to deal with resources separately (on this history, see SEMARNAP 2000; also Gil Corrales 2007).[5] For example, the fisheries sector was governed first in the agriculture ministry (in 1923), before being moved to the maritime ministry (1941), the ministry of industry and commerce (1958), and the ministry of water resources (1971). In 1977, a fisheries agency was created, which was elevated in 1982 to a cabinet-level ministry.

The governance of water resources extends back to the 1761 General Regulation on Water Measurement, prior to independence from Spain (see Gil Corrales 2007: 190–94). A National Irrigation Commission was created in 1926, and the Secretariat of Water Resources was formed in 1946. A National Water Planning Commission was established in 1976 and replaced in 1986 by the Mexican Institute for Water Technology (IMTA). In 1989, the government created the National Commission for Water (Conagua), which along with IMTA was located within the Secretariat for Agriculture and Water Resources (SARH). Conagua was transferred to a new federal environmental agency in 1995, the Secretariat for the Environment, Natural Resources, and Fisheries (SEMARNAP), based on the view that water should be treated as an environmental issue rather than an agricultural issue.

These arrangements were intended to help exploit resources rather than conserve them. An overarching environmental law, known as the Federal Law to Prevent and Control Environmental Pollution, was not created until 1971. Along with this new law, a Secretariat of Environmental Health (SSA) was established, whose main remit was to plan and carry out environmental health policy (SEMARNAP 2000: 66). The priority was the effect of the environment on human health. But according to Mumme (1992: 126), this law was "so general in content and wanting in force that it remained little more than a symbolic document." Enforcement was limited. Manufacturing was a higher priority. Discussion of environmental issues remained confined to academics, scientists, governmental experts, and a small number of conservation groups.

Recognition that environmental governance was too fragmented among different departments, along with growing public opinion on the importance of the environment, led to the creation in 1982 of the Intersecretarial Commission on Environmental Health. Its job was to coordinate among the various departments and agencies. It was accompanied in the same year by a new Federal Law of Environmental Protection. Although the new law did not differ significantly from the 1971 law, a shift was beginning to take place, in that the environment was beginning to be perceived less as a public health issue and more as an issue of urban pollution.

The Secretariat of Urban Development and Ecology (SEDUE) was created at the beginning of the presidency of Miguel de la Madrid in 1982, with an Undersecretariat of Ecology. Its powers covered pollution prevention and control, including water contamination, environmental impacts, protected areas, wildlife, and ecological protection and restoration, a relatively new federal responsibility (Gil Corrales 2007: 162). It was also responsible for some forestry issues (though much of this responsibility remained in the Agriculture Secretariat). Although de la Madrid was eager to expand environmental policies and powers, in practice, his efforts were less than fruitful. Budgets for SEDUE were low because of the financial crisis, the ministry went through four secretaries in his six-year administration, and the effort to co-opt civil society by encouraging the formation of new groups failed to stem a rising chorus of criticism (GAO 1993; Mumme 1992: 128–29).

By the mid-1980s, environmental governance was split between three secretariats: SEDUE, Environmental Health, and Agriculture. A new National Ecology Commission was created in 1985, comprised of the heads of these three secretariats. However, dissatisfaction with existing institutional and legal arrangements continued. Some secretariats had a reputation for incompetence and ineffectiveness. For example, SEDUE failed to address the air quality issue that was the main reason for its creation (Guerra, personal interview, 2008). Likewise, the government continued to try to co-opt civil society groups or marginalize them to reduce their effectiveness.

Legal and Institutional Change in the Early NAFTA Years

Environmental governance went through a dramatic reform process beginning in 1988, when the General Law on Ecological Equilibrium and Environmental Protection (LGEEPA) was passed. Environmental concerns had been rising, and incoming president Salinas was faced with growing media and public dissatisfaction with environmental problems, especially in the capital (Mumme 1992: 129). The new law superseded the Federal Law of Environmental Protection and began to change the approach to environmental politics. Patterned after the powers of the U.S. Environmental Protection Agency, LGEEPA gave greater regulatory and police powers to the Mexican federal environmental agency.[6]

For passage, LGEEPA required a constitutional amendment that made ecological balance and environmental protection an obligation of the state. It also, for the first time, gave states and municipalities legislative authority over pollution prevention and control and allowed them to participate with federal authorities in water pollution control, designation of protected areas, and establishment of environmental impact systems where federal jurisdiction did not preclude their participation (Gil Corrales, 2007: 165). Previously, all legislation had been "federal" rather than "general," respecting the mandate of Article 27 of the Constitution that natural resources were the common property of the nation. Moreover, ecological resources had been treated as economic assets, without a comprehensive consideration of their ecological role.

At the federal level, the new law provided a definition of environmental principles; coordination between federal, state, and municipal authorities; biodiversity protection; encouragement of protection of natural resources; environmental preservation and improvement; prevention and control of air, water, and soil pollution; encouragement of environmental education and social participation; and sanctions for violations of environmental law (Gil Corrales 2007: 166). It also stated that environmental impact assessments should be carried out for potentially polluting industrial development, as well as mining, tourist development, sanitation works, and federal public works (Mumme 1992: 132). New regulations were promulgated, many directed at Mexico City and its pressing environmental needs. In short, LGEEPA heralded a shift in priorities. It was, according to a former head of the environmental enforcement agency (Profepa), "the most important fact in the process of legalizing environmental politics in Mexico" (Azuela 2006: 157).

In April 1992, the Congress passed a further environmental reform and established the Secretariat of Social Development (SEDESOL), which replaced SEDUE. The change was influenced by a study that reported in 1992 that Mexican environmental politics needed to (1) develop a long-term strategic perspective, (2) base its environmental priorities on evaluation of risk, (3) integrate its environmental management, (4) balance application of clean technologies against social and economic costs, and (5) ensure that social and economic development occurs in harmony with public health and environmental protection (Gil Corrales 2007: 179). A further study internal to the Undersecretariat of Ecology examined how to configure a new secretariat to conform to international commitments, including NAFTA.

The Secretariat of Social Development was given authority over ecological planning, environmental standards, natural resource exploitation, and research and technical development. The change was perceived as necessary to bring together regional and urban development standards and capacities; include infrastructure, housing, and other factors in the development agenda; consolidate social participation mechanisms; bring together development and environment issues; and connect social development with education, health, and other development objectives (Gil Corrales 2007: 166–67). The National Ecology Institute (INE) and the Federal Attorney General for Environmental Protection (Profepa) were also created in 1992, as "deconcentrated" units within the Undersecretariat of Ecology (in SEDESOL).[7] The role of INE was to provide research and analysis for the government, to propose standards and provide technical assistance, and to be a point of contact for NGOs and interest groups (Gil Corrales 2007: 168). The new agency had responsibility for permitting and regulating, specifically, ecological planning, environmental standards, oversight of natural resource use, and technological development and research.

Profepa was formed to provide supervisory and enforcement powers and to deal with citizen complaints. Its task was to improve levels of compliance with laws and regulations. In the first five years, its work concentrated on sources of pollution and hazardous waste. One further institutional change was made in 1992, the creation of the National Commission on Biodiversity (Conabio), whose remit was to improve understanding and use of sustainable biodiversity through biological inventories, databases, and information networks (SEMARNAP 2000: 67–68). Conabio's powers included coordinating activities and studies to improve understanding and preservation of species; it also was tasked with exploring, studying, protecting, and using biological resources; with conserving ecosystems; and with designing criteria for their sustainable management.

These new agencies increased federal environmental powers over enforcement, research, and policy making and also for the first time separated the administrative and policy-making functions from enforcement and inspection. However, they did not amount to a full recognition of environmental protection in institutional terms. Environment remained one aspect of social development. Meanwhile, legal reforms in 1992 strengthened federal powers in the areas of forestry, water, and fisheries. These changes required a constitutional amendment, which provided a means for incorporating NAFTA into Mexican law and specified the relationship between Mexican sovereignty over its natural resources and the new free trade agreement (Carmona interview, 2008).

At the end of 1994, the most far-reaching institutional change was made with the formation of a new Secretariat for the Environment, Natural Resources, and Fisheries (SEMARNAP). Interestingly, this occurred only two years after SEDESOL had been created. For the first time, a cabinet-level environmental agency was established, with powers over environmental protection and governance of natural resources, equal in rank (if not in budget or power) to Economía (the economics ministry) and Hacienda (the treasury). Among other things, this new institution was charged with regulating emissions and discharges, environmental pollution, improvements in ecosystem knowledge, environmental impact, research, and economic incentives intended to promote compliance. It was also given the mandate to consider poverty and social participation. Environmental management became cross-sectoral in the sense that SEMARNAP held powers over projects governed by other secretariats (see Gil Corrales 2007: 170–71).

This new secretariat represented a step change, at least from an institutional perspective. It took on powers over social development, agriculture, water resources, and fisheries that were previously within other secretariats. Conagua, previously an independent agency governing water issues, was relocated to SEMARNAP by 1995. Profepa and INE were also brought under its control, although they retained their distinctive roles. Meanwhile, the budget was increased by 48 percent in the first year, from 1994 to 1995, in the face of the peso crisis and a reduction in tax revenue of 20 percent. No cuts were made in the four thousand SEMARNAP staff devoted to environmental management, and the number of technical norms increased from sixty-two in 1994 to eighty-three in 1995 (Husted and Logsdon, 1997). The creation of SEMARNAP also resulted in an increase in the responsibilities of Profepa. By 1997, it had a national inspection and enforcement service with six hundred inspectors, although it admitted that this service was not nearly adequate to ensure full compliance with environmental laws, especially as it began to take on new responsibilities in areas such as forestry (SEMARNAP 2000: 344).

Thus, over a two-year period, environmental institutions were strengthened, with a new stand-alone secretariat, and also became more specialized, as research and enforcement arms were separated from policy-making activities. A new institution was formed to oversee biodiversity issues. Specialization would increase in the years to come, as further agencies were established to govern forests and protected areas. Four regional councils and a federal council that were established in 1995 included representatives from business, NGOs, academics, and the public. Another regional council was added later. According to a brochure produced by SEMARNAT (*Consultative Councils for Sustainable Development*), the councils were created in response to Agenda XXI, adopted at the 1992 Rio summit, although SEMARNAT's head of Social Participation and Transparency also points to the influence of NAFTA in the creation of the regional councils (Castillo interview, 2008).

Typically, the six councils meet with SEMARNAT officials in a day-long session, with input from gender, indigenous, and youth working groups, and SEMARNAT credited the establishment of the regional councils for significant public input. Some 628 public groups with nearly six thousand participants existed by 2000, with further participation from monitoring committees (cited in Torres 2002: 213). Between 2002 and 2004, 60 percent of the recommendations of the regional councils resulted in policy or program changes or in some other environmental action (SEMARNAT 2006: 184). Civil society groups have also been involved in the Climate Change Consultative Council and in various federal agencies such as Conafor and Conabio.[8]

In 1996, LGEEPA was reformed, another major legal change. Of the 194 original articles in the 1988 law, 161 were reformed, sixty new articles were added, and twenty were deleted (SEMARNAP 2000: 68; see also Azuela 2006: 211ff.). Environmental policy was further decentralized. According to the official legislative history, the intent was to introduce economic instruments into the law and include definitions of *biodiversity* and *sustainability*, among other objectives (Chamber of Deputies 1996). The 1996 reforms also provided for increased social participation, a move prompted by the ongoing democratization process, by the growth of Mexican environmental groups, and by the greater participation of social interests in environmental matters internationally. According to a former head of Profepa, when the government enacted the participation reforms, it simply reproduced a 1995 European Union directive on environmental information and transparency (Azuela interview, 2008). However, the new policy was not widely applied because agencies were not sure what criteria to apply, according to Azuela. Agencies dealt with requests on a case-by-case basis and pressured firms as need be to make information available, depending on the exact nature of the request. They were unsure what information to keep secret.

Other legal reforms occurred in subsequent years. Among them were the Sustainable Rural Development Law, enacted in 2001 to address desertification and soil degradation. The Sustainable Forest Development Law (2002) sought to balance conservation and biodiversity aims with social and economic development in the use of forest resources. The National Water Law was reformed in the early 2000s to include within the consultation process a wider group of water users. The General Wildlife Law was passed in 2006 to govern sustainable use and conservation of wildlife habitats. Since LGEEPA, and especially since 1992, the tendency has been for legal authority to grow in specific areas, such as wildlife and forestry, rather than in a general sense (SEMARNAT 2006: 179). Furthermore, all states have their own environmental legislation, usually mirroring federal legislation. What they do not have are resources to fully enforce their laws and, in some cases, the willpower to do so.

In 2000, yet another institutional change was made with the establishment of SEMARNAT, little different from SEMARNAP except that the incoming Fox administration decided to move fisheries to the agriculture ministry, and SEMARNAT was given new responsibilities in the areas of contaminants, forests, soil management, wildlife, protected areas, and water (SEMARNAT 2006: 44). Thus, environmental institutions have grown both in number and in areas of authorization. In 2000, a new agency, Conanp, took control of protected areas, with powers to conserve and protect ecosystems and their biodiversity in natural protected areas. Its budget increased by 400 percent from 2000 to 2008, according to one high-ranking official there (Rabasa interview, 2008), and unlike SEMARNAT, its remit does not require it to consider economic issues when making policy. One year later, Conafor was established to reverse forest degradation and include forest owners and users in the process of protection and sustainable use.

Greener Pastures? Strengthening
Environmental Governance

Through these reforms, Mexican environmental policy has been decentralized in some ways and centralized in others. It has been fragmented into specialized agencies and widened to include new participants. Although on paper new powers were given to subnational authorities, and institutions such as INE and Profepa were partially independent, in reality (at the federal level), the changes strengthened and centralized environmental governance (Gil Corrales 2007: 180). Its human resources and budgetary powers were taken away from INE. By 2000, it was also stripped of its policy-making, regulatory, and environmental management roles and made into a research institute. Profepa was firmly under the control of SEMARNAP and, later, SEMARNAT.

Yet with this centralization came further environmental responsibilities. In its 2006 report, SEMARNAT reported a new policy of "transversality," where environmental issues were addressed in other policy areas, and it launched a number of new initiatives, such as the Intersecretarial Commission on Climate Change (SEMARNAT 2006: 180–84). It began work on the National Biodiversity Strategy and established a national system of protected areas. It created the Priority Species Recovery and Conservation Projects, through which it safeguarded 522 species under threat of extinction, although it acknowledged that this effort was only a start. In 2005, the government formed the National System to Counter Desertification and Natural Resource Degradation, operated by both SEMARNAT and Conafor and established by federal and state government officials, along with civil society representatives.

In its 2007 to 2012 strategy, SEMARNAT outlined further actions it was planning in biodiversity, pollution prevention, remediation of contaminated sites, hazardous waste, water conservation, and other areas. It developed what it called a horizontal agenda on climate change, education, sustainable development, ecotourism, and environmental management systems (see SEMARNAT 2007). Its strategy involved citizen participation, environmental justice, and access to information. It also developed an audit of researchers and postgraduate academic programs on the environment in Mexico.

In addition to institutional and legal reforms, some other indicators also suggest increased commitment to the environment. Prior to 1994, because the budget for the environment was contained in various departments, precise numbers are elusive, but the environmental budget as a percentage of the federal budget was fairly steady from 1995 to 2003 (about 2 to 3 percent). Thereafter, it appears to have jumped quickly, at least in raw figures, from 17.7 billion pesos in 2003 to 39 billion pesos in 2008.[9] A further sign of environmental commitment is the growth in audits. In 1995, an audit program was established to encourage voluntary compliance with environmental standards. Some 629 audits were conducted by Profepa from 1995 to 1998, as well as thousands of inspections (Hufbauer et al. 2000: 52). According to a Profepa official, by 2007, the agency had made a total of 15,000 inspections (Hernández interview, 2008).

In addition, environmental norms grew cumulatively by 114 from 1993 to 2008. Norms on energy efficiency increased from one in 1994 to seventeen in 2004, and norms on biodiversity increased from one in 1993 to nine in 2004 (SEMARNAT 2006: 64, 111). In terms of environmental land use codes, Mexico had thirteen in 2000 and 39 at the end of 2006 (SEMARNAT 2007: 111). According to various editions of the *Directorio Verde,* the number of natural protected areas in Mexico grew from 52 in 2001 to 97 by 2008 (FMCN, various editions). Thus, notwithstanding the enormous environmental challenges, on some measures environmental institutions and programs grew in importance over a period of years from the 1990s to the 2000s. New agencies and policies were established, budgets grew or were not cut, and new programs were set in place. However, the budget for environmental agencies remains far lower than for ministries with a development or economic management role.

NAFTA and the Acceleration of Institutional Change

In the space of a few short years in the early 1990s, Mexico completely transformed the institutional landscape governing the environment. What explains these striking changes? Many Mexicans were deeply critical of the negotiations leading to the creation of the NAAEC. The negotiations were driven by U.S. political concerns, and the outcome reflected an American agenda, namely, that Mexico represented a pollution haven in which environmental regulations went unenforced (Torres 2002). So concerned was the Mexican government over U.S. criticism that as NAFTA was being negotiated and debated, the undersecretary of Ecology created a nineteen-page briefing paper explaining Mexican environmental policy and institutional development. The paper was circulated among U.S. officials to show Mexico's commitment to the environment. Mexican officials were worried that NAAEC's obligations would leave it vulnerable to further criticism because it did not have the resources to finance joint institutions and environmental infrastructure investment or to enforce environmental laws. So it sought to convince the United States that its standards were already strong.

Mexican priorities were already shifting toward greater environmental protection by the early 1990s, as we have seen. A report from the U.S. General Accounting Office points to 1989 as the beginning of efforts to increase funding and staffing for the environment (GAO 1993; also Gallagher 2004; Husted and Logsdon 1997). By the early 1990s, Mexico was rapidly developing environmental institutions and policies, although it has also been criticized for its lack of commitment and resources (Gallagher 2004: 68). The federal budget for the environment jumped from $4.3 million in 1989 to $66.8 million in 1992, of which about half was directed toward infrastructure improvements. The ranks of enforcement personnel increased over the same period from 81 to 250, and the number of inspections grew from 3,713 to 21,685 in the eighteen-month period ending in June 1994 (Husted and Logsdon 1997). On balance, Husted and Logsdon (1997) conclude that enforcement led to improvements in environmental quality in some urban areas, though not all, and the record was uneven.

A variety of domestic crises and issues in the 1990s, including a disastrous gasoline explosion in Guadalajara in 1992, growing air quality problems, and broader efforts to democratize and open the political system, intensified pressures to do something about the environment (Gilbreath 2003: 51–52). Internationally, the 1992 Rio conference and membership in the Organization for Economic Cooperation and Development (OECD) and NAFTA also exerted reform pressures. Observers tend to agree that international obligations were ultimately responsible for institutional change in the 1990s, and although it remains debatable exactly how much is related to NAFTA, most attribute the lion's share of causal impact to NAFTA. The present environment ministry claims that NAFTA "has contributed to the environmental regulatory framework, compliance on the part of producers, and has also encouraged social participation in decisionmaking" (SEMARNAT 2007: 135).

Luis Manuel Guerra, described as the grandfather of the Mexican environmental movement, is adamant that NAFTA was the principal motivating force behind Mexican environmental change. There was growing public sentiment in favor of greater environmental protection in the 1990s, but it was the Salinas government's determination to secure NAFTA and its realization that the Bush administration in the early 1990s could not control the opposition of U.S. environmental groups that prompted Mexico to upgrade its institutions. The Mexi-

can government "became greener with every week that passed" (Guerra interview, 2008). Guerra rejects the claim that the Rio summit made a difference to
the rapid redesign and overhaul of Mexican environmental institutions. "Rio
was a nice thing to go to, there were magazines and publicity, but it didn't have
the teeth of NAFTA." Salinas had invested all his political future in gaining the
passage of NAFTA and was determined that the U.S. Congress would approve
it. The creation of Profepa and SEMARNAP were signals that the environment
was important to the Mexican government. Another observer claims:

> The transnational political pressure on the Mexican state to implement its
> environmental legislation outweighed the earlier activities of national ENGOs
> and gave way to a rapid political reaction. The risk of losing NAFTA, or having
> to accept strong US conditions, gave Mexico enough motivation to make an
> effort. Between 1991 and 1994 several initiatives were taken to change Mexico's
> poor enforcement record. [E]nvironmental budgets were greatly increased,
> more personnel were recruited, better trained and equipped, and legislation was
> further defined. (Hogenboom 1996: 1002; see also Auer 2001: 450; Fisher 2002)

Gil Corrales claims that changes made to the environmental governance regime were partly to enable the government to respond more directly to the
"political circumstances" of NAFTA (2007: 168, n. 5). However, he also states
that the 1992 creation of SEDESOL and INE were the result of LGEEPA in
1988, the Brundtland report of 1987, and the international consensus surrounding the importance of environmental issues, which brought pressure to
restructure the environmental institutions (2007: 179).

One of Mexico's most experienced environmental bureaucrats stated that
NAFTA made "all the difference"—that many natural resource laws had to be
amended because of NAFTA and that there was a clear causal effect of NAFTA
on legal and constitutional reform, in order to incorporate NAFTA into the
Mexican legal system (Carmona interview, 2008). In 1992, the creation of INE
and Profepa out of the environmental part of SEDESOL was the direct result
of NAFTA, according to SEMARNAT's chief advisor to the secretary, and in
1994, SEMARNAP's creation was also influenced strongly by NAFTA (Guerrero interview, 2007; this was echoed by Fernando Tudela, the ministry's
number two official, in an interview in 2008). Hufbauer and colleagues (2000:
55) claim that "without the NAFTA, the Mexican government would have had
less incentive to pass environmental legislation or to improve its enforcement
efforts, and the achievements, modest though they are . . . would not exist."

Blanca Torres, a long-standing analyst of environmental politics, states that "NAFTA's environmental commitments have contributed to a greater concern for the environment among relevant state and non-state actors in Mexico . . . improved environmental training and research as well as the design of environmental institutions and mechanisms for public participation" (2002: 201–202, 210ff.). She outlines specific ways in which NAFTA has helped Mexico improve its environmental capacity. First, it established incentives to improve data, training, and other elements of environmental work. Second, federal environmental institutions were strengthened, and SEMARNAP brought together environmental responsibilities under one federal ministry. The budget increased from 803.5 million pesos in 1995 to 1,068.8 million pesos in 1997, although it suffered a 20 percent reduction in its budget in 1999 due to economic problems (Torres 2002: 211–12). She also shows that SEMARNAP's power relative to other agencies was increasing.

Third, in terms of policies and programs, the number and size of environmentally important protected areas increased. New legislation included a reformed LGEEPA, a forest law in 1997, and a general wildlife law in 2000. There has been criticism of some laws, and enforcement remains a challenge, but she characterizes these changes as progress, at least in legal terms. These points were echoed by Paolo Solano, a legal officer working in the Commission on Environmental Cooperation's Submissions on Enforcement Matters Unit (interview, 2008). He described an "explosion of laws, regulations and environmental standards" since 1994, as well as increased specialization among law firms and consultancies (see also INE 2000: 110). The quality of application of environmental law is much better. Environmental impact assessments are taken more seriously, and there has been more exchange of information across the border. He claims NAFTA is responsible for these changes.

There is unanimous agreement that the establishment of Profepa was a direct result of the NAFTA negotiations and the desire to demonstrate to skeptical U.S. environmental interests that Mexico was committed to environmental enforcement (see Gil Corrales 2007: 167–68, 187; Azuela 2006: 336). In its report on environmental management (2000: 343), SEMARNAP acknowledges that the creation of Profepa was due largely to NAFTA. It called this a "qualitative change" in environmental management, with enforcement becoming increasingly important (SEMARNAP 2000: 343–44). Most observers also credit NAFTA for the focus on inspections and closures.

According to a former head of Profepa, NAAEC "opened spaces for the discussion of problems in enforcement of Mexican environmental laws, and above all, created political conditions favoring the aggressive program of law enforcement pursued by Profepa after its initiation in 1992, along with its new system of environmental audits" (Azuela 2006: 499). He emphasized that the environmental audits were not the result of the reform of LGEEPA in 1996, but rather the creation of NAAEC. Interestingly, when compliance and enforcement results began to improve, the results were announced not in Mexico but in the United States. President Clinton pointed to environmental audits of 617 plants and agreements that had been concluded with 404 companies to implement improvements in order to comply with the law (cited in Azuela 2006: 369–70).[10]

NAFTA's Trilateral Environmental Institutions

Mexico took it upon itself to upgrade capacity, but the NAAEC institutions brought further incentives and resources to continue the job. There are two important institutional differences between NAAEC and its labor counterpart: one is the Joint Public Advisory Committee (JPAC), a permanent institutionalized citizen advisory body; the second is the relative independence of the NAAEC Secretariat. These small differences prove critical.

The North American Agreement on Environmental Cooperation established a Commission for Environmental Cooperation (CEC), made up of a Council of Ministers, a Secretariat, and JPAC (see Figure 2.2). The council is the environment ministers from the three member states. The Secretariat, led by an executive secretary chosen by the council, provides support for the council and any committees it establishes. At the end of 2009, Secretariat staff numbered fifty-six (twenty-three professionals and thirty-three support staff). The JPAC is made up of five civil society representatives from each member state, whose role is to advise and provide information both to the council and the secretariat (see GAO 1997).

The CEC is responsible for creation of a "trilateral North American environmental community" to coordinate action among the three governments, encourage public participation, promote development of Mexican environmental capacity, and provide information sharing within a neutral forum (TRAC 2004: 4). Its official programs and projects include environment, economy, and trade; conservation of biodiversity; pollutants and health; and law and policy, among others.[11] In terms of enforcement (the main rationale for NAAEC), two avenues exist. The first is through Articles 14 and 15, which permit citizens to complain about lack of enforcement. The second is through Part V, which

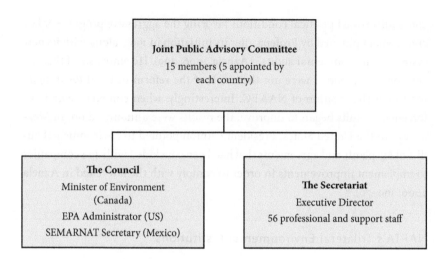

FIGURE 2.2 Commission on Environmental Cooperation

permits governments to consult on problems and disputes. Under the process of Articles 14 and 15, the Secretariat prepares a factual record if the council agrees. The factual record can be made public (the council must agree to this, too). Though citizen submissions and factual records may result in pressure being exerted on governments, there is no formal penalty that may be imposed. I address these mechanisms in more detail later. Under Part V, sanctions for persistent failure to enforce environmental law include monetary penalties or withdrawal of NAFTA benefits (Article 22). As of 2011, it had not been employed.

In the early years of NAFTA, Mexican government officials complained that they did not have enough input into the work programs of the CEC and that some of the work on the border overlapped with what Mexican agencies themselves were doing (GAO 1997). They were also unhappy with the process regarding citizen submissions, particularly in the first case, where they felt the commission acted unduly strictly toward them. They bridled at the intrusion into their sovereignty. How then is it possible to claim that the CEC has had an important impact on Mexican environmental governance? I address that by first considering the access points for civil society and then turning to the border environmental institutions. I assess the role these institutions play in building capacity and how they brought about a change in thinking in environmental agencies.

Public Access—the Joint Public Advisory Committee

The North American Agreement on Environmental Cooperation brought opportunities that proved critical to the development of Mexico's independent environmental NGO movement. One of the opportunities was through JPAC, a transnational body with a remit to promote environmental cooperation, ecosystem protection, and sustainable development. It gives advice to the Council of Ministers (for example, on the enforcement of environmental law) and information to the Secretariat, and it meets three or four times per year with representatives of the public. It also meets with government representatives and has working groups on law enforcement, biodiversity, and energy, among others. It promotes "active public participation and transparency in the actions of the CEC," according to a member of the team reviewing its performance after the first ten years (Dannenmaier 2005: 2). It does not act on behalf of governments, but sets its agenda in response to public input, through its own ideas, and in response to council requests. In the first ten years of its existence (1994–2004), it held ninety-three meetings, made seventy-nine recommendations, and produced various reports (Bourget, 2004).

Although JPAC acts as a strategic partner to the council, it also serves as a watchdog, monitoring the council and providing access and information for interested groups. It also provided funding for participation in the advisory process, which was a great help to Mexican NGOs, according to one JPAC member (Silvan 2005; see also Gallagher 2004).[12] The North American Fund for Environmental Cooperation (NAFEC), although discontinued in 2003, enabled local groups to exchange information, create networks, and participate in the public advocacy process. Between 1995 and 2003, 196 grants were made (TRAC 2004: 41). According to the CEC, in the first ten months of 2003, the CEC provided travel expenses and accommodation for 571 participants in thirty meetings, half of whom were Mexican (TRAC 2004: 15). A total of 109 Mexican environmental interest groups were funded during the lifetime of NAFEC.

The result is that "practitioners are in closer contact with their counterparts, not only in governments but also in NGOs and academia" (TRAC 2004: 15). Awareness of views and positions among stakeholders is better. Moreover, JPAC brings the voice of the public to its interactions with the council (Dannenmaier 2005: 3). It has helped to commit NGOs to the consultation process. Its engagement with environmental NGOs increases NAAEC's legitimacy and credibility. In terms of public participation and input, therefore, JPAC plays a significant role, although its capacity to generate transnational interests and identities is limited by the power of the member state principals. Its recommendations may be ignored by the council. Its effectiveness is also limited by budget constraints and by the fact that much of its work is highly technical. It has argued that its credibility is jeopardized by interference from member state principals and that limiting civil society input "did not advance key issues of accessibility, transparency, independence, balance and impartiality" (Dannenmaier 2005: 13). Activists are concerned that member state control of JPAC's work may eventually tempt civil society interests to abandon the NAAEC arena in favor of national politics.

Public Access—Citizen Submissions
The CEC has two direct avenues to respond to civil society concerns regarding environmental protection. The first is known as Article 13 public reports, which the Secretariat may prepare on any matter within its annual program of activities. Article 13 reports investigate alleged failings (examples include the Silva Reservoir case, the Maize Report, and the Green Building Report). Unlike the more formal Article 14/15 citizen submissions, Article 13 reports avoid the need to exhaust domestic remedies. They can be done by the Secretariat without council approval and thus are an independent source of power for the Secretariat. In the Silva Reservoir case, for example, several U.S. and Mexican NGOs filed a petition regarding the deaths of thousands of migratory birds in the Silva Reservoir in 1994–1995. According to a media report at the time, the investigation was welcomed by the Mexican government and was a sign of increasing openness to international scrutiny.[13] The Secretariat published a report on the case, which in turn was important to the development of NGO capacity in Mexico (Dannenmeier interview, 2008).

The second avenue is the Article 14/15 procedure. Individuals or groups are entitled to petition the Secretariat if they believe national environmental laws are not being enforced, a process known by the formal name Submissions on Enforcement Matters and less formally as "citizen submissions."[14] The Secretariat checks the admissibility requirements (for example, petitioners must first have exhausted domestic remedies). If admissibility requirements are met, the Secretariat then asks for a response from the member state in question. Once the response has been considered, the Secretariat may recommend to the council that a factual record be created. Factual records include information on the history of the case, pertinent facts, the obligations of the relevant member state, and their actions in the case (CEC 2002a). The Secretariat has the power to consider not simply information provided by the member states but also publicly available information submitted by interested parties or generated by the Secretariat itself or by independent experts (NAAEC Treaty, Article 15). The draft is then submitted to the member states for comment. Figure 2.3 shows the steps involved in the process.

The creation of a factual record needs to be approved by a two-thirds council vote, although in practice the decision is always unanimous. There

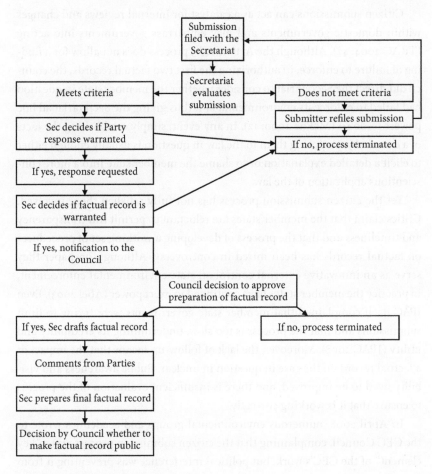

FIGURE 2.3 Citizen submission process

must also be a two-thirds majority in favor of making it public. The Secretariat claims that it always tries to facilitate an understanding between the submitter and the member state, playing the role of a neutral arbiter. For example, in its public information meeting on the Lake Chapala case (in the Mexican state of Jalisco) in November 2008, the Secretariat gathered the views of the public but did not express an opinion. It did not want to portray the meeting as a "hearing" because of sovereignty sensitivities and because of what one CEC official described as a lack of trust between the Secretariat and the council on Article 14/15 issues (Solano interview, 2008). It had taken three years for the member states to approve a factual record in the case, so sensitive was Mexico to perceived intrusion.

Citizen submissions can act as a catalyst for internal reviews and changes within domestic governments and may embarrass governments into acting (TRAC 2004: 42). Although the Article 14/15 process does not allow for a finding of failure to enforce, in authorizing the first two factual records, the council did direct the Secretariat to consider whether the member state in question had failed to enforce its environmental law, thus giving the Secretariat ad hoc powers to do so (McRae 2000: 12). In any event, simply establishing the facts of a case and juxtaposing them to the law in question is usually enough either to elicit a detailed explanation or to shame the member state into a more conscientious application of the law.

Yet the citizen submission process has not fully satisfied those involved. Critics claim that the member states are reluctant to permit full transparency and timeliness and that the process of developing a working set of procedures on factual records has been mired in controversy. Although on paper they serve as an innovative external control on state environmental enforcement, in practice the member states have continued to exert power (Abel 2003). Even JPAC itself complained that member state governments were trying to limit submissions and that the process is too slow, undermining its credibility and utility (JPAC 2008). Moreover, the lack of follow-up means that the impact of a factual record on the case in question in unclear. Public awareness and visibility need to be improved, and there is insufficient evaluation of the process to ensure that it is working correctly.

In April 2008, numerous environmental groups and academics wrote to the CEC Council, complaining that the citizen submission process was a "key element" of the CEC's work, but political interference was preventing it from functioning properly. They pointed to long delays in deciding on factual records and the refusal of the member states to hold votes on their preparation and release, which undermined public confidence and credibility, as well as the motivation to bring submissions in the first place. They complained about the practice of limiting the scope of investigations when factual records *are* agreed and of limiting the timeframe on which investigations can be focused. This can hide the extent to which member states may be failing to enforce environmental laws and mask important contextual information. Nonetheless, despite criticisms of ineffectiveness, I argue that Article 14/15 has in fact been a catalyst for change. The reaction of the Mexican government to cases brought against it suggests it has adapted behavior and accepted rule of law norms. Even if citizen submissions have not resulted in the kinds of changes that NGOs hoped for, there is clear evidence that Mexico reacted to the threat of shaming by improving enforcement procedures.

Article 14/15 Factual Records

Capacity has been built not simply in federal agencies but also in NGOs. Both have become more professionalized: that is, officials of NGOs and public agencies share awareness of problems, as well as expectations, objectives, and values. Their training, education, and experience lead them to similar understandings of challenges and solutions. The citizen submission and factual record processes are central elements of capacity building and professionalization. Despite the lack of dispute resolution powers and the absence of a judgment on the merits of the arguments, a factual record elevates an issue from an obscure local disagreement into an internationally visible dispute. Social pressures are brought to bear on Mexico because it "creates public awareness that the party is knowingly engaging in unlawful activities" (Dorn 2007). Moreover, although factual records were intended to be neutral, a former chief of Profepa pointed out that "the way you word the facts, there is always a judgment implied" (Azuela interview, 2008). Expectations are changed through this process. According to a U.S.-based legal scholar:

> The CEC's access to information policies, decision making records, citizen submission process, and public Council sessions have helped shape Mexican citizens' expectations for the conduct of government business for national agencies and public institutions. That [SEMARNAT] is regarded as one of the more open and transparent Mexican government agencies is in a small, but not

inconsequential way, due to its intense interaction with the CEC and civil society. (Block 2003: 516; see also Herrera 2008)

In this section, I review the completed factual records against Mexico in chronological order. Of the seventy-seven total submissions made, thirty-nine have been against Mexico, resulting in seven completed factual records and one unfinished factual record (see Tables 2.1 and 2.2 for information on the submissions). Twenty-five of the thirty-nine cases did not proceed to a factual record. In one case, the council voted against the Secretariat's recommendation to begin a factual record. In the remainder of the cases, the process had not terminated at the time of writing (November 2011).

Cozumel (SEM-96-001)

In the first citizen submission, the so-called Cozumel pier case, the Mexican authorities had granted a permit to a company to build a pier to accommodate cruise ships at Cozumel, along with related onshore infrastructure. On January 18, 1996, a group of three Mexican environmental organizations filed a citizen submission claiming that the authorities, in granting the permit, failed to enforce environmental law. The government required the company to provide an environmental impact assessment only for the pier itself, rather than for the associated buildings and other works onshore. Moreover, the petitioners claimed that the area of the development was within a protected natural area and that consideration of the environmental consequences of development in the area had not been taken into account.

After reviewing the allegations, the CEC requested a response from the Mexican government. On March 27, 1996, the government responded (see CEC 1996, 1997).[15] It opposed the petition on several grounds, stating that the decisions made to allow the port facilities to be constructed had been taken before the NAAEC came into effect. It also argued that the petitioners had not shown that they suffered harm from the project, that they had not exhausted remedies under Mexican law, and that the petition did not advance the objectives of the NAAEC. The Secretariat rejected all the government's claims and made a recommendation to the council that a factual record be developed. This was accepted by the council; the factual record was duly carried out and presented to the council in 1997 (CEC 1997).

In the factual record, the Secretariat recapped the arguments of the petitioners and the Mexican government. It reviewed technical and scientific reports on the project and its possible impact on the local environment (especially

TABLE 2.1 Citizen submissions to the CEC

Against	Mexico	USA	Canada	Totals
Submissions	39	10	28	77
Active files	5	1	4	10
Factual records	7 (plus 1 in process)	1	8	16

TABLE 2.2 Submissions against Mexico

Date filed	Name of case	Reference	Status	Action
17/01/1996	Cozumel	SEM-96-001	Closed	Factual record
15/03/1997	Río Magdalena	SEM-97-002	Closed	Factual record
10/10/1997	Lake Chapala	SEM-97-007	Closed	The Secretariat determined not to recommend the preparation of a factual record
14/10/1997	Ortiz Martínez	SEM-98-002	Closed	Dismissed
9/01/1998	Guadalajara	SEM-98-001	Closed	Dismissed
11/08/1998	Cytrar I	SEM-98-005	Closed	Process terminated without recommendation of factual record
20/10/1998	Aquanova	SEM-98-006	Closed	Factual record
23/10/1998	Metales y Derivados	SEM-98-007	Closed	Factual record
27/01/2000	Molymex I	SEM-00-001	Closed	Dismissed
6/04/2000	Molymex II	SEM-00-005	Closed	Factual record
9/06/2000	Tarahumara	SEM-00-006	Closed	Factual record
14/02/2001	Cytrar II	SEM-01-001	Closed	Secretariat recommends factual record but council votes against
14/06/2001	Dermet	SEM-01-003	Closed	Dismissed
7/02/2002	Mexico City Airport	SEM-02-002	Closed	The Secretariat determined not to recommend the preparation of a factual record
23/08/2002	El Boludo Project	SEM-02-004	Closed	Submitter(s) requested the Secretariat to withdraw the submission
25/11/2002	ALCA-Iztapalapa	SEM-02-005	Closed	Dismissed—submission did not conform to requirements under Art 14(1)

(continued)

TABLE 2.2 (*continued*)

Date filed	Name of case	Reference	Status	Action
14/05/2003	Home Port Xcaret	SEM-03-002	Closed	Dismissed
23/05/2003	Lake Chapala II	SEM-03-003	Active	Secretariat posted a request for information relevant to the factual record on its Web site (4/09/2008)
17/06/2003	ALCA-Iztapalapa II	SEM-03-004	Closed	Factual record
15/08/2003	Cytrar III	SEM-03-006	Closed	Secretariat determined not to recommend the preparation of a factual record
27/01/2004	Hazardous waste in Arteaga	SEM-04-001	Closed	Secretariat determined not to recommend the preparation of a factual record
14/07/2004	Environmental pollution in Hermosillo	SEM-04-002	Closed	Secretariat determined not to request a response from the concerned government party
7/09/2004	Gasoline spill in Tehuantepec	SEM-04-003	Closed	Dismissed
12/01/2005	Crushed gravel in Puerto Peñasco	SEM-05-001	Closed	Process terminated without recommenda-tion of factual record
3/05/2005	Coronado Islands	SEM-05-002	Closed	Secretariat requested approval for factual record, but process is terminated before it is produced
30/08/2005	Environmental pollution in Hermosillo II	SEM-05-003	Active	Council informed that the Secretariat considers that the submission warrants development of a factual record (4/04/2007)
26/01/2006	Ex Hacienda El Hospital	SEM-06-001	Closed	Submitter(s) requested the Secretariat to withdraw the submission
17/07/2006	Ex Hacienda El Hospital II	SEM-06-003	Active	CEC seeking factual record
22/09/2006	Ex Hacienda El Hospital III	SEM-06-004	Active	The Secretariat informed council that the Secretariat considers that the submission warrants development of a factual record (12/05/2008)

TABLE 2.2 (*continued*)

Date filed	Name of case	Reference	Status	Action
9/11/2006	Los Remedios National Park	SEM-06-006	Closed	The Secretariat determined not to recommend the preparation of a factual record
5/02/2007	Minera San Xavier	SEM-07-001	Closed	The Secretariat determined not to recommend the preparation of a factual record
26/07/2007	Drilling waste in Cunduacán	SEM-07-005	Closed	Secretariat determined to proceed no further because the matter is the subject of a pending judicial or administrative proceeding
22/02/2008	La Ciudadela project	SEM-08-001	Closed	The Secretariat determined not to request a factual record
17/11/2008	Jetty construction in Cancun	SEM-08-003	Closed	Dismissed
28/01/2009	Transgenic maize in Chihuahua	SEM-09-001	Closed	The Secretariat determined not to request a factual record
4/02/2009	Wetlands in Manzanillo	SEM-09-002	Active	Considering whether to recommend a factual record
16/07/2009	Los Remedios National Park II	SEM-09-003	Active	The Secretariat began reviewing the submission under Article 14(1) (10/08/2009)
25/02/2010	Sumidero Canyon	SEM-10-001	Closed	Dismissed
20/12/2010	Bicentennial Bridge	SEM-10-004	Closed	Dismissed

SOURCE: Compiled by author from CEC Web site. www.cec.org/Page.asp?PageID=751 &SiteNodeID=250. See also JPAC 2008.

the coral reefs), as well as relevant laws and regulations. It described evidence that the firm had inadequately responded to requirements to minimize environmental impact. The factual report also described communications between federal and local agencies, such as the request in late 1994 by the government of the state of Quintana Roo to relocate the pier project to reduce environmental damage (because its technical reports showed there would be damage) and the response by the federal agency INE that there was insufficient evidence to require such a change (CEC 1997: 37). In the wake of the factual record, the federal government changed its position and required the firm to scale back its plans. It also changed the status of the area to give it greater protection as an ecological zone.

Río Magdalena (SEM-97-002)
The Río Magdalena case involved river pollution in the state of Sonora, where municipal authorities were permitting wastewater (including sewage) to flow untreated into water supplies used for drinking and irrigation (CEC 2003a). The submitters complained about the failure of both federal and state authorities to enforce provisions on monitoring wastewater discharges and ensuring they conform to standards. The federal water agency Conagua had begun building a sewage treatment facility in 1988 but stopped construction following complaints. It then authorized a temporary (forty-five-day) discharge into an area that had been excavated for the purposes of the treatment plant. Discharges were still happening nine years later (in 1997), when the complaint was filed.

The Mexican government responded that discharge of wastewater into bodies of water was a federal issue, not a state issue, and that enforcement did occur where it was required. It rejected complaints about issues that arose before the entry into force of the NAFTA treaty. However, the response did acknowledge problems in wastewater treatment and discharge, saying that budgetary shortfalls limited construction of treatment facilities, although they remained an objective. It also acknowledged that the municipalities in question did not possess the discharge permits they required but said that the authorities were rectifying the situation. The CEC Secretariat found that monitoring and enforcement by Conagua were indeed faulty in several respects. The municipalities had not monitored or reported discharges and had not paid fees for discharge permits. The reaction to the case was swift. Conagua began in 1998 to construct or complete wastewater treatment plants and regularly monitor the discharges. The timing of the construction projects and the fact that Conagua began bimonthly testing of effluents (in 1999) both suggest they were a strategic response to the submission on the government's part.

Aquanova (SEM-98-006)

The Aquanova case was filed in 1998 by Grupo Ecológico Manglar regarding environmental damage caused by a shrimp farm in the state of Nayarit (CEC 2003b). The company had obtained relevant permits and authorizations from INE to establish the farm and cultivate shrimp and had undergone thirteen site inspections by Profepa between 1995 and 2002. The company was fined twice for failure to meet the conditions of the environmental impact assessment, for changing land use without permission, and for destroying mangrove forest, filling wetlands, and uprooting coconut palms. Also, it diverted water courses (though these were authorized) and began wastewater discharge two years before applying for permission. A criminal investigation was begun but terminated because the company had received authorization for its project. Independent experts studying the environmental effect of the project decided that the positive effects of Aquanova's restoration programs depended on their being maintained. The company also made an effort to engage in cooperative activities with local environmental groups to deal with opposition to its operation.

The response of the Mexican government indicated that it was aware of environmental problems associated with Aquanova and was using its legal powers to address them. A number of instances were alleged in which the company failed to obtain permits or authorizations, as well as cases where water-quality monitoring was not carried out. The government rejected many of the allegations; it conceded damage had occurred but said that the damage had been noted and the company had been fined and/or had agreed to rectify damages. In some cases, the government stated that damages were caused prior to the 1996 reform of LGEEPA, and relevant law did not apply at the time. It also stated that some reports of investigations carried out by the authorities could not be made public, and so the Secretariat was not able to gain access to them.

The factual record detailed the environmental impact assessment, permitting, and authorization requirements under Mexican law. The Secretariat requested a copy of the company's environmental impact statement from INE, though it did not receive it. It did obtain a copy of the environmental impact assessment issued by INE, along with the forty-three conditions the company was required to observe. Profepa's site visit revealed violations of some of these conditions. Penalties were issued, some of which were later reduced. For phases two and three of the project, INE again issued an environmental impact assessment, this time with forty-nine conditions. Profepa noted some violations of these conditions in a site visit but signed an agreement with the company that the company would conduct studies to determine the impact on affected areas.

Some reactions by Mexico again suggest that the government was reacting strategically to the NAAEC filing. It denied some of the allegations, while admitting there had been problems in enforcement. Moreover, the council dragged its feet on approving the Secretariat's request to create a factual record: fifteen months elapsed in the Aquanova case between the Secretariat's request and approval by the council. In the first two cases, about one month elapsed between the requests and the authorizations. However, the government also agreed that there were problems with the site and with the company's compliance, and it is clear that Profepa took enforcement action.

Metales y Derivados (SEM-98-007)
This case was filed in 1998 by two groups who were concerned about a site abandoned by the firm Metales y Derivados (a subsidiary of a San Diego–based firm) in the state of Baja California. The site had been used to process refined lead and phosphorized copper granulates (CEC 2002c: 21). Following its closure in 1994 (and arrest warrants against its owner), the submission asserted that the toxic waste was not returned to the United States as required and that steps were not taken to secure the site, prevent contamination of local villages, or warn residents of the dangers. The submitters claimed that these represented failures to enforce Mexican environmental law. In its response, the government indicated that it was also concerned about the site, and it explained the actions it had taken, including filing criminal charges, visits to inspect the site by the state Profepa office, and both temporary and permanent closure orders. It claimed that it had looked into transferring the contaminated soil to an authorized facility and restoring the site to a safe condition but did not have the resources to do so. The Secretariat did not receive responses from SEMARNAT to three subsequent letters requesting detailed information.

About two and a half months elapsed between the recommendation of a factual record in this case and its approval by the council. The factual record confirmed that the soil was contaminated by hazardous substances, including antimony, arsenic, cadmium, and lead (CEC 2002c). It found that the site had not been restored to a condition corresponding to local zoning (light industry), nor had access to the site been secured to reduce possible ill effects to public health and the local environment. The factual record implied that Profepa and SEMARNAT knew of the public health risk of the company's operations. A study conducted by experts from the University of California, Irvine found that blood lead levels were acceptable but that there were long-term health risks. The Secretariat pointed out that enforcing environmental law in the maquiladora sector is stymied by inadequate resources and the offenders' ability to flee across the border. However, it also noted that it had not received information from Mexico on exactly how these factors interfered with enforcement in the Metales y Derivados case.

The Secretariat concluded that the response from Mexico to the petition "did not allow dismissing the Submitters' assertions" (CEC 2002c: 49). It detailed the actions conducted by the authorities, noted the limitations, and also listed possible enforcement actions they did not pursue, such as civil action against the owners. In addition, failures to measure levels of toxicity and pursue cleanup options were noted. It strongly implied that these shortcomings amounted to enforcement failures:

> The site abandoned by *Metales y Derivados* is a case of soil contamination by hazardous waste in relation to which measures taken to date have not prevented the dispersal of pollutants or prevented access to the site, which relates to the issue of whether Mexico is effectively enforcing LGEEPA Article 170. It also reveals that, as a matter of fact, no actions have been taken to restore the soil to a condition in which it can be used in the industrial activities corresponding to the zoning of the area . . . in order to enforce effectively LGEEPA Article 134. (CEC 2002c: 59–60)

Molymex II (SEM-00-005)

The Molymex II case was brought in 2000 by a human rights organization and an individual against a molybdenum roasting company in the state of Sonora (CEC 2004). Civic groups and local residents accused the company of contaminating the local area and particularly of dangerous levels of sulfur dioxide emissions, with serious effects on both human health and the environment more widely (through acid rain). In this case, five months elapsed between the recommendation of a factual record and its approval by the council.

The petitioners claimed that the authorities failed to conduct an environmental impact assessment (EIA) on the company's operations, though the government's response indicated that it was not required because the company's activity began before EIAs were required (in 1982). The Secretariat's report indicates, however, that the law is ambiguous on whether they can be applied retroactively and in fact requires them when in the public interest. It also noted that the Mexican courts were considering the issue and had yet to decide. The Mexican government replied that when the company expanded operations in 1998, it did comply with the environmental impact assessment requirement.

The factual record also questioned granting a land use permit to the company. The legal requirement is that "general criteria for the protection of air quality be applied in defining, in the rural development plans, the areas where polluting industries may be sited" (CEC 2004: 10). However, the municipal authority that issued the permit stated that the zoning in the specific location was defined by virtue of having granted the land use permit to this particular company and by placing a roaster symbol on its development map. In other words, instead of a general zoning plan defining areas where polluting industry could be sited, the individual permit to Molymex served as a de facto indication of the zoning.

The third issue related to the enforcement of air emissions. The environmental authorities issued the company an air emissions limit indicating maximum allowable emissions of sulfur dioxide in six-hour average intervals. However, the Secretariat was unable to gain information on monitoring at the plant, and its own independent reports suggested that the total legal limit on ambient levels of sulfur dioxide might be exceeded even if the stack emissions limit set by SEMARNAT was never exceeded. This could occur through peaks in emissions that were disguised by the six-hour averages. It concluded:

> Monthly reports of continuous SO_2 monitoring ... do not in fact demonstrate conclusively that the ambient air SO_2 standards ... were never exceeded. The data were collected with analyzers of insufficient detection range, there were blank records and negative data, and there is no substitute data calculation algorithm to make up for the deficiencies in the data. (CEC 2004: 12)

Tarahumara (SEM-00-006)

The Tarahumara case was filed by a human rights group in 2000, alleging failures by the authorities in dealing with citizen complaints and investigating likely offenses related to logging and other activities in indigenous communities in the state of Chihuahua (CEC 2005). Eight months elapsed between the request from the Secretariat for authorization to produce a factual record and the agreement of the council. The factual record addressed twenty-eight citizen complaints to Profepa, most of which took longer to administer and resolve than the legally allotted time (because of backlogs and other resource constraints or problems with the submissions). In many of the cases in which Profepa ordered fines or corrective measures, the offenders did not comply. In some cases, Profepa did not reply to the Secretariat's request for information, for example, over the consequences for offenders who did not pay their fines and what happened to cases referred to federal prosecutors.

Profepa was accused in the petition of not providing information on enforcement activities related to complaints made to it and of not dealing with illegal processing at a mill. An *ejido* had been ordered by Profepa to carry out reforestation, despite having been the victim of illegal logging and burning activities.[16] The government stated that in some cases it had reported offenses to the federal prosecutors (though the information provided to the Secretariat was limited) and that in other cases it was unnecessary to do so. It also stated that complaints about illegal sand extraction had been dealt with by the authorities, but in its information to the Secretariat, the details did not explain how this happened. The government indicated other ways it had responded to complaints: it acknowledged the *denuncias* it received from complainants; it had established meetings between the authorities and the indigenous communities and NGOs beginning in 2000; it intended to created "participatory surveillance committees" for the region (CEC 2005: 20).

The factual record noted numerous enforcement challenges in this case. One is geographic. Profepa and Conagua inspectors need to travel between eight and twenty-four hours from Chihuahua City to reach the area. Another is the language barrier, as the indigenous communities do not use Spanish as their first language. They are also vulnerable economically and socially, in comparison to the wider population. The report mentioned that there were too few Profepa inspectors and their salaries were lower than federal civil servants more generally. Concern was also expressed regarding the failure by Profepa to follow up on complaints. Even where it is not required to do so, this failure resulted in an impression that the process was not effective (CEC 2005: 14). Finally, the factual record noted the difficulties in coordinating between relevant agencies (SEMARNAT, Conagua, and Profepa) and between the state and federal level. State authorities often lack resources to carry through on plans to crack down on illegal logging.

Although this case, like the others, shows deficiencies in enforcement and follow-up activities by the federal authorities, it is also clear that Profepa (and other agencies) were trying to respond to complaints from the public and also to the CEC investigation. When the factual report was made public, the salaries of Profepa inspectors were raised in response to the point made by the Secretariat in its report. In contrast to what we will see in the labor sector, the reaction by federal environmental authorities to investigations was far more positive: problems were acknowledged, actions were explained, and corrective steps were taken, even if all were tentative.

ALCA-Iztapalapa II (SEM-03-004)

This case was filed in 2003 against a Mexico City manufacturing plant producing polystyrene latex for footwear. The issue involved solvent emissions that affected a neighbor of the facility. The factual record indicated that Profepa conducted site visits on eleven occasions from 1994 to 2005. Partial closings of the plant were ordered in 1994 and 1997. Fines were imposed for violations of air emissions standards, as well as for improper handling of hazardous waste. The second closure was ordered after the plant was found to be continuing improper air emissions. Profepa then imposed new conditions that the plant refused to implement, saying they were impossible to meet and that according to its data it was already meeting emissions standards. Profepa accepted the company's interpretation. Other agencies also took enforcement action. The Mexico City Environment Ministry visited the plant on ten occasions and closed it in 1999, though it was opened again later the same year. The Federal Public Prosecutor sought criminal prosecution against the company four times but was denied an arrest warrant for lack of evidence. The Public Affairs Center of the legislative assembly of Mexico City also filed a complaint regarding the company. The company went out of business at the end of 2005.

In its response to the submission, the government of Mexico stated that the original citizen petition on the matter (dated November 1995) was lost when archives were flooded. The citizen who made the 1995 complaint filed another complaint with the Mexican authorities in 2000. The company was visited in July 2001, which resulted in a small fine (of about $250). All the complaints were then closed. The complainant also filed a petition against Profepa officials, who he said were in collusion with the company. Although SEMARNAT decided the case did not warrant investigation, it did not provide information to the Secretariat as to its reasoning. Mexico responded to the factual record by complaining that the Secretariat had exceeded its scope by considering issues outside the immediate complaint. In a long letter, it also claimed that:

> A factual record cannot establish conclusions, and especially should not contain statements that may be construed as incriminating the Party; it should join and summarize the essences of the submission and the response. Otherwise, the insertion of opinions, viewpoints or judgments as to the Party's actions implicitly make the Secretariat a reviewing agency, a power not conferred by the NAAEC, thereby affecting the impartiality of its actions. (CEC 2007: 142)

In some of the issues surrounding the case—such as the criminal investigation against the company—the Secretariat was unsuccessful in getting a response from Mexican authorities, even to explain why information could not be provided. Thus, it appears that the environmental authorities took strategic actions to limit information about compliance, if not the compliance itself. Moreover, more than nine months elapsed between recommendation of a factual record and council approval. These actions suggest lax enforcement, although it is important to note that the factual record showed a history of enforcement actions against the company in question, even if they were not fully effective.

Capacity Building in Mexican Agencies

The results of the factual records suggest that Mexico reacted strategically to limit criticism, complained on occasion that the Secretariat exceeded its scope, and sometimes delayed agreeing to factual records in the first place. However, it also acted to rectify problems in several cases, admitted failures, and sought to explain how matters would be improved. The limited number of records prevents drawing general conclusions, but evidence suggests that some within the environmental agencies, as well as many NGOs, came to welcome the international attention and used the citizen submissions process as a lever to open the enforcement process to greater scrutiny.

But capacity building takes place in more direct ways, too. The 2004 Puebla Declaration (unsurprisingly) singled out Mexico as the weakest member state in terms of institutional capacity, and the CEC reacted by raising capacity building to one of three priority areas in its 2005–2010 strategy (along with information for decision making, and trade and the environment). Projects within the capacity-building area were intended to improve compliance with wildlife laws; improve the private sector's compliance; strengthen capacities to conserve species and habitats by building planning, tracking, and enforcement capacities; and strengthen capacities to assess and control chemicals of interest.

Projects were established on chemicals, conservation, environmental trade, information tools, law enforcement, protected species, sustainability, and wildlife. They provide training, improvements to scientific quality, and a forum where national officials come together to decide work program priorities. Mexico is at the table with the United States and Canada, and these cooperative mechanisms help build its organizational and institutional capacity. The CEC stated in an undated document that its capacity-building emphasis had changed from being focused on training and education of individuals, such as law enforcement officers, to more "systemic" issues, namely, the "abilities and efficiency of institutions and their instruments," including policy formulation, institutional arrangements, science and technology, infrastructure, funding mechanisms, and public participation.

The CEC identified specific audiences, capacity requirements, and detailed actions. For example, within the priority area "strengthening capacities to improve compliance with wildlife laws," the CEC stated that knowledge needed to be improved regarding priority species, international agreements (such as the Convention on International Trade in Endangered Species), national environmental rules (LGEEPA and federal legal standards), and wildlife species management. This was to be achieved through workshops, informational publications, and educational guides, among other methods, and was targeted at officials from the Attorney General's office, the Navy and National Defense, finance and public credit officials, communications and transport officials, and airports and auxiliary services staff. Similarly detailed plans were created for the other priority areas. The plan included judicial officials as well, although one Secretariat official claimed that they needed to expand their training to include more federal judges (Heredia interview, 2008).

Not all capacity-building activities worked out as planned. For example, the CEC found unsatisfactory a training program on wildlife inspection (established under the 2005–2010 strategy) because many of the inspectors later left their jobs. It thus developed a stakeholder strategy in which interested agencies, such as Profepa, help set the agenda on the wildlife program. They created a new course leading to a certificate from the Mexican National Institute for Penal Sciences that qualifies inspectors as forensic environmental scientists. The qualification was recognized by the Secretariat of Public Administration. The idea was to increase the stake everyone has in the project. Several other CEC sectoral programs are designed to upgrade capacity as well. They include the Pollutant Release and Transfer Registry (PRTR); action plans to decrease or eliminate emission and use of toxic substances; pilot projects on sustainable tourism; promotion of shade-grown coffee; cooperation on marine ecosystem protection; establishment of ecoregions; and development and creation of FIPREV (a fund to prevent contamination by small and medium enterprises) (SEMARNAP 2000: 358–59).

The CEC also influences Mexico's environmental capacity through an annual work program strengthening domestic laws and programs, improving transparency and public participation, increasing the flow of information, improving the availability of funding, providing training, working toward common views on environmental management goals, and helping standardize data collection. The CEC has established guidance on risk assessment, disseminated techniques for collecting information on emissions and baseline data, fostered technical standards, and helped in testing samples of air and water quality (Gilbreath 2003: 54–55). Research sponsored by the CEC suggested that large firms and ones with high levels of contact with consumers were more likely to participate in systems of environmental administration and also in maintaining inventories of toxic substances (CEC 2002b). Firms in competitive industrial sectors and those trying to distinguish themselves from competitors were more likely to participate in environmental improvement programs. Mexican officials have been highly enthusiastic about the role played by the CEC, particularly in programs to identify green markets for Mexican producers to target, build capacity to preserve threatened species, improve public participation, manage toxic chemicals, and establish an environmental technology fund (Gilbreath 2003: 56–57).

A Mexican JPAC member listed numerous environmental improvements in Mexico in the first ten years of NAFTA, including banning DDT; a toxic waste registry; sustainable energy, agriculture, and tourism projects; cooperation on tracking transboundary hazardous waste shipments; and creating habitats for endangered species. She directly credits the collaboration flowing from the CEC and NAAEC for these advances (Silvan 2005; also, Garver, personal communication 2007). But bilateral cooperation between the United

States and Mexico also increased in the wake of NAAEC. Mexican and U.S. agencies (including AID and Department of the Interior on the U.S. side) entered into agreements that had capacity-building results, including information exchange; joint research on ecosystem stress, resulting in new data on indicators of environmental quality and stress; technical assistance in terms of training, planning, and assessment; and assistance in designing and implementing outreach programs that increase public participation. In 1992–93, the United States and Mexico sponsored more than seventy projects, and by 1996, the number had increased to 188, of which forty-one were started under NAFTA initiatives on trade and the environment. As one example, the U.S. Fish and Wildlife Service sponsored 107 initiatives under its Wildlife Without Borders program, with 41 percent of the projects aimed at capacity building in response to SEMARNAP's claim that lack of trained personnel was an important obstacle for Mexico (Gilbreath 2003: 61).

Managing Pollutants

One of the most important capacity-building programs, cited by numerous interviewees and reports, is the Pollutant Release and Transfer Registry (PRTR), dating from 1994. Under PRTR, firms report emissions and movements of specified chemical substances. The resulting database is made available to the public. According to the CEC Secretariat, Mexico initiated its PRTR program because of international agreements such as Agenda 21, the OECD, and a pilot project of the UN Institute for Training and Research activities and also because of an internal commitment to its environmental program (CEC 2001: 4). For its part, SEMARNAT claims that its participation in the program is due to "the commitments entered into by Mexico with its adhesion to the NAFTA treaty."[17]

A pilot project was designed and executed in the state of Querétaro during 1995–96. Eighty manufacturing facilities were invited to participate, though the CEC stated in its 2001 report that the quality of the reporting was not high. The CEC involvement in the Querétaro project came at the behest of the state government, which felt it had insufficient resources (Serrato interview, 2008). The Secretariat initially provided workshops, technical assistance, and computer equipment. After the pilot project, the Secretariat withdrew support, although financial support continued for other projects, such as greening the supply chain and legal reform. Querétaro receives about $30,000 a year from the CEC, and, according to the local SEMARNAT official, its capacity in environmental politics has increased in terms of resources and technical ability (Serrato interview, 2008).[18]

Following the pilot project, a National Coordinating Group requested that all firms in Querétaro with thirty or more employees engaged in full-time activities in certain sectors (those that emit any of 178 specific substances) register and report emissions. Therefore, 1997 marked the first year of voluntary registry and also the creation of the annual operation certificate (COA). The program was still not mandatory nationally, and issues over public access to data were left unresolved. Moreover, only 5 percent of eligible firms registered in the first year. By the end of 1999, the first report on emissions was issued, with 1,893 firms participating. The following year the report contained information on 2,308 firms, though these firms' reports contained many omissions. In an effort to improve data quality, the federal agency INE created a manual on how to complete the COA and, along with SEMARNAT, academics, industrial groups, and associations, began to offer training courses. Also, INE published a voluntary standard, setting out which facilities PRTR applied to, a list of substances that needed to be reported (down from 178 to 104), and the format of the report, among other aspects (CEC 2001: 6).

The change of federal government in 2000 made a difference to Mexico's commitment to the PRTR. The former director of the CEC Secretariat, Victor Lichtinger, became head of the Mexican environmental agency and in June 2001 signaled his support for a mandatory and publicly available PRTR in Mexico (Winfield 2003: 46). By 2002, following consultations with industry groups, Mexico had passed a new law requiring reporting of emissions at federal, state, and municipal levels. In 2006, SEMARNAT published mandatory data for the first time (from the year 2004), although only nine states plus Mexico City participated with state-level data. This year was also the first time that Mexico's data was published in the CEC's *Taking Stock* report.

Pollutant Release and Transfer Registry data are now collected at all three levels of Mexican government—national, state, and municipal—with national level data collected in higher-risk industries, such as chemicals, and municipal data collected for low-risk industries, such as companies involved in commerce and mechanical workshops. Reporting is difficult because firms often do not know what their emissions levels are, do not want to report them, or lack the capacity to collect information. State authorities likewise often lack the capacity or resources to force firms to report. Reporting has been patchy, although the government can withhold the single environmental license (a regulatory instrument for firms in certain heavily polluting sectors) to pressure firms to hand over information.

The CEC creates an annual report using PRTR data from SEMARNAT and the other member states. However, SEMARNAT reporting is slow. In November 2008, it had just published the 2005 annual report. The CEC has sought to automate the process of data collection, working with SEMARNAT to improve the database and the domestic capacity to collect data. The CEC obtained money from the Canadian government to provide SEMARNAT with resources to develop software to speed this process up, which will be done in coordination with the United States and Canada in order to harmonize data. The CEC also provides money to SEMARNAT to analyze PRTR data, which included the petrochemical industry for first time in the 2006 report. In addition, SEMARNAT now monitors chemical substances in the air, especially dioxins and furines. The Secretariat pays to transport monitoring equipment within Mexico, and EPA pays for testing and analysis (Garcia interview, 2008).

How influential was the CEC in the development of PRTR capacity? Winfield (2003: 38) states that "the North American PRTR story is emerging as one of the best examples of upward environmental policy convergence in the post-NAFTA period." The role of the CEC has been crucial in this experience—a "strong trinational policy network" brought about by the CEC has been instrumental in policy transfer and learning. It performed this role both by capacity-building work and by publishing its annual *Taking Stock* report, which makes information on emissions available to the public. Likewise, council resolutions in 1999 and 2000 called on all member states to have mandatory reporting systems in place and to report results to the public (see council resolutions 99-02 and 00-07). Resolution 00-07 sought to strengthen the compatibility and quality of reporting. The resolution declared that to be effective, there would be reporting on individual substances and by individual facilities on a regular basis, covering releases into all media (air, water, etc.), that the reporting would be standardized and available to the public, and that there would be opportunities for public comment and input. The CEC has provided outreach and training, technical assistance, seminars, and other activities designed to improve Mexico's ability to implement the PRTR program (Winfield 2003: 47).

In addition to these PRTR activities, there is a broader effort involving the Mexican government and the CEC to develop a chemicals inventory as part of the Sound Management of Chemicals initiative. Council Regulation 95-05 provided the authority to develop this inventory, which SEMARNAT is creating. The purpose is to make information available more widely among ministries and between member states; facilitate trade, information, and knowledge on the location and levels of hazardous substances in member states; harmonize standards; and facilitate adoption of other international agreements on chemical substances. The CEC is working with Mexican officials in both SEMARNAT and SALUD (the health ministry) on knowledge transfer and data classification and identification processes, including laboratory testing procedures. This is an effort to build quality assurance and improve methods and protocol in labs, especially in the areas of toxic pollutants and human health.

The CEC helps by facilitating meetings, administering funds, and organizing seminars, workshops, and training. It locates consultants on projects and follows up on performance indicators, as well as suggesting activities that need development. Within the chemical inventory program are two main activities: a technical report and a legal framework. To carry out the technical report, SEMARNAT and representatives from the Mexican Chamber of Chemical Companies visited the United States and Canada to review (with consultants and industry officials) how they manage their inventory systems. The Mexican Chamber is responsible for providing much of the information necessary to complete the report, but SEMARNAT also helps develop the report. The CEC remains the project manager, acting as coordinator and catalyst, leading, organizing, and managing the program. It also holds workshops on capacity building in this area.

A revised legal framework is also necessary to require firms to provide data, and in late 2008, the CEC was working with a SEMARNAT nominee to develop terms of reference and put out a call for Mexican legal advisors. The CEC's role was to provide funds and manage the contractor, as well as bring together other Mexican ministries (Garcia interview, 2008). Further capacity-building work is aimed at creating a national air emissions inventory to establish baseline data on air quality. The CEC hired contractors to work with SEMARNAT on this issue. Other training activities on data management are designed to upgrade Mexican capacity in terms of reporting data and to harmonize North American data management and reporting standards.

In 2011, the CEC reported on the legal requirements and processes in the three member states for transborder hazardous waste shipments (CEC 2011). It singled out the inefficiency of the paper-based information-collection system, inadequate data sharing, and administrative burdens to industry and government agencies, among other issues. It also created a project spanning 2011–12 worth more than $600,000 Canadian to improve law enforcement related to shipments of environmentally regulated materials (electronic wastes, ozone-depleting substances, small engines, and hazardous waste) and vulnerable wildlife. The purpose was to improve information collection and sharing among the member states and to improve common enforcement actions.

Evan Lloyd (Director of Programs at the Secretariat and the number two official), explained that the development of the PRTR registry "clearly would not have happened without NAFTA. There has been a raising of the bar in terms of environmental standards in Mexico" (interview, 2008; Garver, personal communication 2007). He also pointed to some shortcomings in the capacity-building process. The CEC sometimes feels that it does so much direct capacity building through training programs that it becomes capacity supply and wonders whether it has the desired effect (Lloyd interview, 2008). As yet, they have no method of measuring capacity-building results. A related concern (as discussed earlier) is that the method of providing training courses often has the perverse effect that newly trained officials leave shortly afterward to pursue other opportunities, having had their economic prospects improved by the training. Moreover, the CEC is concerned to encourage law clinics in order to create more domestic legal capacity.

Capacity Building in Mexican Environmental Civil Society

The North American Agreement on Environmental Cooperation created a new source of power for the Mexican environmental movement because civil society groups were given an opportunity to challenge enforcement inadequacies within Mexico through the trilateral institution. The Mexican government was now faced with scrutiny not only from the United States and Canada (as well as some of the side agreement agencies and other international organizations) but also from its own citizens. Scrutiny from independent civil society groups was a new experience and initially uncomfortable.

Until the 1990s, Mexico lacked a professional, technocratic, legally sophisticated group of NGOs who were able to articulate reasonable and convincing positions to government officials. Largely because of NAFTA, such groups became increasingly common, although they face challenges both because their leaders are increasingly called on to fill government posts and because they need to improve salaries in the face of recruitment competition from corporate law firms (Puentes interview, 2008). But the rise of professional environmental interests is one of the great success stories of the past two decades.

The story begins in the early 1980s, as the administration of President Miguel de la Madrid encouraged the formation of popular environmental groups. By the mid-1980s, with the slow strengthening of environmental regulation and the gradual realization that environmental stress had become serious, there were several dozen environmental NGOs in Mexico. In 1988, fifty groups signed a joint statement outlining Mexico's environmental problems, and by the middle of the 1990s, an estimated four hundred environmental groups were active throughout Mexico (Torres 2002: 217–18, n. 23, 211).

Environmental groups fell into three categories, most of which tended to be comprised of elites in Mexico City or the border region.[19] The first was researchers and academics who carried out technical and scientific studies and therefore contributed to measurement and awareness raising. Among these were INAINE, a group of scientists, and the Group of 100, a loose collection of intellectuals. The second category was conservation groups, which worked closely with the government on restoration and conservation projects. Conservation groups were stable, professional, and sophisticated fund-raisers but not engaged in the policy process (at least to the extent that it clashed with government priorities).

The third category was activist groups, which tended to take direct action. They were more confrontational and spontaneous, often amateurs with specific, local interests, according to Sergio Reyes, a scientist and former head of INE. Many groups never transcended the "one person's dream" syndrome, focusing on a single not-in-my-backyard issue, advocating radical reforms, and putting forward unrealistic proposals (Puentes interview, 2008; also Martin interview, 2008; Guerra interview, 2008; Mumme 1992). Their knowledge of public policy processes was poor.

Environmental interests played no part in bringing about the domestic legal and institutional changes in the early 1990s. The most influential civil society groups were the researchers and academics, but they produced scientific studies rather than lobbying for change (Reyes interview, 2008). The Salinas administration (1988–94) co-opted or silenced environmental groups through press censorship, job offers, and intimidation. Although formal access to government grew, in practice groups that were politicized or critical of the government were restricted in terms of influence and access. Thus, despite significant institutional reform, Salinas's government did not improve the ability of environmental groups to influence government policy (Mumme 1992: 137). In other words, although environmental groups had become more numerous and more active, they remained ineffective. This point is very important in determining the influence of NAFTA on civil society because it shows that despite institutional and legal reform, and despite growing numbers of NGOs, at the time of the negotiation of NAFTA, Mexican environmental NGOs remained weak vis-à-vis the state.

> Evidence from environmental leaders and government officials and data on government performance point toward an effort to contain and manage environmental criticism and dissent, channelling it through official consultative forums of a corporative nature by which environmental criticism can be filtered and softened. The structure of the new arenas of environmental participation is consistent with government-dominated modes of participation found in other policy sectors; it is designed to confine participation and criticism to system-sustaining modalities rather than encouraging the development of independent movements. (Mumme 1992: 137–38)

Yet both the number and the technical capacity of environmental NGOs were about to grow. According to the *Directorio Verde,* the number of environmental groups working on projects in Mexico increased from 216 in 1997 to 321 in 2008 (FMCN, various editions). The same source indicates that the number of private and public institutions in Mexico working to support environmental projects numbered twenty-nine in 1997 but by 2008 had increased to sixty-three. Of these groups, many are single issue, are restricted to a specific geographic area, or become inactive after a short period of time. Only a few are national and organized in such a way as to be effective. Two of the most significant are Pronatura and CEMDA. In the following paragraphs, I review them to provide a picture of their development and remit.

Pronatura was formed in 1981 with a meeting of several individuals who were concerned about the loss of bird habitat and the ineffective response of the authorities and civil society groups. By 2006, the organization had a total of seven hundred staff, consultants, directors, and others. Its strategies are (1) conservation and sustainable management of ecosystems, (2) environmental education and communication, (3) sustainable community development, (4) environmental policy and management, (5) information management and production, and (6) institutional development (Pronatura 2006). Pronatura personnel include biologists, oceanographers, and lawyers. The director (since 2006) is a lawyer. Pronatura also has specialists in environmental education. Former employees of Pronatura have moved to government, including Ernesto Enkerlin and Flavio Chazzaro, both in Conanp (the former became its director). Ex-employees have also gone to other NGOs, and Pronatura acts as a seedbed for talent and capacity building.

Pronatura is an insider group, working closely with the government. It is part of the National Forest Council (Conafor) and other government advisory bodies. In its 2007 annual report, Pronatura highlighted some of its capacity-building work, such as training and educating more than six thousand rural farm workers, civil society representatives, and local and state officials. It also educated nearly 15,000 children in its environmental programs (representing a 15 percent increase from the year before). The southern regional office in Chiapas works with Colorado State University, Conanp, and NGOs to offer an international course on management and conservation of natural protected areas. Money for this comes from the Nature Conservancy, among other groups. Along with governmental and other organizations, it has produced documentation on environmental needs and cooperated with businesses to design and operate Mexico's first carbon emissions neutralization program. More than a hundred NGOs have been trained by Pronatura on, for example, private conservation tools, water conservation, private and *ejidal* (communal) land management, and technologies such as geographic information systems (Salazar interview, 2008).

Pronatura's sources of funding include corporations such as Cemex, Bancomer, Grupo Modelo, and Televisa, as well as major U.S.-based foundations. In 2008, Pronatura undertook a project with Coca-Cola and the federal agencies Conanp and Conafor on restoration of 25,000 hectares of watershed. Thirty million trees were to be planted, with a budget of $12 million. The central Pronatura office was expanded to include regional offices in the 1990s. The Yucatan office was formed in 1990, after beginning its conservation work in the 1980s. Another office was opened in Chiapas in 1989, and the Veracruz office was established in 1991. In 2006, an office was created in Hermosillo, Sonora, bringing together regional offices in Sonora, Sinaloa, and Baja California that had operated separately since 1993. Finally, an office was established in 1998 in Monterrey. Institutional changes underway were intended to establish a more consistent and contractual relationship with the traditionally independent regional offices in order to professionalize them and ensure consistency in financial administration, media messages, and image.

The Mexican Center for Environmental Law (CEMDA) was formed in 1993 as a direct result of NAFTA (Alanís interview, 2005). It has twenty-four staff and receives 85–90 percent of its funding from U.S. foundations, with other funds coming from consulting, publications, courses, seminars, and training workshops. It is committed to participating in the governance of the NAAEC, and despite being much smaller than Pronatura, CEMDA is the principal NGO using litigation as a tool to bring about policy change (Puentes interview, 2008). Its director, Gustavo Alanís, has twice been a member of JPAC, and the organization has been party to groundbreaking complaints against the Mexican government before NAAEC institutions. Alanís believes NAAEC has been very important to the development of Mexican civil society. Mexican interests have fewer alternatives for satisfaction of their demands than U.S. or Canadian NGOs and therefore more to gain.

The organization is also involved in capacity-building work, giving training workshops and creating manuals on environmental law that explain legislation, rights, and responsibilities (for example, on forestry and water management for *ejidatarios* and local communities). They also create TV programs for adolescents and other materials covering Principle 10 issues to demystify the law and make it more accessible. Juan Carlos Carrillo, a CEMDA lawyer, explained that he gives talks on these issues in local communities and organizes environmental law training workshops in universities and technical academies (Carrillo interview, 2008). It collaborates with CEJA—the Center for Juridical and Environmental Studies—in an environmental law course at the National Autonomous University of Mexico.

Like Pronatura, CEMDA created regional offices in several locations throughout the country. A Cancun office was opened in 2001, with one lawyer. An assistant was hired in 2004. In 2006–2007, the office hired three more lawyers. A similar office was opened in the northwest city of La Paz in 2005, after four years of seeking funds. The director of the La Paz office, Pablo Uribe, started alone but in 2006 hired another lawyer and an assistant (who later also became a lawyer). In 2008, they added another assistant and another lawyer. It is supported by the Packard Foundation and the Sandler Family Foundation, from which it gets about 45 percent of its funds, as well as the Hewlett Foundation, the Marisla Foundation, the Mexican Fund for Nature Conservation, and the Loreto Bay Foundation. Coalition building with external foundations and international organizations helped build CEMDA, which does not receive support from the government except for targeted funding to pay for services, such as design of new regulations.

The links between CEMDA and external environmental organizations are part of a pattern in which European and North American foundations and NGOs have become increasingly involved in support of Mexican environmental NGOs. Much of this interaction was prompted by NAFTA. The World Wildlife Fund began to operate in Mexico in 1993. Along with other North American groups such as the Hewlett Foundation, it was pivotal in bringing foundation money and advice to Mexico. Outside conservation organizations and foundations tend not to do legal work or engage in the political process; instead, they do scientific research or buy land. However, CEMDA believes this is not enough and that more legal capacity is needed (Uribe interview, 2008).[20] At the time of the interview (October 2008), there were eight lawyers in the northwest area, including those in CEMDA's office. Community participation is slowly growing, NGOs are winning court cases, and requests for scientific data are resulting in higher quality information. Interest among students is growing, but the amount and quality of law school training in the northwest region remains poor. Likewise, judges need training in environmental law to improve the quality of environmental justice. Thus, despite positive signs (institutional avenues of public participation and growing legal capacity), the region also needs more training and a stronger network.

In terms of reviewing and challenging applications for development permits, Uribe explained that although public input has increased, 90 percent of public participation in Mexico is promoted by CEMDA, and individuals rarely use the processes available to them. Interested parties need to review the weekly public gazette of SEMARNAT to learn about proposed development projects and then prepare a letter requesting a public meeting. Very few actually request hearings to participate in environmental impact assessments. By late 2008, CEMDA La Paz had been involved in six public meetings and twenty-five public consultations. Public meetings are sessions with project developers, for explanation and feedback. At public meetings, SEMARNAT listens to developers' presentations and responses to questions from the public. Public consultations are an opportunity for the community to present concerns in the environmental impact assessment process. These meetings are important parts of the process of civil society input, and SEMARNAT responds to requests, but if no one asks for a public meeting, they do not conduct one.

NAFTA at the Border

In 1965, Mexico initiated a new policy known as the Border Industrialization Plan, allowing foreign firms to import raw materials and unfinished products for assembly and reexport. These so-called maquiladora plants were limited to a distance of twelve miles from the northern border, although restrictions were relaxed after 1972 (Husted and Logsdon, 1997). The policy proved very popular. The number of maquiladora plants and their workers grew from 102 plants and 36,943 employees in 1980 to 254 plants and 216,945 employees in March 1999 (GAO 2000). In the early 1980s, a time when employment declined in Mexico, employment in maquiladoras increased by 78 percent (Goldrich and Carruthers 1992: 106).

However, the explosion in development resulted in serious environmental stress in the border area: rapid population growth and industrialization put enormous pressure on existing infrastructure, especially water supply, sewage treatment, and hazardous and solid waste treatment (Hufbauer et al. 2000: 39; Husted and Logsdon, 1997; Hufbauer and Schott 2005). In 1980, the border population as a whole stood at roughly 4 million, but by 1997 it had increased to 10.5 million. In the border city of Ciudad Juarez, the population grew from little more than 260,000 in 1960 to about 1.1 million in 1999. By 2020, the border population was projected to double in size from its 1997 level (GAO 2000). Existing infrastructure was unable to cope. As late as 1996, only 88 percent of border households in Mexico had clean water, 69 percent were connected to sewers, and 34 percent were connected to wastewater treatment facilities.[21]

Domestic mechanisms for developing environmental infrastructure come mainly from Conagua, which provides funds for water supply and wastewater treatment, with matching funds from local and state authorities. The social development agency SEDESOL has generally provided the funding for solid waste projects (Lehman 2001: 6). Communities have the alternative of applying to the National Bank of Public Works and Services for loans, although many cannot afford its interest rates. Moreover, tax breaks for the maquiladoras have left border communities with few resources to pay for public projects. Environmental infrastructure development on the border is also hampered by lack of long-term stable communities (since many workers are temporary), high poverty levels, and the absence of foreign capital (Hufbauer et al. 2000; Hufbauer and Schott 2005). Local authorities are dependent on federal funding appropriations and have little opportunity to raise capital through local taxes or bonds.

Thus, the border region was a priority for both the United States and Mexico.[22] In addition to the NAAEC, two bilateral institutions were established, the Border Environmental Cooperation Commission (BECC) and the North American Development Bank (NADB). The role of the BECC is to provide technical assistance to border communities and to certify proposed projects for funding by the NADB. The BECC's initial priorities were in the areas of wastewater treatment, drinking water, and municipal solid waste projects. Projects seeking funding must meet environmental, health, technical, financial, community participation, and sustainable development criteria. The intent is to assist local communities in developing projects and undertaking environmental assessment, as well as build institutional capacity.[23]

Before submitting their proposals to the BECC for certification, project sponsors may call upon funding assistance programs to carry out preliminary engineering work, designs, planning studies, and environmental impact statements. Such assistance was initially limited to water and wastewater treatment projects, although since 2000, funding has been available for air quality and hazardous waste, too. Up to 2008, the BECC had provided $34.9 million in grants (some of this money coming from the EPA) to 147 communities through these programs (BECC & NADB 2008: 5). In addition to the funding, the BECC also provides advice and guidance on sustainable development plans, public participation, and coordination among the different projects and it works with EPA and SEMARNAT on long-term border plans.

The role of the NADB is to aid these projects by providing financial and managerial guidance, loans on its own account, help in structuring financial packages (including loans or grants from other sources), and guarantees to help secure outside financing. It also administers U.S. EPA grant funds (BECC & NADB 2008: 3). By mid-2008, the NADB had contracted loan funds of $238.6 million (BECC & NADB 2008: 9). The NADB also helps manage the EPA-funded Border Environment Infrastructure Fund (BEIF) for water and wastewater infrastructure and administers two newer funds providing grants for water conservation and solid waste projects. In addition, it provides technical assistance and training in conjunction with the BECC. As of mid-2008, the BECC had certified 138 projects, mainly in water and wastewater infrastructure. Of the 138, seventy-five were in the United States, and sixty-three were in Mexico. At the same point in time, the NADB had approved financing for 119 projects, with a total cost of $2.8 billion. More of these projects were located in the United States (sixty-four) than in Mexico (fifty-five), but the funding level was higher for Mexico ($1.8 billion versus $1 billion for the United States) (BECC & NADB 2008: 14).

The border plan was strengthened in 1996 with the so-called Border XXI program, with new working groups on environmental information resources, natural resources, and environmental health. The purposes of Border XXI were to promote public participation in environmental issues along the border, build local human capacity, and increase interagency cooperation to avoid duplication of effort and make the best use of resources (GAO 2000: 17). Border 2012, which replaced Border XXI in 2002, involves EPA and SEMARNAT, border states, tribes, and related federal agencies, and seeks to foster upward harmonization. It is informed by ten principles related to public health risks; local capacity, participation, and transparency; information; and tribal issues. Its goals are to reduce water, air, and land pollution; improve environmental health; provide emergency preparedness; and promote environmental stewardship.[24]

Despite institutional and financial achievements, NAFTA's border institutions were not a panacea. A GAO report in March 2000 outlined the daunting problems on both sides of the border. It identified a lack of sufficient hazardous waste facilities (only one existed in Mexico in 2000) and the failure to treat or return to origin much hazardous waste. Air pollution was a growing problem. Many communities lack safe drinking water or sewage treatment facilities, and in some locations, untreated sewage was finding its way into drinking water supplies that serve communities on both sides of the border.[25] Citing a study from 1999, the GAO estimated that $3.3 billion would be needed over ten years to bring water, wastewater, and solid waste infrastructure improvements to both sides of the border and that 77 percent of this figure should be directed toward wastewater treatment facilities (GAO 2000). However, this figure has been disputed. An independent report for the NADB in 2001 suggested that $3.1 billion would be needed over the following five years alone (Lehman 2001). Hufbauer and colleagues (2000) claimed the figure could be as much as $20 billion.

Whatever the funding level needed, Mexican communities found it hard to take advantage of the border programs. The NADB charged higher rates of interest to Mexican communities to cover for currency conversion costs and higher risk. In 1999, the rate of interest charged for a fifteen-year peso loan was between 25.5 and 27.1 percent (GAO 2000: 23). Local communities' access to capital at affordable rates was therefore limited. Further, although the BEIF made grants available to these communities, their use was restricted to water and wastewater projects. In 1998, the NADB and the Mexican government created a public company to act as an agent for the NADB in Mexico to channel funds to local communities. This initiative brought $3.69 million to local communities by September 1999, but it was far below their long-term needs (GAO 2000: 25).

Mexican responses to border growth and industrialization have also been retarded by lack of adequate urban planning (partly because of turnover among administrative staff) (Hufbauer et al. 2000: 39). Human capacity limitations mean local communities have limited ability to carry out infrastructure projects, undermining their ability to plan, implement, and maintain environmental infrastructure. One problem is that senior Mexican administrators leave office with changes in government every three years and take with them any experience gained during their tenure. According to the BECC, technical personnel such as utility directors stay in office on average less than two years (cited in GAO 2000: 21).

The BECC and NADB scope initially extended to one hundred kilometers on either side of the border in the areas of water, wastewater, and municipal solid waste, but both the geographical and program areas have been expanded. The eligible border area on the Mexican side was extended to three hundred kilometers, and in 1999, the Solid Waste Environmental Program was created in the NADB because one of the weaknesses of the border programs was the failure to provide assistance for solid waste projects. Thus, the NADB Board of Directors decided to create a program whereby $5 million of earnings on capital would be used as grants for the construction of solid waste disposal projects.

In 2000, the boards of directors of the BECC and NADB approved an extension beyond the traditional priority areas of water, wastewater, and municipal solid waste to include improvements in air quality, public transportation, clean energy, municipal planning, development, and water management (BECC & NADB 2008: 3). Also in 2000, the Value Lending Program was approved by the NADB board, providing lending at lower interest rates in water, wastewater, and municipal solid waste projects. As noted previously, the BEIF was established in 1997 with funds from the EPA to facilitate grant financing of Mexican border projects. In addition, the Utility Management Institute was created within the NADB, as part of its Institutional Development Cooperation Program, to train officials in financial administration and utilities planning. In 2002, the Water Conservation Investment Fund was created in the NADB. In the same year, the NADB established the Project Development

Program to assist local entities in planning their environmental infrastructure projects.

Building Capacity at the Border

In its 2000 report on the state of environmental management in Mexico, SEMARNAP argued that significant achievements had been brought about in the border region, due to the Border XXI agreement along with the NADB and BECC. The achievements included increases in drinking water availability, wastewater treatment, improvements in air quality, management of hazardous wastes, information exchange, and designation of firms as "Clean Industry" in voluntary cooperation with Profepa. Data indicate that from 1995 to 2005 the coverage of drinking water and wastewater treatment facilities on the Mexican side of the border increased, respectively, from 89 percent to 96 percent, and 63 percent to 88 percent (Balarezo and Ramírez 2008). Others were less sanguine, noting that despite the achievements, "the progress is in no way proportionate to the depth of the problem" (Hufbauer et al. 2000: 46; Hufbauer and Schott 2005).

From 1994 to 2000, the United States and Mexico together invested $3.1 billion in border environmental infrastructure projects. The largest amount came from the U.S. EPA ($1.2 billion), with roughly 20 percent coming from Mexico ($648 million) (GAO 2000). The International Boundary and Water Commission contributed resources, too. The constraints on local Mexican authorities' tax-raising powers, the poverty of these communities, the inability of most of them to afford commercial borrowing costs, and their lack of human capacity show how reliant they are on the border institutions for environmental improvements. Data from the GAO (2000) show that the NADB was responsible for roughly 21 percent of U.S. project costs and provided 50 percent of Mexican project costs (mainly through EPA grants, but a small portion through loans as well). In other words, Mexican projects were far more heavily dependent on NADB-administered funding. Without it, many projects would not have been pursued.

Commitment by the EPA to the BEIF made an enormous difference to project financing. Prior to BEIF funding, the NADB provided $4 million in loans (over the 1995–96 period). However, from 1997 to 2000, with the backing of BEIF grant funding (the NADB is unable under its charter to make grants from its own funds, as opposed to loans), the NADB made loans and grants totaling $270 million (Lehman 2001: 1). Institutional commitment is critical to the success of environmental infrastructure development measured in financial terms. However, technical assistance is also important. Without funding and technical assistance, border communities, especially in the poorer regions in Mexico, are unlikely to be able to afford environmental improvements. Border environmental institutions' favorable lending terms have enhanced the creditworthiness of borrowers. In addition, they have upgraded the technical abilities of border communities and improved human capital through the training program focusing on utility management, finance, administration, and organization.

Moreover, the decisions to expand the scope of the program beyond water and wastewater extended project development, too. Perhaps most important, while U.S. projects have turned to non-NADB sources, Mexican communities are less well placed to do so because their creditworthiness is lower, and virtually all BEIF projects in Mexico were partially funded by NADB loans. Mexican border environmental development was made easier by the border institutions; without capital from them on favorable terms, they would not have been able to afford infrastructure improvements. The border institutions were a means by which the Mexican government could secure international funding for infrastructure development (Gilbreath 2003).

Border institutions have also made an impact on human capacity building. Aside from meeting technical, economic, and financial viability criteria, projects must foster community participation. According to the BECC's head of Communications and Community Management, the process by which the rules and procedures of projects are defined and applied has been opened (Bravo 2008). Public participation is mandatory, and information is disseminated to communities. Consultation activities have brought together SEMARNAT, Conagua, EPA, the Boundary and Water Commission, NADB, state and municipal governments, and communities on both sides of the border, but especially on the Mexican side.[26]

In the planning stages, citizen committees are formed, and information is provided through public campaigns, media outlets, public meetings, and education (Bravo 2008: 43). At least two public meetings must be held in the consultation phase. Moreover, a plan needs to be developed specifying how community participation will continue in the operation and maintenance phases later. As of late 2008, 337 public meetings had been held in Mexico, 115 citizen committees had been established, and more than a thousand local organizations had received information regarding projects and certification (Bravo 2008: 45). The benefits include transparent planning procedures, better continuity, wider consensus, and more legitimacy. Social participation is a mechanism that fosters capacity.

Javier Cabrera, the head of BECC from 1997 to 2005, explained that Mexican local authorities eventually accepted the idea of citizen participation, although it took time. The initial strategy of Mexico was to limit the influence of the border environmental institutions ("to close as many doors as possible," in his words) when negotiating the mandates of the BECC and NADB (Cabrera interview, 2008). Mexico was unhappy with the requirement for public meetings and community participation and also with U.S. involvement in investment decisions. Mexican officials wanted funds to flow directly to Mexican communities with as little interference as possible. There were cultural differences between Mexicans and Americans inside the BECC. The rules of operation were modeled on U.S. organizations, but for Mexico the idea was simply to bring money and technological support to Mexico rather than be concerned with following established procedures. Mexican staff did things "Mexican style"—arriving late, leaving late, and making decisions without following procedures (Cabrera interview, 2008).

The bottom-up idea of determining community needs from communities themselves was anathema to Mexico's municipal and state authorities, and there was a great deal of conflict in the early years, as state governments clashed with the BECC over procedures. The same was true with Conagua, which did not want to hold public sessions on its projects at the border. Cabrera recalled an example in 2003, when Conagua rejected public participation on a water project. But the head of SEMARNAT supported the BECC and required Conagua to include public participation, despite strong resistance.

Mexico initially succeeded in limiting the influence of citizens. It required would-be participants in public meetings to request permission to attend. The local authority could then filter participants and control dissent in the planning stages, as they put together funding applications. However, filtering participation was impractical because the authority could not read all requests for participation. "With time the Mexican authorities saw that public participation wasn't dangerous, they could cope with the criticism" (Cabrera interview, 2008). Now the doors are open, anyone can participate, and there is much more interest in taking part in these meetings among Mexican citizens than among U.S. citizens. One of the important advantages of the work of BECC, SEMARNAT (2001: 104) also emphasized, was to channel the participation of local social groups, suggesting that the federal government had come to accept the institutionalization of this input before northern state and municipal authorities. In some Mexican cities, the institutionalization of citizen input served as a catalyst for wider citizen involvement in environmental issues (Kelly 2002). Environmental groups were given legitimacy.

Thus, while the BECC negotiated with state governments to take into account their priorities and programs, it also insisted that they comply with the public participation requirements. The United States was adamant that public participation be respected. Local authorities requesting BECC and NADB support were forced to create community committees. State governments wanted to screen members of these committees, but the BECC decided whether the community committee and its working plan were acceptable, and they rejected the idea of stuffing the membership of committees with political cronies. Cabrera explained the significance of this development: "Things could no longer be done in the traditional way, and it took them time to understand. This is the big contribution of BECC. We have taught local governments and communities that things could be better. And I think it is a lasting change." Projects have more coherence and continuity because the EPA (the source of much of the funding through the BEIF) insists on overall strategic plans rather than one-off projects. Communities were required to think strategically and develop long-term integrated programs. Continuity also came about through the public consultation process. Governments understood that because they were getting the support of the public, it had become more difficult to cancel projects with a change in government.

But despite improved planning, there are still problems. For example, although the NADB paid for the training of sanitation and utilities technical staff, changes in municipal and state government meant changes in managers, who then sacked the technical staff to appoint political allies. Without depoliticized career positions for technical staff, the training benefits are lost (Cabrera interview, 2008). Other problems interfere with the exercise of local powers over funding and planning in Mexican border communities. Asymmetries in education, income, and social status affect the processes of communication and awareness raising. Poor populations in urban centers who find themselves next to proposed treatment plants, for example, often feel isolated and harmed by the process of development. Likewise, the traditional work of garbage collectors and recyclers can be affected by the construction of municipal waste facilities. Better grassroots social mobilization, group leadership, and more institutionalization of public discussion would lead to wider participation (Bravo 2008).

Conclusion

Mexico is not an environmental miracle. It has serious problems and many needs, and there is little doubt that major challenges confront its environmental institutions. Although it is often believed that economic development leads to greater concern for and attention to the environment, these things do not happen automatically. Legislation and institutions need to be created. Interests need to be mobilized and resources targeted at problems. Communication needs to be fostered. Though much remains to be done, NAAEC and the border institutions have begun to encourage these changes in environmental governance.

The capacity-building programs discussed here—limited though they are—strengthen institutions, fund infrastructure, provide information, and give civil society a chance to participate in decision making. Technical capacity and professionalization have been built. The CEC and the border institutions provided resources for capacity building and institutional development, both in SEMARNAT and in other federal and border authorities. Programs incentivized or required public participation through JPAC and border consultative committees. These changes helped professionalize civil servants and also civil society. The expansion of SEMARNAT and other agencies drew in trained NGO officials, which further strengthened the agencies. And the independent fact-finding powers of the CEC often drew positive responses from SEMARNAT (see Table 2.3). Unlike the experience in labor agencies, SEMARNAT admitted problems and took it upon itself to search for solutions. And it did this publicly.

In certain cases, there is evidence that Mexico reacted strategically to safeguard rule of law only when forced to do so. It occasionally anticipated outcomes in the citizen submissions process and responded in ways that suggest it wanted to avoid negative publicity. The involvement of the CEC raised the profile of all the cases it investigated, and the ensuing media attention on processes (often carried out at local levels) that were incomplete and slanted toward development embarrassed the government. The government dislikes seeing issues in international news that portray it in a bad light, so the citizen submission and fact-finding processes are very effective threats (Carrillo interview, 2008).

In the Cozumel case, less than two months passed between the determination by the Secretariat that a factual record was warranted and the unanimous

TABLE 2.3 Government reaction to complaints about environmental enforcement

Case	Initial reaction to allegations	No. of months to approve factual record*	Admission of problem in enforcement?	Follow-up change to policy or practice
Cozumel	Rejected.	2	No.	Created natural reserve and limited development plans at the site.
Río Magdalena	Acknowledged wastewater treatment and discharge problems. Blamed budgetary shortfalls.	2	Yes. Accepted that the issue was a federal responsibility.	Within one year began construction (or completion) of wastewater treatment plants. Within two years began a bimonthly effluent testing program.
Aquanova	Indicated awareness of problems at site. Rejected some allegations.	15	Yes. Claimed it was using legal powers to address shortcomings.	N/A
Metales y Derivados	Accepted there were enforcement problems. Also indicated how it had made site visits, issued closure orders, and filed criminal charges.	2.5	Yes.	N/A
Molymex II	Rejected allegations saying that the company did comply with Environmental Impact requirement when it expanded in 1998.	5	No.	N/A
Tarahumara	Acknowledged problems. Indicated it had reported offenses to prosecutors. Indicated it had received *denuncias* from complainants.	8	Yes.	Meetings established between authorities and indigenous communities/NGOs beginning in 2000; created "participatory surveillance committees" for the region. Pay levels raised for inspectors.
ALCA-Iztapalapa II	Acknowledged problems, explained its enforcement actions against company, including site visits, closure orders, and criminal charges.	10	No. Complained that the CEC exceeded its scope in this case.	The case involved an individual company, which closed in 2005.

*In three further cases, the CEC requested the council to approve creation of a factual record (one in 2007 and two in 2008), but at the time of writing (December 2011), the council had not acted.

SOURCE: Data from CEC; table compiled by author.

decision by the council to approve its creation. It may be that Mexico miscalculated by thinking that the Secretariat would accept its arguments and that the factual record would exonerate it, which it did not. Mexico (along with the other member states) now drags its feet on decision making, allowing far more time to go by before deciding whether to accept creation of a factual record by the Secretariat. It also seeks to limit their scope. It has failed to respond to some requests for information from the CEC and complained that the CEC exceeded its authority. Numerous environmental groups, academics, and others (including employees of the CEC, in private) have complained that the member states are ignoring their obligation to decide on the establishment of a factual record in a timely fashion.

Yet Mexico is not alone in reacting strategically, and in fact, the strategic responses can have beneficial outcomes, too. The government raised the salaries of environmental investigators when a CEC factual record claimed that low salaries were part of the problem of poor enforcement. In the Cozumel case, the original development permit was withdrawn as a result of the case. Shortly after the factual record was made public, President Zedillo declared the reef a protected natural area (Garver 2001). Also bear in mind that priorities differ among federal, state, and municipal authorities. State and municipal governments face greater resource constraints and rely on alliances with the private sector for growth. Economic development often takes higher priority than environmental protection.

Moreover, SEMARNAT acknowledged that despite decentralization, sufficient mechanisms to resolve social conflict between different interests and between the three levels of government do not yet exist (SEMARNAP 2000: 326). The agencies lack funds for enforcement, and there is too much corruption. In addition, access to environmental justice is constrained in a number of ways, including the fact that courts lack judges with expertise in environmental cases. (For a wider discussion, see SEMARNAP 2000: 343–49.) The CEC Secretariat has found enormous frustration among citizens, for example, in its public meetings at Lake Chapala over wastewater treatment, industrial use of water, and enforcement. Citizens have become very outspoken (Solano interview, 2008). There is criticism of SEMARNAT's bureaucratization and at the loss of the NAAEC travel funds that were important to mobilizing Mexican NGOs in the early years. Much remains to be done between Profepa and PGR (the federal attorney general's office) to improve enforcement results. Specialization among inspectors needs to be increased, along with compensation: Profepa lawyers receive 7,000 pesos per month (less than $700) and are competing against high-paid lawyers.

At the same time, the government has clearly been sensitized to environmental complaints and the issues surrounding them. It has acknowledged shortcomings in enforcement and given explanations. In 2007, during a CEC investigation, SEMARNAT admitted that the Lerma-Chapala watershed, which includes Mexico's largest lake, had suffered serious environmental degradation in a number of respects. Economic growth in the region had put pressure on natural resources. Although much of the region remains agricultural, changes in land use resulted in loss of natural vegetation, fragmentation in forest cover, soil degradation, worsening water quality in Lake Chapala, and heavy metals in water bodies (SEMARNAT 2007: 99–100).

Despite frustrations with the process, the very first case (Cozumel) helped prepare the way for future petitions and demonstrated that the citizen submission process can work (Garver 2001). Initially breaking off relations with CEMDA because of its submission, SEMARNAT eventually came around to the idea that independent NGOs were helping to strengthen environmental governance. According to the director of CEMDA, Cozumel resulted in improvements in protection for coral reefs and in environmental law, but it also resulted in a better exercise of power in Mexico (Alanís interview, 2008). Cristina Martin of the UN Development Program stated that Cozumel began to introduce the concept of legal process into Mexican environmental politics (interview, 2008). Mateo Castillo, SEMARNAT's head of Social Participation and Transparency, cited the Cozumel case as important not just for sustainable tourism and ecological protection but also because it represented an important turning point for transparency, law enforcement, institutional infrastructure, and strengthening of rules (Castillo interview, 2008). It gave NGOs an instrument and forced the government to pay attention.

The central conclusions of this chapter are that despite problems, Mexican environmental governance *has* improved. Relatively independent NAAEC institutions generated pressures on the Mexican government to account for its practices. Unlike the labor institutions, in which member states investigate each other, NAAEC is an independent organization staffed in part by Mexicans themselves, with responsibility for investigating complaints. Moreover, agenda-setting capabilities, funding programs, and other capacity-building activities kept Mexican bureaucrats and NGOs committed to the NAAEC and learning from it. Legal proficiency grew among Mexican NGOs through their experience in the NAAEC and through interaction with foreign foundations. Nongovernmental organization personnel have moved into leadership positions within federal environmental agencies, and officials have also moved between federal agencies and the CEC Secretariat. Rule of law and public participation improved as a result. Targeted programs built capacity within the environmental agencies by providing funding for information gathering, analysis, training, and participation. Likewise, despite weak institutions and low levels of resources, the border region improved in terms of infrastructure development and public participation. Attitudes evolved, and expertise has grown. The contribution of the NAAEC to capacity building and normative change is underacknowledged. In the final chapter, I return to this topic to examine the evidence of normative change. First, I look at the evolution of labor politics.

3 Mordida Politics

Governing Mexico's Workplace

MEXICAN LABOR POLITICS—IN SHARP CONTRAST WITH ITS ENVI-
ronmental counterpart—is a deeply murky world of institutionalized conflict of interest and inappropriate political influence peddling. Unlike environmental politics, with its energetic reform process, labor institutions
are hardened by years of rent seeking. Reforms are piecemeal, grudging, and
reactive. Attitudes remain unbending among large segments of labor bureaucrats and co-opted confederations. Changes to governance have been retarded
by the weakness of NAFTA's labor oversight regime, by the lack of professionalism among many civil servants and civil society groups, and by the imper-
viousness of the labor agencies. Yet surprisingly—at the margins—there have
been some NAFTA-inspired capacity building, new forms of public participation, and new policies designed to improve workers' rights.

Labor politics has a long, stable history. Its foundations can be traced to
Article 123 of the Constitution and a subsequent 1931 federal labor law, which
was amended substantially in 1970 but not significantly since then. Mexico is
a signatory to international labor accords, and many workers are represented
by trade unions. However, labor law often goes unobserved. Although there is
a legal guarantee of workers' rights, in practice, labor politics is a delicate balance between employers, who want to control costs; the state, which wants to
attract investment; and the leaders of traditional unions, who purport to represent workers but who help to maintain the delicate balance (and are hand-
somely rewarded for doing so).

This "corporatist" system was institutionalized during the presidency of Lázaro Cárdenas (1934–1940). Powerful trade union confederations became affiliated with the PRI, the main political party, and supported the party by mobilizing union members to vote. Party candidates were recruited through the unions. These "official" unions endorsed government policy, bringing "legitimacy" to policy making and stifling dissent. Union leaders enforced worker peace in exchange for consistent wage increases above inflation and guarantees of a specific number of jobs regardless of the demand for labor. These leaders were granted public offices, concessions, and other privileges. Import substitution industrialization protected domestic industry through high tariffs, import permits, and exchange controls. Governments maintained control over unions by granting or withholding official recognition (depending on the friendliness of the unions) and by controlling who sat on the union boards. They also influenced firms by encouraging or suppressing worker protests and other direct action, depending on the government's aims and whether the company in question was supportive of the government (de Buen Unna 2002: 410ff.).

The principal confederation benefiting from this *triángulo de hierro* (or Mexican-style iron triangle) was the Mexican Workers Confederation (CTM). The CTM was founded in 1936, with roots going back to earlier confederations such as the General Confederation of Workers and Peasants of Mexico and the Mexican Regional Workers Confederation. Rank-and-file members of CTM-affiliated unions were also members of PRI and, of course, voted for PRI candidates. Although some important unions, such as railway employees, telephone operators, and electrical workers, remained outside the CTM umbrella, they still remained connected to the PRI and thus were part of the system perpetuating the power of the PRI and the union bosses. The CTM remains by far the most important of the major confederations, and most government-connected unions are affiliated with it.[1] Collectively, they became known as *charro* unions.[2] Within the unions, members are required to elect their leaders through open ballots in which their votes are recorded. Meanwhile, the leaders hide their activity (including kickbacks and special favors). Cults of personality are common, and it is not unusual for unions to be led by octogenarians who have held the same position for decades and accrued great wealth in the process.[3] Little wonder that they are described as "despotic," a "cancer," and a "mafia" by those most closely involved.[4]

Mexican unionism is totally corrupt. Huge amounts of money flow into union leaders' pockets from sweetheart alliances with owners and employers at the

> expense of workers' interests; from underground deals to get contracts and concessions from government agencies; from the sale of jobs in governmental institutions; from participation in corrupt practices involving public officials; and more generally, from threats, blackmail, and illegal pressure placed on employers. In addition to all this, union fiscal immunity has allowed them to charge many expenses, real or fictional, to the national treasury, generating a huge tax-free income for them. (de Buen Unna, 2002: 412)

Traditional *charro* unions are more prevalent in the state sector and in large firms. But they stifle productivity growth and innovation, and their inflexibility does not suit smaller companies or inward investors. Thus, many of the latter have entered into contracts with "ghost unions" that offer firms a protection contract whose sole purpose is to allow companies to signal that their workforce is unionized. Ghost union leaders (often nothing more than racketeers) are paid by the firms, not the workers. Their aim is to keep the labor peace and keep other unions at bay, rather than benefit or protect employees (Bouzas 2006: 115). Protection contracts are common in foreign-owned enterprises, including maquiladoras, and in small and medium-size companies (Bouzas 2006: 117).

Whether of the *charro* or ghost variety, the majority of unions fail to respond to workers' demands, instead operating as "the property of their leaders" (Alcalde 2006: 162). Despite the fact that workers have the legal right to choose which union represents them, in practice they are marginalized, do not have a say in electing the leadership, have no access to the accounts or management of the union, and often have no idea that they are even represented. Article 373 of the Federal Labor Law requires unions to provide a "complete and detailed account of the administration of the union," such as biannual reports on management and finances, but there are no sanctions for failure to report, and only in exceptional cases is there compliance (Giménez Cacho 2007: 34; Alcalde 2006: 169). Most unions are highly resistant to opening accounts, showing financial records, allowing money flows to be traced, or demonstrating what their activities are and how union subscriptions are used. Accountability occurs only in the sense that unions deposit copies of their collective contracts with the relevant authorities, indicating their memberships, boards of directors, and bylaws.

Corrupt racketeers have succeeded in registering paper unions and gaining legal standing, through which they have constructed semipermanent monopolies. The registry process confers on them a property right they use to sell labor, without the reciprocal duty of safeguarding workers' rights. They are often connected to local labor authorities through political, economic, or family links, so that "their impunity is guaranteed from the start" (Bensusán 2007: 24). Along with business organizations, lawyers, and others, they have been able to veto reforms that would open and democratize the system (Bensusán 2007: 13). The federalization of labor law from 1931 institutionalized this system: controls over union registry, exclusion clauses, and arranged contracts between unions, businesses, and political leaders.[5] Labor civil servants share the culture of authority over labor administration: union registration is supposed to be a simple administrative act, rather than a process in which unions prove their loyalty to politicians or governments. Instead, the authorities grant workers the right to organize, as though registry was a scarce resource, and unions have been denied registration for not supporting government policy.

The key institutional components of this system are the federal Secretariat of Labor and Social Provision (STPS), established in 1941, and the federal and local Conciliation and Arbitration Boards (CABs). The role of CABs was codified by the federal labor law in 1931, although they were recognized by the courts in 1924 and had operated in several states even earlier. At the state level, the CABs control union registration and also serve as tribunals, resolving disputes between workers and employers (including decisions over which union represents the workers in a given workplace). At the federal level, unions are registered with the STPS, but disputes are resolved in the federal CABs. (Unions representing workers in certain sectors are registered at the federal level, before the STPS. All others are registered in the state-level CABs.) The *toma de nota,* or union registry, happens when the union hands over to federal or state authorities certain documents: (1) a certified copy of the minutes of the general meeting at which the union was established, (2) a list of the names of the members and their employers, (3) a certified copy of the bylaws, and (4) a certified copy of the minutes of the meeting at which the board of directors was elected.

The various CABs operate quite differently, including their connections to or autonomy from the corresponding government (see Bensusán 2006b: 367ff.). They apply different criteria to dispute resolution. Decisions can be highly politicized, corrupt, arbitrary, and unprofessional. In fact, their inconsistency and lack of professionalism became an important issue in public reports on their performance. Information on the operation of CABs is difficult to get and often contradictory. Yet they are central to the union registration and dispute resolution process because local CABs deal with 74 percent of labor disputes; the Mexico City CAB alone deals with 20 percent of all local disputes. Details of collective contracts—including the identity of union leaders, their work addresses, and the rules by which the union is constituted— were guarded by state and federal authorities until a 2007 policy change at the federal level, the main argument for this secrecy being that the documents contained private information that should not be made public (Giménez Cacho 2007; Alcalde 2006: 168). Even when workers sought information about their own unions, the authorities still denied them, making it difficult for workers to know whether they were in fact represented. In some cases, the STPS decided that handing over information would be prejudicial to the internal functioning of the union.

Despite the sorry state of labor administration, independent unions and labor rights organizations *have* emerged, and they *do* seek to promote workers' rights. But to do so, they must first be registered as a union and then win a representation vote (called a *recuento*) in the relevant CAB. Both steps present formidable obstacles. First, CABs often delay or reject registration by new unions on spurious grounds. Only 27 percent of new union registrations are accepted at the federal level, and 12 percent at the local level (Bensusán 2006b: 377). The reason for such difficulty in registering a new union is apparent from the structure of the CABs. State CABs are comprised of three representatives: one from the state labor ministry, one from business, and one from labor. They have the power to accept or reject applications for union registration.

The most important obstacle is that the labor representative on the CAB invariably comes from one of the major co-opted union confederations, and agreeing to the registration of a *new* union is the first step in the *old* union being replaced: new unions register in order to fight for representation in companies in which workers are struggling for better terms. In other words, if the labor representative on the CAB accepts the registry of a new union, that new union is likely to try to oust the labor representative's own union (or an affiliated union) from the workplace. This blatant conflict of interest is exacerbated by the fact that many state governors do not want to register what they perceive to be militant unions because they fear the consequences on investment. The same is true for businesses, which sometimes threaten plant closure or fire dissident workers who organize better representation. Meanwhile, unions attempting to register at the federal level in STPS are routinely denied if they have not already been co-opted.

But the circus does not end there. Even if independent unions *do* manage to register, they must still win the *recuento* vote within the workplace to gain the right to represent the workforce, and the vote is often rife with intimidation. For many years, workers were required to vote openly for union registration, and CABs permitted hired thugs to police the procedure, threatening those who opted for independent unions.[6] Thus, although the law established CABs as places where workers represented themselves, in fact the co-opted unions were represented there (Robles et al. 2009: 20). Independent unions were excluded, often violently. As we shall see later, independent unions and NGOs have used the complaint procedure in the NAALC to take these legal violations to an international tribunal. Nonetheless, they continue to face pressures from corrupt rent-seeking unions and government officials—as well as employers— who will not recognize them for fear of their militancy.

Evidence of violations of rule of law is so overwhelming that a report published by IFAI (the government transparency and information agency) noted the unanimous view that there was a "severe deformation" of labor laws and norms (Giménez Cacho 2007: 23). Relying on widely respected lawyers and academic analysts, the report stated that laws have been broken with impunity by both employers and state agencies, who apply them in a discretionary manner to their advantage. The CABs are corrupt, slow, and ignorant (Giménez Cacho 2007: 22). Where private economic interests are important to the government, legal justice attends to their interests rather than upholding the law, and leaders of government-connected unions treat the unions as their personal businesses. The report noted that injustice is most noteworthy in the areas of legal recognition of unions and exercise of their collective rights.

> The CABs are rife with corruption, mainly in the areas of union registration, strike procedures, and titularity judgments regarding collective contracts, all of which are generally resolved contrary to the legitimate interests of workers, because to respect them would affect the government's corporatist control, as well as the interests of corporatist unions and companies involved in protection contracts. (Giménez Cacho 2007: 23)[7]

Citing a labor researcher, Héctor Barba, the author claimed that more than 90 percent of the collective contracts throughout the country (estimated at more than 700,000) are "legal fronts" (Giménez Cacho 2007: 42). It is impossible to know the number for certain, as the majority are deposited with local CABs and their existence is considered secret, but in the Mexico City CAB (where research has been done), only 7,000 of the 105,000 contracts on deposit are not protection contracts.

Graciela Bensusán's exhaustive study of the institutional and legal design of labor politics also revealed a litany of abuses of power at both federal and local levels, arbitrary and unprofessional decisions, clear favoritism and corruption (Bensusán 2006b: 330ff.). The system of labor justice is widely considered to be characterized by "discretion and corruption," a conclusion shared by company lawyers, unions, and even the UN High Commission on Human Rights (Bensusán 2006b: 365). A great deal of the power of the CTM comes from its role within the CABs, and there has been no attempt to resolve the conflict of interest in which the CTM is both interested party and judge. Governors perpetuate the problems because they appoint state CAB representatives who favor business interests and corporatist unions. Business provides investment, and unions provide political support. The lack of impartiality is striking.

Even those defending the system do so by pointing out its greater good, not by denying the rampant corruption. One of Mexico's most influential historians acknowledged the problems but claimed that the CTM brought stability and growth, helping Mexico avoid the cycles of anarchy and dictatorship that gripped much of Latin America in the twentieth century (Krauze 2000: 7). What others describe as "corrupted class conscience" on the part of co-opted union leaders, he interprets as an attitude of pragmatism geared toward material improvement in workers' lives (Krauze 2000: 9). The late Fidel Velázquez—powerful leader of the CTM for many years—acknowledged that corruption had affected the CTM but said that it was less of a problem in the CTM than in society more generally (Krauze 2000: 118).

In short, whatever its glaring shortcomings, the system is seen as a solution to the problem of labor governability, given globalization and external competitive challenges. A strict application of the law would give too much power to labor, and therefore it is applied selectively (and in so doing, political opposition is managed). Controlling labor facilitates inward investment, protects against "fraudulent strikes," and offers employers a way to shield themselves against competing and extortionate union claims. For investors, strict application of the law would be a "nightmare that undermines competitiveness" (Diaz 2004: 555). Indeed, legal requirements on employers in the formal sector, such as vacations, pensions, and other costs, add up to 50 percent to the cost of labor. Strikes that do take place often continue for long periods because of the inability to impose arbitration. Strikes are relatively easy to call but hard to end, so companies go to great lengths to avoid them. This tricky balancing act has proved easier to manage than wholesale reform (Bensusán 2007: 24).

Thus, although the labor regime embodies high legal standards for workers (guarantees against unilateral modification of working conditions, compensation for dismissal, and other rights), it was designed with "important doses of ambiguity" that give the authorities wide discretion to apply the law and intervene in disputes (Bensusán 2006b: 315). The 1931 reform sought to strengthen the capacity of the state to intervene in labor matters but also limit adverse effects on employers by guarding against claims by labor that would destroy companies. Strong legal protection of workers was offset both by lower wages and by weaker enforcement (Bensusán 2006b: 321). Since then, it has proved extremely difficult to reform the system.

Cracks started to appear in the 1980s. Following the 1982 debt crisis, Mexico began to make a transition from a protected economy with an import-substitution model of development and a strong state role to an economy more open to external influence and to the market. Under Carlos Salinas, who was president from 1988 to 1994, a group of technocrats and economists reformed economic policy, opening Mexico to international competition, selling or closing many state-owned businesses, reducing inflation and the budget deficit, curbing subsidies and social expenditures, and orienting manufacturing toward external markets. The impact of these changes on labor was significant. The level of unionization declined, workers' purchasing power dropped, many collective agreements were altered or terminated, and the voice of labor in government and in the Congress was diminished (Gutiérrez 2006: 36–37). Union density between 1984 and 2000 declined from 30 percent to 20 percent (Bensusán 2006a: 266). Labor insurgency grew as workers became dissatisfied with poor economic performance, the closed labor union system, and the evident corruption of their union bosses. Independent unions were formed and sought to displace the co-opted unions.

Meanwhile, greater party competition from 1988 resulted in more openness for critics of the corporatist system, as new legislators entered Congress. Many were labor activists, linked not to the PRI but to other parties. Traditional unions with formal links to the PRI weakened, and individuals with their own agendas were strengthened. The 1990s saw further economic restructuring, growing power in opposition parties (especially the PAN and

PRD), and external pressures such as NAFTA. The PRI lost control of Congress in 1997. In 2000, Vicente Fox broke the stranglehold of the PRI and became the first non-PRI president in seventy years. He campaigned on a platform of anticorporatism: because of its strong connections to business, the Fox administration was loath to see an expansion of union power (Bensusán 2006a: 259). Yet his government failed to enact labor reform in part because state governors—PRI and others—feared loss of inward investment. Following the election, the CTM and other co-opted confederations sought to build ties to the PAN party, despite having fought against Fox's campaign and, in some cases, having threatened strike action if he was elected. The corruption and vice of union leaderships remained.

The corporatist system of industrial relations proved enduring. It was not swept aside with the new PAN government, which accepted the system under which labor peace was guaranteed in exchange for state protection of union monopolies (de la Garza 2006: 326). Protection contracts continued, not because the unions delivered votes, but rather because they helped attract inward investment. Even as PRI power declined, the system continued to privilege official unions because companies believed that this system was the most efficient way to safeguard their interests (Gutiérrez 2003: 112). At the same time, the government had less ability to provide special favors to government-friendly unions. It lacked the ability to repress worker discontent that it had enjoyed in previous decades.

NAFTA and Labor Governance

Clearly, the rule of law was weak, and the system of labor politics needed reform. The question was whether NAALC would help Mexico achieve it. The NAALC provided opportunities to bring complaints and collaborate with like-minded organizations in other member states. But unlike the environmental sector, labor politics was more established at the outset of NAFTA. There was a federal cabinet-level ministry for labor, as well as well-established official labor unions, most of which favored NAFTA but opposed any external influence in labor politics. Thus, although Mexico faced pressures from NAALC to enforce its own laws, it was resistant to interference. The ministry and the CABs were less porous than the environmental agencies, they were not going through a process of expansion, and powerful domestic labor interests were opposed to modernization. Labor ministry politics conformed to a model of path dependence: historical design and practice constrained adaptation so that new pressures from outside were not easily translated into new designs or practices within the institution (Thelen and Steinmo 1992). Change was blocked by powerful interests that had grown around existing structures and practices, and norms of sovereignty and development were used to justify defense of the status quo.

To read most accounts of the NAALC, one would judge it an obvious failure. Disillusionment over its effectiveness in addressing workplace compliance problems is widespread. The NAALC is certainly a weak institution, reflecting deep opposition in Mexico and the United States to supranational labor authority. Preserving national sovereignty was paramount. For most observers, the issue boiled down to a zero-sum competition for jobs. The term most frequently associated with NAALC seems to be *toothless,* used repeatedly in interviews, academic analyses, and NGO reports. It has failed to bring about meaningful change in Mexican labor politics, it has not safeguarded the rights of workers, it has not changed the byzantine ways of the CABs, and it has not rectified injustices visited on hapless Mexican workers.

Most of this criticism is true. Nevertheless, it is also unfair: NAALC was never intended to come to the rescue of individual workers or to reform Mexican labor legislation. Early complaints show that this was a common misunderstanding.[8] Instead, NAALC was first and foremost an instrument through which the member states would be required to enforce their own law. In this sense, it was the same as NAAEC, its environmental counterpart. The rule of law logic meant that companies could not improve their competitive positions by evading the requirements of Mexican labor law. The beneficiaries, in theory, were not simply Mexican workers but also workers *outside* Mexico, in the United States and Canada, who would not lose their jobs due to unfair competition resulting from lax enforcement.

It is true that NAALC provides weaker enforcement oversight than NAAEC. In addition, adjustment has been hampered by the opposition of the main Mexican trade union confederations to modernizing labor practices. However, the very fact that Mexico agreed to this weak scrutiny mechanism is itself significant. It (grudgingly) acceded to periodic inspections of its labor regime by the other member states. Moreover, despite the apparent obstacles, and much to the surprise of those who have looked closely, Mexico *has* benefited from the labor accord. It has taken advantage of expertise from the United States and Canada to improve information systems and strengthen capabilities in occupational safety and health, among others. Capacity building, though limited, has been most apparent in technical, nonpolitical areas. Independent unions, who are a thorn in the side of the corrupt CABs and who brought the cases to NAALC, have forged links with unions and NGOs in other member states. These links, plus strategic responses by Mexican agencies to NAALC-origin pressures, have strengthened independent unions.

To be sure, these changes are relatively small, and the responses of the federal and state agencies to investigations have been strategic and instrumental. They have responded only when the spotlight is shining on them, and not always then. In some cases, the spotlight came from another authority within Mexico, such as the transparency agency IFAI or the federal courts (often emboldened by NAALC decisions). However, in contrast to the environmental sector, the evidence of normative socialization—a process of acceptance of rule of law norms—is virtually nonexistent. In the sections that follow, I briefly describe the NAALC institutions before reviewing the effects of cases brought before it and describing the capacity-building changes wrought by this process.

NAFTA's Trilateral Labor Institutions

The NAALC enumerated several objectives, including improvement of working conditions and living standards, promoting key labor principles, encouraging cooperation on innovation and productivity, promoting research and exchange of information, promoting cooperation on related activities, and encouraging compliance with national labor law as well as transparency in its administration. Eleven labor principles were specifically enumerated in the agreement.[9] Article 3 requires governments to "promote compliance with and effectively enforce its labor law through appropriate government action." They must also endeavor to improve labor law, give "due consideration" to requests for investigations of violations, and ensure that workers have access to justice domestically, that enforcement is fair and transparent, and that there is recourse to appeal as well as remedies; that laws, regulations, and other instruments are publicly available; and that information is disseminated to the public. These requirements were to become the focus of many of the investigations under NAALC. The agreement also calls for cooperative activities in areas such as occupational safety and health, child labor, migrant workers, gender equality, and others (see Article 11 for a full list). These are to be carried out through seminars, training sessions, conferences, joint research projects, technical assistance, and other means, though section 3 of Article 11 calls for "due regard" to be given to national differences in economic, social, cultural, and legislative areas.

The NAALC created a Commission for Labor Cooperation (CLC), with a slightly different organizational structure than CEC. In addition to a council, made up of the heads of the labor ministries in each government, and the Secretariat, the National Administrative Office (NAO) was established in the labor ministry of each country. No counterpart to the environmental JPAC was included, in which civil society was made part of the institution. Unlike the NAAEC, a complaint (known formally as a "public communication") must go to an NAO in a different member state from where the violation allegedly occurred, and not to the CLC Secretariat. The NAO receiving the complaint may then conduct an investigation of the case if it so decides. The Secretariat plays no role in investigations.

There are three stages in the dispute process. In the first stage, the NAO receiving the communication undertakes an information-gathering and consultation exercise and reports its findings. It can recommend ministerial consultations if it so chooses. If ministerial consultations do not resolve the dispute, an evaluation committee of experts is formed, which also reports to the council, though its remit is confined; it may not consider issues related to the rights to collective bargaining, freedom of association and organization, or strike action. The final stage is establishment of an independent arbitral panel of five members. The arbitral panel can consider only three of the eleven labor principles: labor protection for children and young persons, minimum employment standards, and prevention of occupational injuries and illnesses. The agreement provides for the possibility of monetary sanctions and, ultimately, suspension of trade privileges, but only in limited cases. The member states have never come close to such a decision.

The differences between the secretariats of the CLC and the CEC reflect the higher political sensitivity associated with labor issues and the deep reluctance to permit any independent authority to emerge. The CEC Secretariat has the authority to collect facts and information and to issue factual records and reports, but the CLC Secretariat does not have these powers. Public communications are channeled through national governments. The CLC Secretariat is not part of the public communication process. It must communicate with NAOs to get information, and communications tend to be on routine administrative issues only. The Secretariat plays a limited role in forming relationships with the public and NGOs, and there is no direct official contact.[10] Staff must get permission for meetings and approval for their research. In fact, privately, Secretariat staff complain about their lack of independence and the political nature of their leadership. Speaking during the Bush administration, they stressed that the Secretariat needed a leader with a technocratic knowledge of issues, sensitivity to problems, willingness to be more active, and good contacts in the three countries.

The level of funding for the CLC was always lower than for the CEC, but funding is only one of the many signs of weak commitment to labor issues at the trilateral level.[11] Until its closure in mid-2010, the staff working for the CLC included an executive director, a director of administration and cooperative consultation, an executive assistant, a financial officer, a research director (vacant in early 2010), a research specialist, and a cooperative activities specialist. The only other posts were three temporary positions. With only six permanent staff, there were obvious limits to its ability to contribute to capacity building.[12]

The closure of the office was undertaken to allow the NAOs to look for ways "to improve the implementation" of NAALC, according to the Web site. Its main contribution has been its research in three main areas: labor law, industrial relations, and labor economics. It published biannual reports, trends, employment statistics, and other information and followed twenty general labor market indicators. It also occasionally published studies, for example, on women or migration. Its labor law research included a series on cooperative labor law, employment discrimination, union rights, the right to strike, and migrant workers. This work is descriptive only and does not analyze enforcement issues.

Review of NAALC Cases Against Mexico

By 2011, a total of thirty-seven public communications had been made against the three member states, twenty-five of them against Mexico (see Table 3.1).[13] However, their impact on Mexico was limited. Although the investigations revealed some illegal or questionable practices, pressure was limited to ministerial consultations, exposure in the press, and best practice seminars. In some cases, Mexico refused to permit information to be gathered, or the investigating country (usually the United States) yielded to political pressure to

TABLE 3.1 Labor public communications to United States and Canada on Mexican practices

Case	NAO	Accepted?	Allegations	Action
940001 & 940002	USA	April 15, 1994	Violations of freedom of association and right to organize.	U.S. NAO held public hearings. Issued report. NAOs held trinational workshops on freedom of association and right to organize.
940003	USA	October 13, 1994	Violations of freedom of association and right to organize.	U.S. NAO held public hearings. Issued report. U.S. and Mexican ministerial consultations, 3 public seminars on union registration and certification, study by Mexican authorities regarding union registration, meetings between Mexican authorities and complainants.
940004	USA	November 4, 1994	Violations of freedom of association and right to organize.	Withdrawn by complainants.
9601	USA	July 29, 1996	Representation of federal employees not guaranteed.	U.S. NAO held public hearing, commissioned studies on Mexican labor law enforcement in federal government, released report. Seminar held on labor laws in 3 member states.
9602	USA	December 10, 1996	Violations of freedom of association.	U.S. NAO held public hearing, but communication withdrawn after the union was registered and other actions were taken by the firm in question.
9701	USA	July 14, 1997	Employment discrimination: pregnancy testing of workers.	U.S. NAO held public hearing, issued report, held ministerial consultations. Seminars and conference held to publicize rights of women.
9702	USA	November 17, 1997	Violations of freedom of association, occupational safety and health, minimum employment standards.	U.S. NAO held public hearing, issued report, held ministerial consultations. Seminar held to promote principles of freedom of association and right to collective bargaining. Mexican government committed to promote registry of collective agreements and information, secret ballots, etc. Trilateral public seminar on labor boards.

TABLE 3.1 (*continued*)

Case	NAO	Accepted?	Allegations	Action
9703	USA (also filed in Canada as CAN 98-1)	January 30, 1998	Violations of freedom of association, right to organize, bargain collectively, occupational safety and health	U.S. NAO held public hearing, issued report, held ministerial consultations. Seminar held to promote principles of freedom of association and right to collective bargaining, in conjunction with case 9702.
9801	USA	No	Failure to enforce right to strike.	U.S. NAO held public hearing, issued report, held ministerial consultations.
9802	USA	No	Child labor practices on Mexican farms	
9901	USA	January 7, 2000	Violations of freedom of association, right to organize, bargain collectively, minimum labor standards	U.S. NAO held public hearing, issued report. Bilateral working group created on occupational safety and health issues. Public seminar and information exchange on differences in labor rights, union types.
2000-01	USA	September 1, 2000	Failure to enforce occupational safety and health and injury compensation laws	U.S. NAO held public hearing, issued report, held ministerial consultations. Bilateral working group created on occupational safety and health issues (to consider case 9901 as well). Technical cooperation projects identified.
2001-01	USA	No	Mexico failed to fulfill commitment in prior ministerial agreement (May 2000) to promote the use of eligible voter lists, secret ballots, and neutral voting places in union elections, as well as other NAALC commitments	
2003-01	USA (also filed in Canada)	February 5, 2004	Violations of freedom of association, right to organize, bargain collectively, minimum labor standards, and occupational safety and health standards	Web site contains no further details.
2004-01	USA	Withdrawn	Violations of minimum employment and occupational safety and health standards	

(*continued*)

TABLE 3.1 *(continued)*

Case	NAO	Accepted?	Allegations	Action
2005-01	Can	No	Violations of freedom of association, right to organize, bargain collectively	
2005-01	USA	No	Proposed labor reforms would weaken existing legal protections	
2005-02	USA	No	Nonenforcement of freedom of association, right to organize, bargain collectively	
2005-03	USA	January 6, 2006	Nonenforcement of freedom of association, right to organize, bargain collectively, the right to strike, prohibition of forced labor, labor protections for children and young persons, minimum employment standards, elimination of employment discrimination, prevention of occupational injuries and illnesses, and compensation in cases of occupational injuries and illnesses, and under Article 5 with respect to fair, equitable, and transparent labor tribunal proceedings	Report issued, ministerial consultations recommended.
2006-01	USA	No	Denial of freedom of association rights and proper access to appropriate labor tribunals	
2010-01	USA	Pending	Denial of freedom of association and collective bargaining rights	

SOURCE: Compiled by author from NAALC and Department of Labor Web sites. See http://new.naalc.org/index.cfm?page=229; see also www.dol.gov/ILAB/programs/nao/status.htm#iia1.

reject or downplay the investigation. In contrast to the NAAEC, there was no facility for a public report to be made by an independent trilateral agency. In fact, Mexico complained bitterly about U.S. incursions into its sovereignty. Unlike SEMARNAT, which owned up to enforcement weaknesses and often made immediate efforts to rectify problems, STPS consistently denied problems.

For their part, workers felt abandoned when the Bush administration sharply reduced the number of investigations, and they stopped bringing complaints. Follow-up reports by the U.S. NAO often revealed that consultations, workshops, and best practice seminars did not result in change to Mexican labor practices at all; similar patterns of poor enforcement were uncovered in later investigations. They found that lack of professionalism among labor agency officials was the root of much of the poor administration of labor justice.

Yet Mexican institutions themselves—especially the courts and the information agency IFAI—were bringing pressure on the labor authorities. According to some, their pressures were indirectly attributable to NAALC investigations, which had highlighted problems and caused, for example, the courts to take a stricter enforcement line on domestic labor law (Bouzas interview, 2010). A Supreme Court decision in 2008 ordered that secret ballots should be allowed to elect union leaders. Another court decision ruled that the requirement for public employees to be part of a union was unconstitutional. Then IFAI, brought into being by a 2002 law guaranteeing transparency, also brought new pressures on the secretive world of industrial relations by opening previously closed sources of information to the light of day.

In this section, I briefly review the public communications against Mexico before exploring how they have led to changes in Mexican labor politics. In every case, the NAO doing the investigation was trying to determine whether Mexico was complying with its own labor law. The majority of complaints made about Mexican labor practices dealt with issues of freedom of association and the right to bargain collectively, although some cases also concerned the rights of pregnant employees, child labor, the right to strike, minimum employment standards, and occupational safety and health. In two cases, a complaint was filed jointly in the United States and Canada, and in one case a complaint was filed in Canada (but rejected). So the majority of this discussion refers to the actions of the U.S. NAO and the responses of the Mexican government. The U.S. NAO recommended some of the submissions be subject to ministerial consultation, which pushed them up to the top political level, but in other cases, it rejected the submissions. Some of the complaints resulted in conferences or workshops in one or more of the member states and led to agreements being signed to promulgate information to employers about workers' rights.

In eleven of the cases (nine of them during the Clinton administration and two during the Bush administration), the U.S. government took some kind of action, including ministerial consultations, public hearings, and follow-up information dissemination events. In some cases, the complaint was withdrawn or was refused by the NAO, and I do not review them here. The Maxi-Switch case, for example, involved a maquiladora in the state of Sonora whose workers were represented by a protection contract without their knowledge. Efforts to represent the workers by the Mexican Telephone Workers' Union were blocked by the local CAB. However, the complaint was withdrawn after the federal government exerted pressure on the local CAB, which reversed its decision (Compa 1999: 88; see also Nolan 2009).

The GE/Honeywell Case (US 940001 and US 940002)[14]

The first two cases were filed on the same day in February 1994 by the Teamsters and the United Electrical Workers unions and concerned practices at the Honeywell plant in Chihuahua and the General Electric plant in Cuidad Juarez, both in the northern state of Chihuahua. The allegation against Honeywell by the Teamsters stated that several employees were fired by the company for organizing an independent union. Likewise, in the GE case, the complaint alleged infringements of freedom of association and collective bargaining rights, as well as violations of health and safety rules. Workers who had been attempting to organize representation by an independent union were fired and pressured to accept severance pay, which negated their rights to reinstatement. The unions filing the complaints raised a number of related issues concerning Mexican labor practices, including the difficulties facing independent unions in gaining legal recognition, the support of the government for "official unions," the blacklisting of union activists by companies, and the practice whereby employees are required to sign blank sheets that may later be converted into statements of resignation (U.S. NAO 1994).

The U.S. NAO accepted the cases for review and issued a single report for both. The purpose of the review, as established in its guidelines and in the NAALC treaty, was to "gather information to assist the NAO to better understand and publicly report on the Government of Mexico's promotion of compliance with, and effective enforcement of, its labor law through appropriate government action" (U.S. NAO 1994). Among other sources of information, the NAO conducted a public hearing in Washington, D.C., to get the input of interested members of the public.

Benedicto Martínez of the Authentic Workers' Front (FAT), who was involved in organizing the union in the Honeywell case, alleged political interference in the process of registration (interview, 2010). Martínez had successfully organized about forty new unions prior to this case. According to his account, workers took a petition to the local CAB three times on the same day, trying to gain recognition for STIMAHCS (an independent union, part of FAT, known for protecting workers' rights). The first two times the petition was rejected on very technical grounds. Each time, FAT corrected the application. Finally, the CAB explained that the governor did not want them to be allowed to organize. Subsequently, FAT representatives met with the governor, who explained that the company was opposed to the FAT, and he (the governor) felt that if FAT was allowed in, their organizing would spread through the area, making businesses less competitive and threatening inward investment.

The governor said they could appeal, but it would take months. The appeal would also have to be at local level, since the industry was not designated as a federal industry. Eventually, the union did succeed in gaining recognition, and it was allowed to compete for recognition as the representative of the Honeywell workers. A *recuento* procedure was held, at which participants agreed to allow a secret vote. However, the workers voted against affiliation with STIMAHCS. According to Martínez, the company put on a very convincing show, holding barbecues and parties and saying it would improve the offer made by STIMAHCS to the workers. Essentially, the company convinced its workers to vote no. Martínez believes that deference to the company is due in part to the fact that the workers are poor migrants from southern Mexico who have no local roots and are accustomed to a culture of hierarchy. There is little in the way of a culture of unionization in the north, which, combined with business and government antipathy, makes it hard for independent unions to succeed. The FAT response was to set up a local research office in Ciudad Juarez.

The U.S. NAO decided that there was not enough evidence to state that Mexico had failed to enforce its labor laws because most of the workers who had been fired chose to accept severance pay in lieu of a challenge, and for the workers who challenged the companies' decisions, the cases were pending before the relevant CAB. However, the report did point out insufficient publicly available information regarding the rights of workers to organize and bargain collectively. Thus, although not recommending ministerial consultations, it did recommend cooperative programs and public information activities to promote understanding of relevant national labor law, as well as of the NAALC itself. Government representatives of the member states subsequently met in March and September 1995 to discuss union organization and representation, protection against antiunion activity, procedural guarantees, and union democracy (Compa 1999: 84). Fired workers were reinstated in the GE and Honeywell cases, though it is not clear whether the Mexican labor authorities pressured the companies or whether the companies took it upon themselves to respond.

Sony (US 940003)

The Sony case was filed in 1994 by four NGOs, including the National Association of Democratic Lawyers (ANAD) from Mexico, an independent group representing workers' rights, usually in direct opposition to co-opted unions. It involved a Sony subsidiary located in Nuevo Laredo in the northern state of Tamaulipas, where the workers were represented by a collective agreement with a CTM-affiliated union. The submitters claimed there were violations of freedom of association and organization rights, as well as of minimum employment standards. They claimed that the CTM union was compliant with management and that both interfered in a *recuento* on April 15, 1994, in which the workers sought to change their representation. Dissident workers were fired or demoted. Voting in the election was open, supporters of the alternative (independent) union were identified, and the official union organized intimidation and reprisals to dissuade workers from voting in favor of changing unions. A subsequent work stoppage was violently suppressed and dispersed by police, according to the submission. The independent union was also denied registration by the local CAB for technical reasons, such as not including precise legal language and because the workers were already represented by another union.

In its review, the U.S. NAO considered the claim that the local CAB incorrectly denied registration of the new union (U.S. NAO 1995). According to the CAB, denial was because (1) the secretary-general of the CTM union in Nuevo Laredo submitted evidence that another union already existed at the plant,

(2) the objectives of the putative replacement union were insufficiently stated, (3) the necessary documentation was not submitted in duplicate, and (4) there were other general (unspecified) deficiencies in the required supporting documentation (U.S. NAO 1995: 10). A local district court heard an appeal and found that the first two reasons were not legally legitimate, but the latter two were legitimate. It upheld the denial, despite the fact that the deficiencies indicated in the last point were not spelled out. Later expert advice provided to the NAO indicated that local CABs are empowered to remedy the lack of duplicate copies of documentation (presumably by making copies themselves). The NAO report criticized the reasons given by the CAB as "hyper-technical" and sounded a note of concern about the time lag, stating that delays prejudiced workers who sought to establish a new union. It also criticized the fact that the CAB allowed the local head of the existing union confederation, CTM, to become involved in the process.

Although several workers who had been dismissed accepted severance pay (negating their ability to challenge the dismissal), the submitters made the point that economic hardship often dictates that workers take this option because they cannot afford the long appeals process. Two workers who did appeal, charging unfair dismissal, were denied their appeal by the local CAB, after which they were not entitled to collect severance pay. In its review of this case, the NAO stated that it "cannot ignore the similarities of these accounts and of those . . . in the first two submissions" (U.S. NAO 1995: 11). It declared that the submitters' allegations were corroborated by other evidence, such as the timing of union organizing activities.

Ministerial consultations followed, along with public meetings on registration and certification of unions, a study on Mexican law relating to union registration, and meetings between STPS, Sony workers, the local CAB authorities, and the company (see Compa 1999, 85ff.). In a follow-up report in 1996, the U.S. NAO indicated that there were potentially significant ongoing developments in the areas of labor legislation, court decisions, and industrial relations. It made the following points: (1) it is difficult for independent unions to register at the local level, (2) CABs "complicate the registration of an independent union" because their membership usually contains a representative from an established union that would be harmed by the existence of a new union, and (3) union registration laws are not applied consistently by different CABs (U.S. NAO 1996). There are not only conflicts of interest but also uncertainty among experts as to the proper application of laws on registration, which adds to the confusion among workers and unions; moreover, the law is applied differently in different CABs.

SUTSP (US 9601)

This case was submitted on June 13, 1996, by three NGOs, including ANAD from the Mexican side, and again raised questions over freedom of association and procedural guarantees for union recognition. The case involved a tangled web of disagreements over representation of federal workers transferred from one ministry to another during a restructuring. The existing union, SUTSP, represented less than 10 percent of the workers in the new consolidated ministry and so was unable to win a majority vote to represent the workforce. The new ministry, SEMARNAP, declared that it was illegal for its workers to be represented by two unions. The federal CAB agreed and canceled SUTSP's registration as a federal union. However, a subsequent court case negated this ruling, and SUTSP had its registration restored. Another court ruling declared that the new union had been registered wrongly. So the federal CAB canceled the registration of the *new* union, leaving SUTSP as the only legitimate union. Continuing the farcical process, the CAB then held elections, which the new union won, and canceled (again) the registration of SUTSP.

In brief, a pool of workers transferred to a new ministry was represented by two separate unions, one of them brought from the old ministry to the new one. Like earlier submissions, the issue was the conditions for determining union representation when there was a conflict between two unions. The U.S. NAO report stated that all four decisions made by the federal CAB were contrary to SUTSP. It called for ministerial consultations to clarify points of legal doctrine, but its report also made clear that in this case, unlike some of the others, SUTSP was unlikely to have been harmed by noncompliance with the law. Appeals rectified most of the rulings issued against SUTSP by the federal CAB, and the composition of the board, which was claimed to be biased, was not found to be a contributing factor to the outcome, in that both unions belonged to the same confederation, and the confederation had a seat on the board.

The Gender Case (US 9701)

The gender case was filed by three NGOs—Human Rights Watch, the International Labor Rights Fund, and ANAD—on May 16, 1996, and concerned discrimination against female employees at maquiladora processing plants. Research by Human Rights Watch had revealed that companies engaged in widespread preemployment pregnancy testing of job applicants and later pregnancy screening during employment. Pregnant job applicants were not hired, and those becoming pregnant while working for the firms were pressured into resigning so that the employers could avoid paying statutory maternity leave. The Mexican federal authorities responded by claiming that a review of the petition by the U.S. NAO would exceed the scope of the NAALC, that the cases of abuse were limited, and that women have sufficient legal protection in Mexico against discrimination on the basis of sex (U.S. NAO 1998a).[15] Later, the federal government (largely as a result of this case) would go on to argue in favor of strengthening institutional and legal protections for women. In 2003, the Federal Prevention and Elimination of Discrimination Act came into force, formally ending forced pregnancy testing (Nolan 2009; also U.S. NAO 2007).

In its review, the NAO indicated that the legality of preemployment pregnancy testing was ambiguous. However, the report also stated that the secretary of STPS met on one occasion with the National Council of the Maquiladora Industry to urge them to end preemployment pregnancy testing, though it is not clear whether that occurred as a result of the NAALC case. Despite the assertions of the Mexican NAO that pregnancy screening was not widespread or illegal, testimony from workers and human rights and labor researchers contradicted the NAO. The report found that the efforts of STPS to get voluntary cooperation from the maquiladora sector to end testing were a sign that it regarded the practice as inappropriate, if not illegal. Moreover, the Mexico City Human Rights Commission had found that preemployment screening was in violation of the Mexican Constitution. On balance, while acknowledging the legal uncertainty, the U.S. NAO report sided with those who claimed that testing and screening should be stopped. Ironically, a federal policy entitled Alliance for Equality acknowledged that both preemployment screening and postemployment testing were widespread and of concern. On postemployment screening, the evidence of impropriety was clear.

Han Young (US 9702)
The Han Young case is one of the clearest examples of abusive practices in the maquiladora sector. It involved a Korean-owned factory in the state of Baja California, where workers attempted to change their union affiliation from the CROC confederation to STIMAHCS. As in so many other factories, the Han Young owners had arranged that the workers would be represented by CROC without allowing them the opportunity to choose. Conditions were poor, and

workers engaged in a wildcat strike because their efforts to affiliate with the independent union were rejected by the local Tijuana CAB (Robles et al. 2009). In a *recuento* in the local CAB on October 6, 1997, the authorities rejected the vote in favor of STIMAHCS, stating that STIMAHCS lacked the proper registration to represent workers (U.S. NAO 1998b: 12). The company subsequently fired a number of workers. Industrial action followed, including a hunger strike, and STIMAHCS took the case to the U.S. NAO.

This time the U.S. NAO report pulled no punches. Its criticism of the Tijuana CAB was scathing. It noted the evidence of irregularities in the election, such as "changing the election date with little notice, threats to the workers supporting STIMAHCS, and the ability of persons without proper credentials to enter the voting premises and cast ballots" (U.S. NAO 1998b: 11). It examined the reasoning of the local CAB, which had decided that the results of the first *recuento* election (which STIMAHCS won) were invalid because the union did not have the correct registration. Incredibly, the same CAB had granted recognition to STIMAHCS in a hearing only eleven days earlier, and thus the reversal seemed "inexplicable. The decision of the CAB overturning the election result made no mention of this earlier decision which allowed the vote to take place and offered no explanation for the reversal" (U.S. NAO 1998b: 12–13).

Under pressure from the federal authorities, the Tijuana CAB held another *recuento* on December 16, 1997. Again, STIMAHCS won, and with federal officials as well as international advocates looking on, the CAB had little choice but to recognize the new union. But it continued to fail in its legal duties by not informing the company in a timely manner of this decision. Moreover, the company refused to acknowledge the new union, instead continuing with layoffs, possibly because of pressure from other maquiladoras (Nolan 2009).

The irregularities that the Tijuana CAB permitted to take place during the first representation election, its reasoning in not recognizing STIMAHCS as the bargaining representative, and its delay in formally notifying Han Young of the results of the December 16 representation election, raise questions about its enforcement of [labor law and] about the impartiality of the CAB, particularly with regard to its duty to enforce the provisions of the [federal labor law] protecting workers from employer retaliation for the exercise of their freedom of association rights, and from employer interference in the establishment of a union. . . . The Parties to the NAALC have a duty to promote labor rights by ensuring not only accessibility to tribunals but also that tribunals are impartial, independent and fair in applying the law. It is difficult to conceive of a legitimate reason why the CAB delayed until March 2 to officially inform the parties of the January 12 finding confirming the December 16 election result. This action by the CAB is troubling. (U.S. NAO 1998b: 14–15)

It is important to reiterate that these findings were not new. The NAO had consistently found that CABs disregarded the law, applied it inconsistently, and apparently did not understand some aspects of labor regulation. Moreover, entrenched conflicts of interest within CABs led to unfair treatment of unions not officially recognized by the governments or that posed a challenge to the existing order. In earlier reports, the U.S. NAO had been clear in its analysis of the problems facing independent unions and workers seeking to affiliate with them. All except one of the cases reviewed to that point involved problems related to freedom of association and the right to establish union representation, as well as the obligation by the authorities to respect procedural guarantees.

Itapsa (US 9703; also Canada 98-1)[16]

This case involved a plant manufacturing car parts in Ciudad de los Reyes in the State of Mexico, near Mexico City. The complaint concerned freedom of association and health and safety issues. It was filed by a group of unions, human rights groups, and other NGOs from Mexico, the United States, and Canada on December 15, 1997. The U.S. NAO recommended ministerial consultations on the case, as did the Canadian NAO (see Canadian NAO 1999). The petition raised now-familiar issues of workplace intimidation against employees trying to organize better union representation. The existing union, a member of the CTM confederation, along with plant management, allegedly fired and discriminated against workers who supported the alternative union, STIMAHCS. At an election to determine which union would represent the workforce, workers had to vote openly, in the presence of the existing union, management, and more than a hundred thugs hired to intimidate them. Some of the thugs voted as well, despite not working at the plant; STIMAHCS lost the vote; and those voting for STIMAHCS were fired. In addition, the complaint argued that Mexico had failed to enforce workplace health and safety rules and that workers were exposed to dangerous substances without adequate protection.

Other allegations included that the federal CAB changed the date of the *recuento* election without notifying STIMAHCS supporters, that CAB officials were present at the *recuento* and observed the atmosphere of intimidation without acting, and in a later review of the allegations of improper conduct at the vote, that they did not invite STIMAHCS or its supporters. The CAB ruled that the CTM union had won the election. An appeal to the federal circuit court by STIMAHCS resulted in a ruling in its favor, and the CAB was ordered to conduct another hearing. The Mexican NAO stated that the federal CAB had no information regarding the accusations of intimidation against STIMAHCS supporters, either before or during the election. It denied that violence and intimidation had taken place.

Without saying so directly, the U.S. NAO clearly did not believe the denials of company management regarding intimidation, violence, and firings. It noted the similarities to other cases, and it noted the consistency in the testimony of workers, as well as the gaps in explanation by the company. It stated that "the information reviewed by the NAO is strongly indicative that the company engaged in prohibited activities, including surveillance, threats and intimidation, and outright dismissal, for the purpose of affecting the outcome of the representation election." As to the evidence of election day intimidation on the part of the CTM union, the company, and the federal CAB, it described the testimony as "consistent, convincing, and disturbing."

The Mexican NAO said that notice of the postelection hearing at the federal CAB was published in the official bulletin of the labor tribunal, and therefore failure to notify STIMAHCS directly was nothing more than a technical issue. Noting the legal requirement, the U.S. NAO wrote that "the failure to notify an interested party of an administrative hearing in which it has an interest does not appear to constitute simply a technical issue" (all quotes are from U.S. NAO 1998c). It also pointed out that the court decision disagreed with the logic of the Mexican NAO and the federal CAB. The report concluded that the case raised serious questions about the impartiality, independence, and neutrality of the CAB. With respect to health and safety inspections and conditions, which were the original reasons that the workers wanted new union representation, the U.S. NAO stated that there appeared to be deficiencies at the plant. Although inspections had taken place, the fines imposed were minimal, and it was unclear whether they had been collected.

TAESA (US 9901)

The TAESA case was filed on November 10, 1999, by two flight attendants' unions and concerned freedom of association and collective bargaining rights, health and safety issues, and minimum employment standards. The complaint alleged that training was poor, compensation was low, and aircraft health and safety standards were lax. The Mexican flight attendants' union ASSA, associated with the independent union confederation UNT, attempted to organize flight attendants at the airline. However, all TAESA employees were already represented by another union, SNTETA, which was part of the CTM. The federal CAB, which had jurisdiction in the case, initially refused to allow a *recuento* vote to determine who should represent the flight attendants. Its reasoning was that ASSA, as a "craft union" specializing in flight attendants, could not represent a fraction of the employees of the company because a companywide contract already existed. It cited Supreme Court decisions that representation in a given company could not be fragmented.

Arguing that it should have been allowed a hearing before a ruling was issued by the CAB, ASSA appealed the decision. The courts twice ruled in its favor. Eventually, the CAB was forced to abandon its opposition, and it scheduled a vote on representation. A *recuento* was held, at which allegedly there was intimidation and forced open voting, in the presence of the CAB. When ASSA lost the election, those who supported it were fired. The submitters stated that the CAB officials should have suspended the vote, given the atmosphere of intimidation, but did not. They also claimed that TAESA employees who were not flight attendants should not have been allowed to vote and that people voted who did not work for the company.

The U.S. NAO said in its report that the CAB appeared to have followed Mexican legal precedent in denying to ASSA (as a craft union) the right to gain title to represent a fraction of the workforce once there was a company-wide contract in place. On the vote itself, it found evidence of intimidation in the *recuento* vote to be credible; that the CAB officials present should have, but did not, prevent the intimidation; and that workers who had voted for ASSA were fired afterward for their vote. The report stated that the airline had failed to pay its required pension, housing, and other contributions and that there were probably safety deficiencies on its aircraft. A TAESA aircraft crashed in November 1999, and all eighteen people on board died. The report also found that the Mexican government did take action against the company for its failure to pay taxes and payroll contributions to employees' pensions, social security, and other funds.

The Mexican government did not respond to a request to supply records on its enforcement history with regard to the company's compliance on overtime regulations. This omission made it hard for the U.S. NAO to be certain whether the government had met its obligations. The same is true of records regarding safety inspections. The U.S. NAO's opinion weighed heavily in favor of the use of secret ballots in *recuentos* to avoid the intimidation witnessed in this case. It also said that the STPS had given assurances following cases 9702 and 9703 that it would promote secret ballots. Likewise, a Mexican policy document known as the New Labor Culture included business and labor endorsements of secret ballots. Nonetheless, more than two years later, open voting and intimidation were still the modus operandi, and the fact that the TAESA case was located before a federal CAB and in a high-profile sector of the economy made no difference. Ministerial consultations to discuss the issues raised in the case were recommended by the U.S. NAO.

Auto Trim (US 2000-01)

This case concerned occupational health and safety issues at two plants in the state of Tamaulipas: Auto Trim (in Matamoros) and Custom Trim/Breed Mexicana (in Valle Hermoso) (U.S. NAO 2001). Workers complained that inspections were not carried out by the authorities, despite their requests, and that they suffered illnesses due to the workplace conditions. The U.S. NAO conducted a site visit of the plants, as well as a public hearing in Texas. It met with CTM-affiliated unions representing workers, and it corresponded with the Mexican NAO, as it does on every case it accepts. In its report, the U.S. NAO determined that numerous site inspections had been carried out by the state STPS authorities. Also, the environmental enforcement agency Profepa had been working with company management on occupational safety and health issues. However, the report was critical of the STPS inspections, saying they appeared to be completing checklists, with little in the way of detail or additional comments. Most of the inspections seemed to be of warning signs, lighting, and related issues, rather than exposure to harmful substances. Likewise, the inspectors tended to review paperwork from the company rather than make direct observations of equipment and procedures.

Companies whose employees had workplace-related injuries or illnesses were liable to pay higher levels of compensation than if the sickness was caused by other factors. Thus, company doctors tended to tell employees that their problems were "general" rather than workplace-specific to minimize the cost to the company. The report also indicated that although inspections had been carried out by both STPS and IMSS (the social security agency), certain procedures were lacking. Employees were not protected by confidentiality, the agencies did not test health and safety equipment independently, and no follow-up with employees occurred. Moreover, in some cases the agencies did not respond to (or denied the existence of) petitions by employees for inspections, even though the petitioners possessed copies of their petitions that had been stamped as having been received by the same authorities. These failures, according to the U.S. NAO, were inconsistent with Mexico's obligations under the NAALC. It recommended ministerial consultations. Its report stated:

> The workers' claim that they did not receive a proper response from the authorities is supported. The fact that the Mexican authorities apparently have not communicated with the submitters is a cause of concern [and] raises questions about the Mexican government's compliance with its commitments. (U.S. NAO 2001)

Puebla (US 2003-01; also Canada 2003-1)[17]

The Puebla case again dealt with freedom of association and right to collective bargaining and also involved occupational safety and health issues and minimum employment standards (see U.S. NAO 2004). The complaints concerned activities at the Matamoros Garment and Tarrant México garment factories in the state of Puebla, where the petition claimed that working conditions were poor and that workers were not paid for overtime. They tried to create independent unions and then learned they were already represented without their knowledge. They took their case to the local Puebla CAB and tried to register an independent union, but they were rejected on what seemed to be "hyper-technical grounds" (U.S. NAO 2004). The U.S. NAO report gave an example of what it meant by hypertechnical grounds:

> On January 20, 2003, workers filed a union registration petition signed by 162 workers with the [local CAB]. On March 26, 2003, the [local CAB] issued a decision denying [the] petition for union registration, citing the following reasons: 1) the two lists of members names are not identical (the name of one union committee member is written incorrectly), the reason for forming the union is not written on one of the lists, and one list is not properly authorized;

2) the lists submitted do not authenticate that all members attending the union formation assembly were over 14 years of age as required by law; 3) one of the workers whose name is on the list denied he had ratified his signature; and 4) the legally mandated minimum of 20 workers required to register a union could not be confirmed because the factory was closed when the [CAB] visited the factory (March 18, 2003) as part of its analysis. (U.S. NAO 2004)

In other words, the Puebla CAB visited the factory on a day it was closed (a temporary work stoppage had been imposed) and, finding it closed, denied registration because it was unable to confirm the proposed union's membership details, among other reasons. Later that year, the same CAB denied union registration at the Tarrant plant, giving five reasons for doing so:

1) failure to submit two copies of the original petition; 2) failure to form the union and elect its executive committee on two separate dates; 3) misspelling one of the 728 workers' names on the petition; 4) failure to establish by-laws regarding the union's assets; and 5) unclear by-laws regarding member discipline. (U.S. NAO 2004)

Again, the U.S. NAO roundly criticized the CAB. It noted that the same issues of obstacles to union registration and denial of freedom of association rights had been raised consistently over the ten years in which it had considered cases. "It would appear that despite the passage of 10 years, the same enforcement deficiencies persist in Mexico" (U.S. NAO 2004). It also noted the evidence that the Mexican government was aware of the complaints at various levels, and it requested information (in vain) on what their response had been to workers' requests for action.

The U.S. NAO report described the shortcomings in information available to workers regarding their union representation. It mentioned that STPS manages a publicly available list of registered federal-level unions, but interested individuals cannot access the list by employer name, and it does not show whether a given company has union representation (U.S. NAO 2004). The report mentioned that only the local Mexico City CAB ensured that workers had access to collective bargaining agreements affecting their workplaces, despite assurances given during ministerial consultations four years earlier that workers would be guaranteed access to this information.

The Canadian NAO report was equally damning. Among other things, it noted that workers' concerns about minimum employment standards were known to the local CAB, but that when they were informally raised with CAB officials, their response "was passive and discouraging to the workers . . . informal interactions with workers may be discouraging workers from using appropriate enforcement procedures" (Canadian NAO 2005: vi). Like its U.S. counterpart, it had not received all the information it requested from the Mexican NAO.

Hidalgo (2005-03)

The Hidalgo case concerned workers at a garment factory known as Rubie's in the state of Hidalgo and was the latest in a long, sorry tale of frustrated union organization, discrimination, and abuse of workers' rights. Workers sought new union representation, believing the CTM affiliate to be ineffective at representing their rights. They complained about lack of health and safety inspections, poor working conditions, lack of overtime pay, discrimination against women (who had to take pregnancy tests), and use of minors in the workplace. The Hidalgo case is interesting in part because it shows that earlier commitments by Mexico to improve certain practices had still not been fulfilled. Neither federal nor local authorities had fully accepted the rule of law. The U.S. NAO report mentioned that the local CAB relied on technical grounds to reject the independent union registration application, that there was little publicly available information on unions and collective bargaining agreements, and that pregnancy testing continued until July 2005, all of which had been raised in earlier reports and which the Mexican authorities had agreed to address.

Clearly exasperated with repeated petitions making reference to the same issues, the U.S. NAO called for consultations to address commitments that had already been entered into, including the talks following Submission 9701 on pregnancy testing some years earlier. It requested information on the work of the Gender and Equity Bureau and on the Federal Prevention and Elimination of Discrimination Act. "We reiterate the request made . . . on numerous occasions for copies of agreements signed between STPS and state governments to end pregnancy testing and promote the rights of working women" (U.S. NAO 2007: 50–51).

The U.S. NAO concluded that there were no inspections undertaken at the plant between 1998 and 2005, but that in May 2005, state and federal authorities conducted a total of four inspections (two each). It believed that all four of the inspections were the result of media reports claiming violations of labor law, and none were in response to complaints by workers to the state or federal authorities (U.S. NAO 2007: 37). Worse, there were discrepancies between the federal and state inspection reports over what they found (all four inspections were carried out within a week of each other). It stated that "such inconsistencies raise questions as to the government's ability to detect and effectively seek appropriate sanctions or remedies for violations of its labor law" (U.S. NAO 2007: 42). Lack of professional standards in the application of the law had again prevented labor justice from being administered.

Capacity Building in Mexican Labor Agencies

What do these cases demonstrate? First, the system of labor politics in Mexico has been virtually impervious to a socialization of pro–rule of law norms, despite a high level of technocratic interaction, periodic shaming, and (admittedly weak) capacity-building activities. The evidence for this comes from interviews in the labor authorities, as well as with academic observers, NGO and union officials, and others. Evidence of the failure to internalize pro–rule of law norms also comes from the fact that NAO investigations into complaints revealed that there was a pattern of labor rights violations, and that despite claims by the federal ministry that improvements would be made, similar violations were uncovered in later investigations (see Table 3.2). The message did not sink in. Those public officials responsible for ensuring the rights of workers under the law did not, through their actions or their views, indicate that they thought existing practices to be wrong.

Some of the worst offenses took place in state-level CABs. In response, STPS sometimes claimed it had no authority to intervene and at other times pressured state authorities through informal political channels. Voting to determine union representation continued to be rife with intimidation: leaders used physical and other threats to coerce workers to vote for them. Opposition to secret ballots among the corporatist unions is "obviously not based on freedom or autonomy, but rather on the fear of losing control of the workers" (Alcalde 2006: 173). Two NAALC cases (9702 and 9703) resulted in a declaration in May 2000, whereby the governments of the three member states committed themselves to ensuring secret votes and open information regarding collective contracts. However, Mexico did not comply with this for several years. Eventually, under pressure, STPS established a Web site listing all approved unions, the companies whose workers they represent, and their

TABLE 3.2 Government reaction to complaints about labor enforcement

Case	Initial reaction to allegations	Admission of problem in enforcement?	Follow-up change to policy or practice	U.S. Administration in which case was considered
GE/Honeywell	Rejected	No	U.S. NAO said there was insufficient evidence to state that laws had not been enforced. Follow-up meetings between government representatives suggested changes to improve availability of information. Little real change if any.	Clinton
Sony	Rejected	No	Meetings again between governments to discuss workers' rights and information.	Clinton
SUTSP	N/A	No	N/A	Clinton
Gender	Rejected	No: denial that problem of pregnancy screening was widespread	Some pressure exerted by Mexican federal authorities in individual cases. Eventual legislative change to protect women. Enforcement remained weak in practice.	Clinton
Han Young	N/A	N/A	Federal authorities pressured local CAB to correct mistakes. Claimed it would promote secret ballots but did not.	Clinton
Itapsa	Rejected	No; denial of irregularities and intimidation	Federal authorities claimed they would promote secret ballots but did not.	Clinton
TAESA	Withheld information from U.S. NAO	No	N/A	Clinton
Auto Trim	N/A	N/A	N/A	Clinton
Puebla	Withheld information from U.S. NAO and access to individuals	No	Earlier guarantees to allow access to collective contracts had not been followed up.	G. H. W. Bush
Hidalgo	N/A	No	Plant inspections by federal authorities followed the complaint.	G. H. W. Bush

leadership. This is partly the result of IFAI pressures, but it also stems from NAALC consultations between Mexico and its partners (Alcalde 2006: 170–71).[18] Government information on these unions (and on all unions) has been sparse. Although approval by federal or state authorities is required in order to form and operate a union, the government itself has been extremely reluctant to provide transparent systems whereby workers can identify their union leaders, much less require that union accounts be open or that elections be held fairly and without intimidation (Bouzas 2006).

Despite these experiences, there are positive interpretations of NAALC as well. Compa (1999: 91ff.) points out that it is not a mechanism to right specific injustices or complaints. Rather, it is designed as a "review mechanism by which member countries open themselves up to investigation, reports, evaluations, recommendations, and other measures so that, over time, such enhanced oversight and scrutiny will generate more effective labor law enforcement" (Compa 2001: 453–54). It brought a sunlight effect to labor practices. A Mexican labor lawyer claimed that there were positive effects even in the very first NAALC submissions, the so-called GE/Honeywell cases. One was a public airing of union grievances in an international organization, outside the insulated circles of academia and NGOs, where discussions of labor politics had been confined (the U.S. NAO insisted on public hearings, much to the irritation of the Mexican government). Another was that it encouraged unions and labor organizations to follow suit and contact counterparts in the United States and Canada (de Buen Unna 1999: 2).

Díaz claims that NAALC has added to the pressure to modernize Mexican labor regulation, mentioning discussions between the Canadian labor minister, Claudette Bradshaw, and her Mexican counterpart, Carlos Abascal, regarding labor reform. According to a communication from Bradshaw, four ministerial-level meetings occurred in 2001 and 2002 in response to the Itapsa case (cited in Díaz, 2004: 556, n. 4). Díaz states that concrete effects were seen even in the first three years. Companies that had run afoul of investigations were being more careful. Some supporters of independent unions were pleased with the international publicity, believing that it helped their cause. In the Maxi-Switch case, international exposure and the likelihood of a public report resulted in a resolution favorable to the independent union. Also, a Supreme Court decision in the Ministry of Fisheries case that gave legal recognition to the challenging union probably came about because of the NAALC pressure.

In fact, it is clear from a review of NAO reports that the Mexican federal government did respond to allegations both by pressuring individual firms and CABs, and also through a process of strengthening its policies and procedures. At the same time it has been hampered by the recalcitrance of local labor authorities, firms, and the main union confederations. For example, in the Han Young case, the federal government put pressure on the firm and the CAB, which then did allow the independent union. However, local economic forces opposed this and forced dissident workers to leave the firm. More malleable workers replaced the strikers, and the benefits of the case were lost. The pregnancy testing case is another example of strategic reaction. The Mexican government created special offices in 1998 to look into women in the workplace, as well as child labor and disabled workers. It organized an education campaign in the maquiladora zone to educate female workers on their rights regarding pregnancy testing. An office for equality and gender issues was created in 1999.

The federal government continued to urge reform in company practices even after the NAALC case was finished. It signed agreements with state governments. A number of companies committed to ending pregnancy testing. In 2003, a federal law was passed which formally prohibited the practice. In this case a transnational advocacy group was particularly effective at highlighting the discrepancy between Mexico's international commitments and its domestic practice (Nolan 2009). Union registration was a further case of strategic reaction to criticism, albeit somewhat halfhearted. Following the Sony case and subsequent ministerial consultations, Mexico established a panel of labor experts who recommended that the union registration process be depoliticized and made more consistent by giving the authority to state labor departments. The U.S. NAO noted in the Han Young case that the STPS had formed a roster of officially registered unions and put it on its Web site and had created new federal CABs throughout the country.

Compa believes that the acceptance of external scrutiny was itself important. "Gains come obliquely, over time, by pressing companies and governments to change their behavior, by sensitizing public opinion, by building ties of solidarity, and by taking other steps to change the climate for workers' rights advances" (Compa 2001: 457).[19] Nolan (2009) shows that the Mexican government intervened to solve plant-level disputes in some cases. It imposed a fine the day after a public hearing on the Han Young case, and in another case, a state governor pressed the local CAB to recognize an independent union (Graubart 2005: 134–35). Nolan also notes that promoting secret ballots and public information were outcomes of ministerial consultations in the Itapsa case and that internal policy discussions on labor reform began to include the independent union confederation UNT. Teague (2002) points to NAALC cases in which the negative publicity associated with the public communications brought changes in company practices. He cites a case in which employers at maquiladora plants stopped their practice of pregnancy testing prior to hiring female workers. Though NAALC has not resulted in "systemic change" in Mexican labor practices, it has resulted in some companies being shamed and in improvements to labor practices on an ad hoc basis.

Moreover, communication and technical cooperation between STPS and its counterparts in the United States and Canada increased following NAALC. According to both U.S. and Mexican labor officials, there is greater collaboration than ever before, and without the side agreement, there would not be this level of interaction (Karesh interview, 2005; STPS interviews, 2007, 2009). The creation of offices (the NAOs and the CLC) created structures that institutionalized cooperation, including information sharing, expertise building, and outreach and education, among others. The U.S. government has tended to look more legalistically at Mexico following NAFTA to determine whether it is meeting its legal agreements. Also, NAALC increased the level of knowledge and understanding about labor matters in North America, which was one of its objectives (GAO 1997). Although labor cooperation existed before NAFTA, it has been consolidated and formalized.

National sensitivities mean there is often a better working relationship on technical issues than on political issues. Technical assistance personnel in the U.S. Department of Labor are in direct contact with their counterparts in Mexico, which did not occur prior to the NAALC. Contacts have spread beyond the international affairs offices. "Without a doubt contact has grown tremendously" (Karesh interview, 2005). If staff see something of interest in the newspaper or on the Internet, they contact their counterparts in Mexico to discuss it. The Mexican STPS confirmed that contact occurs directly, via e-mails, phone calls, and meetings, without the presence of foreign ministries (interview, 2007). Discussions between the two governments extend beyond NAFTA to ILO issues as well.

At the end of the 1990s, the three member states convened a group on occupational safety and health (OSH) issues to resolve a NAALC complaint against Mexico (STPS interview, 2009). The group dealt with four areas: training, Web pages, hazardous materials, and voluntary protection programs. Experts worked on exchange of best practices for four years. Also, U.S. labor bureaucrats have worked at the technical level with counterparts in Mexico to improve their electronic job banks and employment service centers (Karesh interview, 2005). A further sign of capacity building, according to Karesh, is that Mexico is more committed to women's rights in workplace, combating discrimination and harassment. Mexico must come to international meetings prepared to explain what it's doing. They want positive things to say, and external pressure helps them. Moral suasion and consensus are the modus operandi. Therefore, despite the criticisms of ministerial consultation—its lengthy process, the fact that it has no teeth—placing issues on agenda at high level has important consequences (Karesh interview, 2005).

The CLC also has an impact, albeit very small. It does not have the institutionalized input of civil society that characterizes the CEC, but it does engage in information activities. The CLC conducted early studies (in 1996 and 1997) on the labor legislation and labor markets of the member states, and later on the clothing and confection industries. It produced a study on the effects of sudden closures on the right to organize. By 1997, the member states and the CLC had held a number of cooperative activities, including meetings and workshops between labor bureaucrats, professional and technical exchanges, seminars, conferences, and other activities open to the public. Activities addressed security and hygiene, especially in the construction, chemicals, and electronics industries; employment training; the role of women in the workplace; unregulated labor; child labor; and other issues (Compa 1999: 82; GAO 1997). The NAALC cases led to a better understanding of respective juridical systems. Early activities also included work on freedom of association and right to organize. Some of these studies revealed how "precarious" the Mexican data were and how badly the government needed to build capacity to enable better comparative studies (Bensusán 1999: 189).

Nolan (2009) found that despite many obstacles and incentives to the contrary, Mexican federal authorities have followed up some of the NAALC cases with policy reforms and changes to existing practices. The government agreed to hold consultations following the Itapsa case to address issues of freedom of association and collective bargaining, registration of collective bargaining contracts, and public registration of unions. It agreed to promote secret ballots in *recuento* procedures and began, for the first time, to publish information on levels of unionization, opening up previously opaque systems of information.

Workers could eventually learn whether they were represented by a union (Alcalde interview, 2010).

They also led to secret votes being used in federal *recuentos,* although the federal government did not make secret ballots part of labor law reform. Likewise, the TAESA case, where a secret ballot was not allowed, was followed by a similar airline case in which the flight attendants were allowed a secret vote, and the claim, based on evidence from the U.S. NAO, is that this was to avoid further international scrutiny. Moreover, to the extent that independent unions have more freedom to register, this progress is partly due to NAALC (STPS interview, 2007). Nolan states that the debate over labor reform was changed: independent unions were included in discussions within government, and issues of freedom of association and public union registration were brought onto the agenda (also Graubart 2005: 126; Alcalde interview, 2010).

In addition, the government created policies such as "The New Labor Culture" and the "Program for Employment, Training and the Defense of Labor Rights: 1995–2000." The New Labor Culture was a policy statement calling on unions to respect the law and calling on government to strengthen the CABs by assigning career judges to them instead of government appointees. It also urged the CABs to conform to the law and to act impartially in adjudicating. The Program for Employment, Training and the Defense of Labor Rights recognized, in its background statement, that labor tribunals applied inconsistent criteria in their enforcement of labor standards. It made a series of recommendations for strengthening the CABs, including setting uniform criteria for interpreting and enforcing legislation and improving the professionalism of staff through exams and career-track appointments. The hope was that such measures would reduce the arbitrary application of labor law and increase the professionalism and capacity of the CABs.

But despite these measures, and despite the recognition that professionalization and depoliticization were needed, little real progress was made in changing the culture of labor administration and justice. Although union registration details were published online, few workers had access to the Web site in the 1990s. In any case, the Web site did not contain details of the collective contracts or the union with which individual companies were associated; it showed simply a list of unions and various registration details.[20] Moreover, federal CABs were relevant only to certain industrial sectors, leaving some of the most vulnerable workers (in the maquiladoras, for instance) exposed to the arbitrary and sometimes vicious administration of state labor politics. In the Han Young case, the U.S. NAO sounded a note of caution:

> The results of previous submissions and the Government of Mexico's own efforts to strengthen the professionalism and capabilities of its CABs seem to substantiate the NAO's basis for concern that the actions by the Tijuana CAB may be inconsistent with the [federal labor law]. Registration, which is supposed to be a routine administrative transaction, is sometimes withheld in a manner which grants the administrative authorities (CABs) control over the right of unions to exist. Union representation rights were initially awarded on the basis of criteria that were not impartial and transparent and this was prevented from occurring only by the intervention of the Federal and state governments. It is evident that the Federal Government of Mexico is aware of the problems associated with some of the state CABs and has initiated efforts to achieve improved compliance with the law by the appropriate authorities. Unfortunately, it is further evident from the instant submission, that in spite of serious efforts on the part of Mexican Federal labor authorities, independent unions continue to experience difficulty gaining the authority and ability to exist and function. (U.S. NAO 1998b: 20)

Capacity Building in Mexican Civil Society

The 1990s was a period of change for Mexican unions. A so-called new unionism emerged, prompted by dissatisfaction with the dominant, co-opted confederations (Bensusán 2006a). Democratic opening and economic crises that had begun in the 1980s added to the pressures. New independent unions and social movements were formed, such as the Zapatistas (in 1994) and the union confederation UNT (in 1997). Many individuals within these new groups were nonaligned, separated from the PRI and without other party affiliations. An added (and related) factor contributing to the change was NAFTA. The Zapatista movement rose on the day NAFTA entered into force. In April 1991, RMALC (the Mexican Network Against Free Trade) was formed as a network of farm, labor, environmental, women's, and other groups to oppose the NAFTA negotiations.[21]

The objectives of RMALC changed following NAFTA's entry into force. It began to monitor the agreement and gather evidence of legal violations, consolidating and building on the links that had been established with groups in the

United States and Canada. Its various groups are active in lobbying the Mexican Congress, sending representatives such as maquiladora workers to the United States to speak about conditions, and organizing meetings throughout Mexico. The U.S. counterpart to RMALC is the Alliance for Responsible Trade (ART), a network of diverse groups: the AFL-CIO; Friends of the Earth; family farm, women's, and church groups; and others. It was established in 1992 specifically because of NAFTA, responding to a Canadian initiative (Hansen-Kuhn interview, 2005). Canadian groups include the Anglophone Common Frontiers and the Francophone Quebec Network Alliance for the People.

For independent trade unions and labor NGOs, the most important results of NAALC have not been the findings of cases or the responses of the Mexican government, such as they are, but rather cross-border cooperation, including information and personnel exchanges. With support from U.S. and Canadian sources, Mexican independent unions and NGOs (lawyers, research organizations, and networks of activists) were empowered in their fight against unfair labor practices. Although they found the NAALC public communication procedure unsatisfactory, the process of filing complaints helped them consolidate cooperation and build capacity (Bensusán 2006a: 262). Not only were unions responsible for shedding light on illegal practices but also they benefited from the experience of international cooperation.

The principal cause of strengthened cross-border cooperation was the requirement that a complaint be filed with the NAO of a country *different* from the one in which the alleged infraction occurred. Mexican labor groups wishing to complain about Mexican practices needed to file the complaint in the United States or Canada, which meant locating and working with partners in those countries. This had the unintended and ironic consequence of bringing about greater communication and cooperation among the unions of the member states—expectations had been that NAFTA would generate a nationalistic competition for jobs. Cooperative activities included grassroots mobilizing, lobbying, campaign activities, and planning (Kay 2005). Church groups, workers, farm groups, and others organized tours and speaking engagements, with the intention of raising public awareness and building bridges. American workers traveled to Mexico under the auspices of the Tennessee Highlander Center to investigate working conditions and returned to do speaking tours. Global Exchange, a San Francisco organization, sent a delegation to Mexico, as did Witness for Peace. In all, NAALC created a new opportunity structure within which labor groups could coalesce and build links (Kay 2011).

The Authentic Labor Front (FAT) was quick to establish relationships with major American trade unions, including the United Electrical Workers, the Teamsters, and the AFL-CIO (whose long-standing ally, the CTM, had followed the government's line and taken a more positive view of NAFTA). The United Electrical Workers and FAT formalized cooperation even before NAALC came into effect and then "internationalized their campaign" by filing claims under NAALC (Fox 2004: 264). Likewise, the Communication Workers of America and the Mexican Telephone Workers Union (STRM) began to cooperate on NAALC cases. Hopes were raised when the first two submissions under NAALC resulted in a public airing of union grievances in an international organization. Other labor organizations were encouraged to follow suit and contact U.S. and Canadian counterparts (de Buen Unna 1999: 2).

The NAALC cases forced partners to coordinate their positions (Compa 1999: 95). It has become common for labor lawyers, economists, bureaucrats, union leaders, activists, and academics to meet at conferences and workshops across the three member states. Delegates exchange information on collective negotiation practices, conduct and translate studies, and search for new ways to connect their organizations. Although NAALC created the context for this, it is not the only reason for such activity. It fostered collaboration whereby unions jointly develop work strategies, write complaints and testimony, create press releases, organize demonstrations, and participate in capacity-building activities. All these activities create learning opportunities.

Ben Davis, the head of the AFL-CIO's Mexico City office, explained that cooperation occurs first through the commitment to file a complaint, which creates a need to work together on practical issues, such as agreeing and drafting the complaint. If the complaint is dealt with in the United States, the authorities there hold public hearings, and the Mexican unions attend. They also cooperate on media and public relations strategies. Practical working relationships are formed and developed, and there is now a trinational community of labor leaders and labor lawyers who have a history of working together and who frequently pick up the phone to consult with each other (Davis interview, 2009). Lance Compa, a former member of the CLC and an advisor on several petitions, argued that activists first tried to politicize the process by arguing for formats that included public hearings and judicial proceedings, with the power to subpoena evidence and testimony (cited in Graubart 2005: 112). The U.S. NAO decided to hold public hearings but did not allow cross-examination or demand information. In fact, Graubart indicates that the U.S.

NAO was "deferential" to the Mexican government and tended to give it the benefit of the doubt, at least initially.

In the Sony case, the petitioners were more careful to draw the connections between company practices and government failure to enforce the law, a connection that had not been made in the GE-Honeywell petition. This meant the Sony petition was better grounded in law. They had learned: it was less politicized and more legal. The U.S. NAO effectively endorsed the petition. It was critical of the Mexican government, giving the petitioners a boost and helping legitimize their position (Graubart 2005: 118). Subsequent ministerial consultations gave independent labor activists the chance to appear before Mexican government officials, helping to open the discussion over labor practices. The factual and legal arguments were even better developed in the Itapsa case (Graubart 2005: 123). The networking activity surrounding the case, with support from activists in all three member states, increased the publicity and shaming pressure. The findings of the NAO were so clearly in favor of the petitioners that the Mexican government threatened to withdraw cooperation. It accused the U.S. NAO of "being too intrusive and acting contrary to the cooperative purpose of NAALC" (Graubart 2005: 125).

Thus, as cases were developed, labor groups learned from their experience, grounding arguments more carefully in law and drawing more effectively on the resources of allied groups in the other member states. Mexican labor interests built capacity. The experience gained in connecting with counterparts in the other member states was invaluable and lasting. Trust was built up during the process of coordinating positions and filing NAALC complaints. Independent labor leaders and RMALC groups have an excellent working relationship with partner groups across North America. Every RMALC interviewee and U.S. counterpart, whether in unions or NGOs, confirmed this point.

In short, NAALC's legacies include both capacity building in Mexican labor and cross-national labor cooperation. The AFL-CIO was drawn into this process, too. Its position changed in the mid-1990s from myopic, nationalistic protectionism to greater interest in foreign workers' rights. It sought to raise living standards outside the United States.[22] It strengthened its Mexico City office and downplayed its links to the established PRI-aligned CTM confederation, which was pro-NAFTA but anti-NAALC. It extended its labor contacts to independent unions. Ben Davis is blunt about how this serves the self-interest of the AFL-CIO. Criticizing what he calls the "Can't Affordism" policies of the Mexican government and its failure to create a middle class of consumers, he states that the AFL-CIO is in Mexico "because we think Mexicans should be making more money. A lot more money. The wage gap between Mexican and American workers is a threat to the working class in America" (Davis interview, 2009).

Interviews with NGO representatives revealed their strong perception that cooperation has become permanent. Expectations have changed; they see this international cooperation as far more fruitful than dialogue with the Mexican government, which has not yielded results and has led to fears of co-optation among some of the RMALC leaders (Sandoval interview, 2007). Trinational NAFTA events take place in meetings of the Hemispheric Social Alliance (created to build a post-NAFTA alliance in opposition to the Free Trade Area of the Americas). To participants, they seem like three branches of one organization (Hansen-Kuhn interview, 2005). Their experience has inspired similar groups in other Latin American countries, and they continue to work with North American counterparts on awareness raising, coalition building, advising, support, and similar activities.

Ultimately, independent labor groups found NAALC to be too weak to be effective and universally condemn the complaint procedure. Their claims did not result in significant enforcement advances or acceptance of a rule of law logic in STPS. However, they did help solidify cross-border cooperation. Mexican unions, which had been isolated, are now more active internationally. The NAALC affected independent Mexican unions and labor organizations because they now have access to international standards and to unions outside Mexico, and because their capacity to mount campaigns was strengthened.

Chiseling Open Mexican Labor Politics

The NAALC is clearly a weak agreement. It has three categories of labor rights (described earlier in this chapter), each with different levels of obligation. Enforcement powers vary, depending on which of the labor rights is under consideration. In 1998, the ILO published a simpler set of fundamental principles and rights at work, and since that time, negotiators have used these principles in treaty negotiations. Further, a member state which seeks to use the Evaluation Committee of Experts mechanism in NAALC must open its own practices to examination, in addition to the country which is the target of the complaint. This dissuades member states from using the mechanism, and it has been abandoned in later treaty negotiations (Polaski 2006: 51). The lack of effective enforcement mechanisms means that member states failing to respond to petitions or correct problematic practices are not punished. However, given sovereignty concerns, it is unrealistic to think that the treaty could have forced member states to guarantee freedom of association more effectively.

Yet cracks are appearing in the old system of protected special interests and corrupted officials. One sign of this is the different way federal authorities have responded to scrutiny pressures as compared to state authorities. The federal government has greater incentive to react strategically to NAALC because its efforts to promote democratization leave it susceptible to moral pressure from external actors (Nolan 2009). For the federal level, the reputational cost of being viewed as a laggard on labor rights is higher than for state governments, which have strong incentives to promote investment, and where authoritarianism is often stronger. Nolan showed that responses by the federal and state governments to NAALC cases are triggered by strategic calculations of economic and/or political cost and benefit, rather than a sense that what they are doing is correcting a wrong that should be corrected. Intervention by the federal government in cases where the state boards had allegedly violated freedom of association often did not occur. In other words, a pro–rule of law norm had not taken hold.

By contrast, one local labor authority illustrates how change *can* occur. The Mexico City CAB has the reputation of being the most accessible, transparent, and honest of the CABs, more so than the federal CAB and far more so than the CABs of some northern states. Figures on registrations and *recuentos* reveal differences: the union demanding to be the new representative won in only 5 percent of the federal CAB cases but 11 percent of the Mexico City CAB cases. The federal CAB declares incompetent 58 percent of the registration requests, whereas for the Mexico City CAB the figure is 14 percent (Bensusán 2006b: 377–79). Interviews with Edith Ramírez, a lawyer in the Mexico City CAB, Jesus Campos, the former head of the same CAB, and several independent lawyers, reveal some of the reason for the openness of this agency.

When Andrés Manuel López Obrador was elected as head of the government of Mexico City in 2000, he asked ANAD (the National Association of Democratic Lawyers) to nominate the head of the local CAB. That's when Jesus Campos was made president of the CAB.[23] And I was invited (almost nine years ago) by Jesus Campos to be part of the CAB too. I should point out that

I am also part of ANAD, and eight of us from ANAD joined the CAB, in strategic locations, to work there. Over time, more colleagues joined from ANAD.
The fact that the Mexico City government was democratic and sensitive to the
needs of vulnerable groups, and also that the president of the CAB was a
democratic lawyer, for me was very important, because it represented change
in favor of the workers. Jesus Campos was always in favor of a strict application of the law, and above all, recognition of workers' rights. He resigned in
January 2010, and we have a new president, a politician with little experience
in the area. We'll have to see what his policies are, but if they are contrary to
workers' rights, I would certainly resign my position (Ramírez interviews, 2010).

Asked to provide examples of how the Mexico City CAB differs from other
local CABs and the federal agencies, Ramírez explained that they have autonomy in the sense that they are not given "a line" by the Mexico City government (that is, told what to do in resolving cases), as is the case with many
local CABs. Their independence is also in sharp contrast to the political control exercised by STPS over the federal CAB, despite the fact that such control
has no legal basis (Campos 2009: 153–54). Autonomy was granted by the Mexico City government because of a PRD administration taking power in 2000,
which brought democratization. Campos brought on board other lawyers with
similar experience of representing independent unions. He states that he accepted the position in order to apply labor law on behalf of the workers, and to
preserve the legal autonomy of the CAB (Campos 2009: 143, 154). He formed a
diploma in law and a morning school in law within the CAB to train and professionalize the legal staff (Campos interview, 2010). He also formed collegial
bodies to govern the budget and to oversee operation, and they undertook a
review of operations with a view to publishing these online as well.

The government representatives in this CAB are experienced bureaucrats,
rather than political appointees. The CAB president has the authority internally
to resolve cases without interference from the government, and Campos insisted on honesty and application of the law. Neither the federal government nor
the Mexico City government has the legal authority to interfere in the financial,
administrative or jurisdictional matters of the CAB (Campos 2009: 154). Furthermore, whereas the CAB once imposed solutions, forbade pay-related strikes,
and took instructions from political figures, this is no longer the case. This modus operandi has allowed parties in dispute to negotiate, rather than having
solutions imposed. It has become more technocratic and less political.

Another example is the *recuento* administrative procedure, discussed earlier, which is the means by which the CAB determines which union the workers want. The *recuento* votes (in the CABs) are now secret because of a Supreme Court ruling, but they were secret in the Mexico City CAB even before the ruling. The CAB also acted to forbid *golpeadores* (thugs hired by corrupted unions) from entering the CAB building and intimidating workers who were voting, formerly an open practice. In addition, the Mexico City CAB has begun identifying and analyzing collective contracts that have gone for a long period without a revision, because they are likely to be protection contracts. Details of each contract were to be published on the agency Web site (Campos 2009: 157). Thus, the process in Mexico City of political reform and democratization, combined with committed leadership and importation of technocrats, appears to be the only instance in which normative change came about in labor politics.[24] Prior experience in an organization protecting the legal rights of workers meant that labor lawyers in the CAB were committed to acting in favor of the rule of law. They understand the legal rights of workers and believe they should be respected.

Other domestic political changes were also putting pressure on the Mexican system of labor politics. These pressures may in some cases have been partly related to NAALC, but it is very hard to be certain of an effect. The first is court cases. In a case involving a federal CAB, decided on September 10, 2008, the Supreme Court resolved several conflicting appeals court cases on secret votes and declared that CABs "must ensure personal, free, direct and secret votes" on the part of workers (Suprema Corte 2008). The decision was unanimous among the five members of the court and made it clear that the obligation extends to CABs, not to unions, and applies to *recuentos* on conflicts over titularity, rather than to election of union leaders. This followed an appeals court case earlier in 2008 in the first circuit, which relied on NAALC and other international obligations on the part of Mexico in its decision to require secret votes. The ruling stated that "confidentiality is the guarantee that intimidation during voting will be avoided. It is obvious that open voting, which is common, is subject to pressures from those present, including the employers and the existing union."

Other court cases were also increasing the reform pressures. Exclusion clauses were ruled illegal by the Supreme Court in the mid-2000s, which had effects throughout the country at all levels.[25] Moreover, according to some interpretations, NAALC rulings were "part of the context" for an earlier Mexican Supreme Court ruling in 1996 that prohibitions on more than one union in the workplace were unconstitutional (Herzenberg 1996: 18). In fact, there were two Supreme Court rulings, both on May 21, 1996, and both concerning state laws, in which the court ruled that a prohibition on more than one union per workplace violated freedom of association guarantees. Another significant development for labor politics (as for environmental) was the creation of IFAI to promote transparency and freedom of information. It applies to all branches of government, including STPS and the CABs, even though the latter include nongovernmental actors in addition to public officials. In labor politics, IFAI has forced labor authorities to justify negative decisions, making it harder to shield corrupt, arbitrary practices from scrutiny, a view shared both by those critical of the existing labor regime, such as the author of an IFAI study, and by those in charge of administering labor standards (Giménez Cacho 2007: 32; interview with Mexico NAO, 2010).

Nongovernmental organizations, research institutes, and some unions have used IFAI to try to force more transparency into the system, and increasing numbers of documents were requested in the early years of its operation (Giménez Cacho 2007: 40). Because IFAI insisted that information on union registration and collective contracts be made available to anyone who asks, it has added to the pressure coming from NAALC cases. When Uniroyal employees were denied access to their union contract and other information, IFAI ruled (in case 0448/04) that the information must be made available to them. Likewise, in case 1305/04 (decided in February 2005), IFAI stated that collective contracts must be made available to parties that request them.[26] Under pressure, the secretary of STPS announced in April 2007 that all collective contracts at the federal level (more than 16,000 between the 2,403 federally registered unions) would be considered public information. By August 2007, 594 of these 2,403 unions had updated and publicized information on their executive committees and lists of members (Giménez Cacho 2007: 44).

By taking this step, the STPS followed in the footsteps of the Mexico City CAB, which was the pioneer in publishing electronic information on its collective contracts. Currently, in the Mexico City CAB, for each collective contract, one can learn the company it applies to, the number of workers covered, the date of revision or renegotiation, the length of the contract, and other information that reveals whether it complies with minimum legal standards. The STPS decision will go further in the sense that it will allow scrutiny of the contracts themselves. This important step reduces the margin of discretion and arbitrariness of decision making, and it will put pressure on the protection contract system. However, it has yet to be extended to the state level, and it also does not apply to internal union governance. In addition, note that this change occurred only because of pressure from NAALC and IFAI.

Conclusion

Mexican labor politics is a deeply entrenched system of protection, influence peddling, and institutionalized corruption. Despite pressure from NAALC, IFAI, and the domestic courts and ad hoc pressures from the federal labor ministry, little changed in Mexican labor politics in the first fifteen years of the NAALC agreement. Strategic responses to investigations brought resolution of some specific cases, righted a few individual wrongs, and resulted in some institutional innovations, at least on paper. But the cases examined here reveal a persistent failure to observe norms of good governance. They show that most labor authorities failed to assimilate rule of law norms.

State CABs, in conjunction with state governments, local businesses, and investors, have enormous scope for manipulating labor law implementation (Alcade interview, 2010; Juan interview, 2010). State governments have been opposed to public information on registries, as they claim it would violate commercial privacy (STPS interview, 2010). Some states have agreements with unions that the unions won't demand salary increases or titularity and instead will leave the decision of which union represents their workers to the firms alone. Labor organizations such as STIMAHCS, which are considered proworker, are less likely to be chosen by firms.

The reports of the U.S. NAO make clear a pattern in which workers are represented by "unions" (more accurately, protection contracts) that serve the purposes of management but not labor, because rights are consistently denied, sometimes flagrantly. Workers who complain are threatened and intimidated, not simply with the loss of their jobs but also with blacklisting, making it difficult for them to find further employment. When groups of workers act together to form a new union, registration is denied on technical grounds, meaning that CAB officials contrive spurious reasons to reject the applications. When new unions *are* registered and *recuentos* held, workers are intimidated into rejecting the new union.

The NAALC cases arose mainly within the maquiladora sector. Little difference is apparent between federal and state-level CABs in terms of adherence to rule of law, as both levels were the subject of NAALC cases and both levels were found to be poor defenders of labor justice. There were no cases from the south of the country; all originated in the north or center, where the maquiladoras are concentrated and unionization is low. Both PRI and PAN governments were implicated, suggesting that poor enforcement of labor rights is not affected by party affiliation (although the one positive case of improved governance occurred in a PRD-controlled jurisdiction).

The problem is not with the clarity of Mexican labor law or with the interpretation of it. Writing in 2004, the U.S. NAO stated that "reviews of recent Mexican court decisions appear to support efforts to direct [local CABs] to comply with the law." Rather, the problem is with the conflict of interest institutionalized within the CABs and also with the failure of the federal government to require compliance with the law. The report continued: "The Government of Mexico itself has on several occasions recognized shortcomings in the union registration process, but, if it has taken action to address the matter, the results are not immediately evident."

The federal labor ministry STPS engaged in some self-started capacity building by strengthening its institutions (on gender, for example) and policies (on transparency). Likewise, there was at least a recognition at the federal level that serious compliance problems existed, many of which were due to poor levels of professionalization. The federal government reacted to the pregnancy case by signing agreements with thirteen states (by December 2003) to eliminate workplace discrimination based on pregnancy testing. The Federal Prevention and Elimination of Discrimination Act came into effect in 2003 as well, and it prohibits discrimination on the basis of pregnancy (U.S. NAO 2007: 50). Yet questions were raised as to the efficacy of these and other measures and as to the true commitment of the authorities to improving labor enforcement. The report on the Hidalgo case makes crystal clear the frustration felt by the U.S. NAO at the continuing failures to ensure justice.

> The use of administrative formalities to deny union registration has been raised as a concern in prior reports . . . and has been criticized by the ILO as inconsistent with international standards . . . the [NAO] reiterates its recommendation from prior reports of review that the Mexican government commit to making up-to-date information on unions and collective bargaining agreements available to interested parties through the establishment of a public registry. (U.S. NAO 2007: 30, 33)

One case after another found obstructions to labor justice, mainly in freedom of association and collective bargaining rights. Recalcitrant local CABs ignored independent unions and favored government-recognized unions who were in collusion with company management. Driven by a concern to promote local investment, they tolerated labor injustices. Entrenched economic interests utterly captured the CABs, which continued to make decisions in contravention of the law. The NAALC spotlight was not bright enough or sustained enough to shame them into internalizing rule of law norms. Investigations were conducted by an agency of the U.S. Department of Labor, which was not seen as independent and neutral by Mexico, and was undermined by the waning interest in workers' rights of the Bush administration. Labor investigations were therefore politicized by ideological bias and nationalist sentiments. Mexico denied problems and refused to send information; NAALC proved incapable of overcoming path-dependent decision making. Moreover, unlike the environmental agencies, labor authorities did not benefit from movement of trained NGO personnel through their ranks. Repeatedly, CABs were criticized for their lack of professionalism and knowledge of the law.

Yet against all odds, there were some positive results, too. The one partial exception to widespread lack of professionalism is the Mexico City CAB. Lawyers who had worked with labor groups were invited to join this agency in 2000, and it quickly gained a reputation as the most open and honest CAB in the country. Furthermore, as NGOs received favorable decisions on their complaints, they increased their efforts and made more submissions to the U.S. and Canadian NAOs. These later fell off, partly because the NGOs were dissatisfied with the results but also because the process of accepting complaints was arbitrary and they had no permanent role in the trilateral institutions. Moreover, as I have pointed out in this chapter, some favorable institutional and policy changes were made—sometimes because of NAALC but often due to other internal influences, such as court cases and IFAI. In addition, STPS was sensitized to public criticism, and the NAALC investigations prompted reactions such as including independent unions in reform negotiations (Nolan 2009; Compa 2001; Alcalde interview, 2010).[27]

But strategic responses in individual cases are not the same thing as normative socialization. A strategic response implies that if the scrutiny were to be lifted, practices would revert to the status quo ante. Absorption of rule of law norms signifies a cultural change: with or without international scrutiny, public authorities would follow the rule of law. When we compare the capacity-building and socialization effects of NAALC with those of NAAEC, it is clear that labor has been a relative failure. The NAALC provided pressures that induced the federal government to act strategically in certain labor cases, but without internalizing a logic in favor of the rule of law.

The STPS maintains that it cannot interfere in cases where state CABs violate labor rules, even though it has intervened strategically when NAALC cases highlighted problems (STPS interview, 2010). Most local CABs were even worse than federal CABs or the STPS in terms of rejecting rule of law norms. Then again, the Mexico City CAB, even without NAALC pressures, moved beyond the federal government to adopt pro–rule of laws norms, and the reason was that a top-level political decision was made to import NGO experts with experience in defending workers' rights. Norms were implanted through these personnel.

4 Governance and Attitude Change

Causes and Limits

EMPIRICAL ANALYSIS REVEALS THAT IMPROVEMENTS TO GOVER-nance—notably, attitudes to rule of law—were more substantial and successful in the environmental agencies than in the labor agencies. To be sure, enormous problems remain in both sectors. Progress is painfully slow, and indicators such as enforcement results and implementation suggest much work remains to be done. However, looking only at attitude change—or pro-rule of law norm socialization—we see a pattern emerging. Under pressure, the environmental agencies show signs of adopting pro–rule of law norms. Labor agencies do not. In labor politics, some small institutional change and policy reform occurred, but agency officials resisted rule of law norms and rejected intrusion by NAFTA partners. How do we explain the different rates of norm socialization?

Pressure for change in both sectors comes from three principal sources: (1) international organizations, especially NAAEC and NAALC (and to a much lesser extent, the ILO and the OECD); (2) domestic and international civil society groups; and (3) domestic political institutions such as the courts and IFAI, the freedom of information agency. The mechanisms of norm socialization as commonly understood by international relations scholars were broadly equivalent across the two sectors. The side agreement institutions brought increases in technical communication, persuasion, arguing, convincing, and shaming. The shaming effects of factual records and public reports led to profoundly political pressures on Mexico; simultaneous technical discussions took place in depoliticized, nonconfrontational settings, insulated from public scrutiny. (On the implications of these very different strategies for norm socialization, see Checkel 2001.) Institutional design permitted NGO input and standing in both areas, which gave NGOs an incentive to mobilize and create advocacy networks. They took advantage of these opportunities. Both side agreements provided for independent reports to be made publicly available. Citizen complaints resulted in strategic responses by both STPS (the labor ministry) and SEMARNAT.

In short, socialization mechanisms were apparent in both ministries: (1) consistent, frequent, informal, technical discussions took place between labor and environmental technocrats across the three member states; (2) complaints by NGOs meant that reports were available to the public, who had access to new information on how Mexican authorities tolerated infringements of law; (3) media and public pressure exposed agency behavior to the cold light of day and forced the authorities to respond; and (4) courts and IFAI passed judgment on the agencies that reinforced actions taken by external organizations and by NGOs. A new opportunity structure was made available for activists in both the labor and environmental areas (through the NAAEC and NAALC). Moreover, agencies in both areas were in regular communication with their counterparts in Washington and Ottawa.

Given that the *mechanisms* of norm socialization were equivalent, variation in the *impact* of socialization pressures can be fully explained only by important differences in contextual factors, both domestic and in the side agreement institutions, *not in the mechanisms of socialization per se.* Plausible contextual factors include differences in the design of the side agreements themselves and differences in the domestic institutions or practices within the environment and labor sectors. Without a thorough comparison of these differences, it's hard to know why mechanisms of norm socialization worked better in the environmental area than in the labor area. In this chapter, I turn to a discussion of these issues and how they resulted in different levels of adaption.

In the first chapter, I identified two relevant differences in institutional design and domestic capacity that matter and that vary across these cases: regional institutional design and professionalization among agency and NGO officials. First, the design of NAFTA's environmental institutions (especially NAAEC, but to a lesser extent the border institutions) requires permanent access and standing by civil society groups and permits findings to be made by the institution semi-independently of member state control. The same is not true on the labor side. Second, levels of professionalization vary considerably between the two sectors. Higher levels of education and training among civil society personnel working on environmental issues enabled them to communicate on scientific and legal levels, increasing their influence in SEMARNAT. Likewise, CEC capacity-building programs aimed at Mexican agencies increased their technical proficiency, though results of the programs are highly variable. Nongovernmental organizations and bureaucrats were better able to communicate with each other, and regardless of the fact that their interests were not always in tune, they shared a common understanding of problems and an ability to use mechanisms of consultation, information sharing, and appeal.

The structural condition of ministry permeability, seen in the mobility of officials between NGOs and domestic agencies, made a difference to professionalization. The movement of personnel between NGOs, federal environmental agencies, and the NAFTA institutions created epistemic understandings across these groups. Leadership positions in SEMARNAT and other environmental agencies were filled by NGO leaders and CEC officials, injecting new values into the public authorities. Where leaders promoted new values (of good governance) and filled positions in their agencies with bureaucrats who also supported these values, normative socialization was more successful. But the ability of personnel to move was affected by differences in domestic institutional configurations. The environmental institutions were evolving rapidly in the 1990s, becoming more specialized and adding new personnel, making them permeable to new influences. In the labor sector, strong preexisting domestic economic interests allied to local institutions of labor relations opposed modernizing reform that would lead to internalization of a rule of law logic.

Later in this chapter, I suggest ways these findings may be generalized to provide both a framework for studying other international organizations and policy guidance. For the moment, I want to be clear about some epistemological and methodological limits to my findings. First, our understanding of the effect of variation in design and capacity would benefit from deeper ethnographic-style research (such as embedding in organizations over long periods of time) to test the conclusions presented in this book. For example, we don't know for certain whether NAAEC- or NAALC-led capacity-building programs (including interaction between Mexican agencies and NAFTA counterparts) actually led to real change in governance in Mexico (as opposed to being advertised as achievements), because the trilateral agencies do not measure the effect of capacity building.

On the dependent variable of normative socialization, there is consensus on the labor side that socialization has not occurred, but there are conflicting views on the environmental side. Many analysts and policy makers believe there is clear evidence of pro–rule of law socialization, though some important NGO participants believe the authorities continue to be prone to corruption and prodevelopment interests. Evidence from interviews with more than sixty policy makers, NGOs, civil servants, think tank representatives, academics, and others in both the United States and Mexico—as well as the statements and actions of the agencies and analysis of secondary sources—lead me to the conclusion that norm transformation *has* occurred in the environment agencies. They may not have transformed as much as NGOs would like, but environmental politics is not the same as it was in the mid-1990s.

Comparing the NAAEC and NAALC cases also clarifies the difference between environmental and labor agencies in a number of ways. We were able to see (1) how they initially reacted to allegations of wrongdoing, (2) whether they eventually admitted or rejected the existence of problems in a given case, and (3) how they later reacted in practice (by changing policy or practice, taking action to rectify a wrong, and so forth). In the following sections, I look at evidence of strategic and normative responses by the Mexican government to pressures emanating from NAAEC and NAALC. Normative socialization represents variation on the dependent variable. In later sections, I return to a discussion of the contextual factors (institutional design and domestic capacity), summarizing empirical findings.

Strategic Responses

In both the environment and labor ministries, officials responded in strategic ways to pressures from the NAFTA institutions, and both SEMARNAT and STPS exhibited a tendency to play the role of good partner. For example, in the NAFTA negotiations, Mexico sought to signal that it was committed to environmental policy. Luis Manuel Guerra, one of Mexico's most prominent environmental scientists, claims that the Salinas government's determination to secure NAFTA and its realization that the opposition of American environmental groups threatened the agreement prompted Mexico to upgrade its institutions (interview, 2008).[1] The creation of the environmental enforcement agency Profepa and SEMARNAP was a signal that the environment was important to the Mexican government. Indeed, in the eyes of virtually every observer, Profepa's creation was a direct result of the desire to demonstrate to skeptical American environmentalists that Mexico was committed to environmental enforcement (see Gil Corrales 2007: 167–68, 187; SEMARNAP 2000: 343–44; Azuela 2006: 499). Mexico responded to scrutiny by U.S. lawmakers and environmental groups by devoting considerable efforts to improving its institutions and legal framework; it anticipated opposition in the United States, knowing that the free trade agreement could founder in Congress if it did not take preemptive action.

Once NAAEC was in place, the shadow of scrutiny also generated strategic reactions by the government. Enrique Lendo, SEMARNAT's head of International Affairs, stated that citizen submissions (the NAAEC complaint mechanism) put pressure on the ministry—attention from the media and international actors causes it to study the issue more carefully and/or resolve it more quickly (Lendo interview, 2008). The government tries to reduce possible negative repercussions by addressing complaints immediately. The CEC Secretariat also believes that Mexico is anticipating decisions and outcomes from the NAAEC institutions and is responding in ways that suggest it wants to avoid negative publicity. In the Los Remedios case, for example, the government denied a development permit to a firm after a citizen submission had been made. The denial came within the sixty-day response period after the submission was made, in other words, the period in which the government was expected to respond to the complaint.

The CEC eventually dismissed the submission, and the Mexican government's denial of the permit might have happened anyway, but according to the Secretariat legal officer familiar with the case, it certainly seemed that the government was responding directly to the submission, especially given the speed with which it reacted. Another example is the Tarahumara case, in which one of the points made in the factual record was that there were not enough environmental inspectors and their salaries were too low. After this factual record was completed, Profepa (which had received a copy and which is the agency responsible for inspections) sought to raise the salaries of Profepa inspectors. The issue of low salaries was included in a press release accompanying the factual record and therefore was publicly available. The CEC official responsible for the case believes the link between public criticism and government action is virtually certain.

Strategic behavior is even more widespread in labor. The federal government pressured state authorities, firms, and union confederations on an ad hoc basis in response to NAALC cases. Two NAALC cases (97/02 and 97/03) resulted in a declaration in May 2000, whereby the governments of the three member states committed themselves to ensuring secret votes and open information regarding collective contracts. However, Mexico did not comply with this, at least until collective contracts were required to be made available by IFAI, the transparency and information agency (Alcalde 2006: 170–71). Likewise, the government agreed to end pregnancy testing and publicize the rights of workers, which it did, partially. These steps occurred as a result of pressures from NAALC and domestic oversight institutions. The government also took measures to include independent (not co-opted) unions in reform discussions, as investigations under NAALC repeatedly pointed to their marginalization. However, as the reform process petered out, independent unions again found themselves on the outside. In other words, action was taken and measures agreed to under pressure, but follow-through was often absent.

Normative Change

Mexico acts strategically, playing the role of advanced member state by creating the right institutions, rejecting development applications that have been subject to complaint, pressuring corrupt officials and businesses (when the spotlight is turned on), and delaying decision making in the two NAFTA side agreement councils to avoid bad publicity. But there is also evidence of normative change in the environmental area: agency officials came to accept that the rule of law was a good thing for Mexico, and the scrutiny by both domestic NGOs and international organizations came to be tolerated (at least), and often welcomed.

Evidence of socialization comes from numerous interviews with environmental agency insiders, NGOs, and independent analysts, as well as reviews of official documents, secondary analyses, and accounts written by former top officials in the agencies. The federal ministry SEMARNAT has made a virtue of these external pressures. As early as 2000, a report lists its experience with NAAEC citizen submissions as an *achievement*, even though it had been embarrassed by them, and even though it had argued *against* the initial submission only four years earlier (SEMARNAP 2000: 359). Cozumel (the first submission) placed Mexico under the spotlight and revealed problems in the enforcement and regulatory processes. The submission was greeted with anger by SEMAR-NAP. It accused the CEC Secretariat of interference in internal Mexican affairs and violation of national sovereignty. It denounced CEMDA as anti-Mexican (Alanís interview, 2010). In other words, it acted as Mexican authorities had always acted: civil society was influential when it was co-opted and supportive. If it became critical, it was pushed out.

The break with CEMDA was overcome when the two organizations returned to work on a book they were jointly writing on trade and the environment. The agreement of SEMARNAP to a CEC factual record also began to open the window to dialogue (Alanís interview, 2010). Although Alanís stresses that continuing violations of rule of law, corruption, and pandering to development interests undermine transformation, it is clear from most sources that Mexican environmental officials came to accept the constraints of the NAFTA institutions as part of the process of modernization. They came to believe that business as usual was no longer acceptable. And this evolution went beyond strategic reactions—ministry officials and those from related agencies repeatedly demonstrated a commitment to rule of law norms, even when they acknowledged lapses in the field. (One interviewee stated frankly that when environmental inspectors work directly with developers, there is bound to be at least some corruption.)

In the words of the former general manager of the Border Environment Cooperation Commission, NAFTA was Mexico's "school of democracy" (Cabrera interview, 2008). Mexico was socialized into new attitudes on the environment by the environmental institutions, according to Cabrera. Left to natural processes, socialization would take much longer. Having originally viewed the NAAEC as an *hijo no deseado* (unwanted child), it is now welcomed as a catalyst of better behavior in Mexico, according to the chief advisor to the secretary of SEMARNAT (Guerrero interview, 2007). In an official report, SEMARNAT stated approvingly that NAAEC "has contributed to the environmental regulatory framework, compliance on the part of producers, and has also encouraged social participation in decision-making" (SEMARNAT 2007: 135). The environment agencies have also become more relaxed about criticism from NGOs and abandoned the practice of selecting friendly participants to take part in meetings of the CEC and the border institutions. Block refers to this as a "maturing of the democratic process" and attributes it to Mexico's experience in the CEC (Block 2003: 516). The same did not happen in Mexico's labor politics. Technocratic communication, structures whereby citizens could bring complaints, and a formal set of rules stipulating enforcement of labor standards have not resulted in internalized norms of rule of law (and there is very little public participation).

Evidence of SEMARNAT socialization also comes from its positive reaction to the 2002 creation of IFAI, which made information on permitting for construction projects available, helping environmental NGOs. The agency's effects have been felt in both SEMARNAT and STPS, but they have been viewed very differently by the two agencies. Officials at SEMARNAT are upbeat about IFAI, even though SEMARNAT was so poorly organized that it initially had no idea what information it actually had or how to locate it. It rejected information requests for fear it would be punished. The transparency law and IFAI helped SEMARNAT organize its information systems professionally, funds were available to help, and SEMARNAT now actively supports access to information. In 2003, it signed an accord on access to information and transparency with four civil society organizations, committing itself to open and transparent decision making, inclusion of civil society groups, and access to information. The purpose was to promote Principle 10 issues stemming from the Rio declaration on the environment and development, which advocated citizen access to information, participation in decision making, capacity building, and access to justice.[2]

The ministry claimed that access to information is important (1) for purposes of scrutiny and oversight by the public, including reducing corruption, strengthening the rule of law, and improving accountability; (2) to help change the culture of secrecy and bring greater democratic maturity, which would increase public confidence in institutions and strengthen freedom of expression; and (3) limit the arbitrariness and discretion of authorities, in turn improving the decision-making environment (SEMARNAT 2004: 13–14). A SEMARNAT pamphlet published in 2008 indicated strategies and methods for promoting citizen participation. Numerous committees and consultative groups, both regional and sectoral, provide access to decision making for citizens. There are also avenues through which citizens can take more direct action to complain, such as *denuncia popular*.[3] Officials at SEMARNAT are positive about the effect of the transparency law. "It's a weapon. It changed everything," explained Oscar Callejo, deputy director general for research at SEMARNAT. There is less corruption when officials know they are being watched. Local issues are accessible to citizens, who can check whether permitting, enforcement, authorizations, and other processes are done correctly.

In comparison with the environment, there is no evidence that STPS or most CABs have internalized norms of respect for rule of law. Along with reports from the U.S. Labor Department, which conducted numerous NAALC investigations, IFAI has prompted STPS to create a database of unions so workers can check to see whether they are represented. But the reaction was reluctant and piecemeal, and STPS dragged its feet for years. Moreover, the database lacked important information, making it practically useless to workers seeking to find out whether they were represented by a union and, if so, which union. A community of like-minded officials has not formed among labor bureaucrats and NGOs as it has in the environmental area. Agency officials do not welcome critical voices from civil society or external scrutiny. A pro–rule of law culture is virtually absent. There is little interest in normative change at the ministerial level or among the major co-opted union confederations (CTM, CROC, and CROM) or evidence that mechanisms of shaming or persuasion have been effective (Gambrill interview, 2009). In fact, the government responds to criticism by insisting that Mexican labor law is advanced and that the role of STPS is to communicate Mexican labor policy, rather than to learn or adapt.

Requests for interviews with STPS officials get funneled to one office, where officials are adamant that NAALC has resulted in no change to Mexican labor administration (and where they will speak only off the record). The role of that office is to "explain" Mexican labor law and practice. There is no need for intrusive action by other member states (STPS interviews, 2007, 2009). Mexico does not require transformation by outsiders but rather to improve its presentation, according to the official line. Whatever pressures for normative transformation may be coming from NAFTA, officials do not see it making an impact. The most important result has been a better understanding of Mexican labor standards in the three member states, all of which are part of the ILO but come from different legal traditions. Mexico's protection of workers is now understood better by the other two member states, and there is less criticism from them, according to one official.

But Mexican labor politics is seen in a very different light by those outside the labor ministry. In its investigations, the U.S. NAO has been extremely critical of Mexican labor practices. As late as 2007, a U.S. NAO report stated that pregnancy testing had continued at the plant it was investigating at least until July 2005, despite earlier commitments by Mexico to eliminate the practice, which "raises concern as to whether Mexico is effectively meeting prior commitments" (U.S. NAO 2007: iii). The report also criticized reliance on technical grounds to reject union petitions seeking collective bargaining rights, unwarranted delays resulting from ineffective communication between federal and state labor authorities, and a general lack of transparency as to how Mexican labor law recognizes unions and collective bargaining agreements. (U.S. NAO 2007: ii–iii)

In some cases, the local CABs, which grant recognition to unions at the state level, were claiming that labor law permitted only one registered union per workplace, though the U.S. NAO found this to be incorrect when it issued a report on a case involving Sony in Nuevo Laredo (U.S. NAO 1996). In other cases, the Mexican NAO denied the U.S. NAO access to some officials it wished to interview. Not surprisingly, given these contrasting attitudes, misunderstandings between the member states are rife. In a report in the late 1990s, the Mexican NAO complained bitterly about perceived attacks from the U.S. NAO:

> The [Mexican] authorities are denounced in a false and distorted manner. National Administrative Offices should be more careful when analyzing and accepting potential public communications.[4]

Neither politicization nor technical discussions were sufficient to bring about acceptance of rule of law norms in labor politics. The head of the AFL-CIO's Mexico City office explained, "The STPS looks at the NAALC as a necessary burden, an offense to Mexican sovereignty, something they have to put up with" (Davis interview, 2009). Mexico is still at the denial stage, the basis of which is that its labor rights regime is advanced and interference is a violation of its national sovereignty. Instead of accepting rule of law norms and taking action when laws or rights are violated, the government refers to sovereignty, intergovernmental cooperation, and preexisting Mexican labor standards. The kinds of failures necessary to promote a new culture of governance have not taken place, at least in the eyes of STPS officials.

Conduits of Socialization

In this part, I look in more detail at the factors that affect the reception of norms by public officials. We may think of these as conduits of socialization because they are channels through which mechanisms of socialization flow, and they can be broader or narrower, constraining or facilitating socialization. There are two: (1) the independence of the international organization from which the norms flow and the access they provide for NGOs and (2) the level of scientific, technical, or legal professionalization of public officials and NGOs. Professionalization is facilitated by "shuffling," that is, movement of key personnel between NGOs, international organizations, and domestic agencies. Shuffling is in turn affected by leadership, permeability of public agencies, and the extent to which they are captured by powerful economic interests.

Independent International Organizations

Variation in the design of the NAAEC and NAALC institutions affects pro–rule of law norm socialization. Recall from the discussion in Chapter 1 that research findings in international relations and sociology led us to deduce that independent institutions and institutionalized access for civil society would lead to greater levels of legitimacy and commitment (Keohane et al. 2000; Goldstein et al. 2000; Kay 2005; Reimann 2006; Pevehouse 2002). Where institutions and interests gain legitimacy, the messages they communicate are more credible and effective (Zimbardo and Ebbesen 1969; Cialdini and Trost 1998).

On both the independence and access measures, NAAEC is stronger than NAALC. The NAAEC's Secretariat has more operational independence than the NAALC's Secretariat (indeed, the latter was closed in 2010!). The former needs the approval of two of the three member states for some investigations and factual records but can do others without approval. Moreover, because civil society participation was institutionalized through JPAC and the citizen submission processes, environmental NGOs were more committed to the NAAEC process. Mandatory public participation is also evident in border projects funded by the NADB, which are required to have local community groups in various stages of the projects. This provides forums for debate, transparency, access to information, and inclusion in decision making. Public input was a new experience for Mexican local authorities and government ministries, who were accustomed either to excluding public input or packing consultative committees with political cronies. It has increased legitimacy and support for projects and often spills over into other forms of local governance, increasing awareness of rights and access to information (see Abel and Sayoc 2006; Cabrera interview, 2008).

Nongovernmental organization participation in the CEC's JPAC (a permanent agenda-setting body of environmental NGO representatives) brought them recognition and standing, increased the legitimacy of public participation in Mexican environmental politics, and strengthened the environmental movement. The CEC helped to institutionalize a transnational environmental advocacy network that included the CEC itself and then had a boomerang effect on SEMARNAT (Keck and Sikkink 1998). This committed civil society groups to the process and to the institution—it locked them in, because even if they disagree with certain findings or outcomes, their membership in the trilateral agency makes it harder to back out and forces state actors to take them into account. Their participation is less ad hoc. For example, the head of CEMDA, Gustavo Alanís, became a JPAC member for the second time in 2008, despite being critical of the way it is treated by member states.

The CEC's success in prompting civil society participation was evident even in the early years. It created new opportunities for NGOs to participate in the process and to gain recognition. "Funding and technical support have allowed Mexican NGOs and indigenous peoples to . . . speak up in international fora, exchange information and technical expertise with American and Canadian NGOs and build capacity at the local level" (Silvan 2005: 2). "NAFTA undoubtedly provided an impetus" to increased public participation in Mexico (Torres 2002: 213). Both enforcement and private sector attitudes have improved as a result.

Moreover, the process of mandatory consultation was replicated at the domestic level. A GAO report indicated that it gave Mexico "the political will to include citizen input" (GAO 1997: 22). According to SEMARNAT's coordinator of transparency and social participation, the 1996 reforms of LGEEPA provided an avenue to include citizens in decisions (de Buen interview, 2008). It opened space for participation, from planning to evaluation, and created regional councils as part of the consultation process. Public consultation (for example, when creating a new protected area) is now mandatory (Rabasa interview, 2008).

In the labor sector, the lack of an independent trilateral agency with power similar to the NAAEC had observable implications. Investigations are carried out by an agency in another member state (from which the complaint is made), robbing them of a sense of neutrality and politicizing them in two ways. First, there is a predictably nationalistic reaction to the effect that "our system is fine, what we need to do is explain it better" (STPS interviews, 2007, 2009, 2010). Mexico resisted pressures from the United States and on some occasions refused to provide information or permit access to certain individuals. In fact, the ad hoc nature of nationalized investigations some-times worked to Mexico's benefit because civil society groups often felt the U.S. agency was overly deferential to its Mexican counterpart. On some occa-sions, the U.S. NAO decided not to hold public hearings as it conducted re-views of cases, instead simply reviewing documents submitted to it by both sides. Nonetheless, in its report on the first four years of the operation of the NAALC, the Mexican NAO complained about the actions of the U.S. NAO in stark terms.

> We are concerned by the fact that declarations made by Party officials have led to a certain degree of public misunderstanding and have subsequently given rise to the assumption that the mechanisms set down in the NAALC effec-tively circumvent internal policy or serve for the *exertion of pressure between the Parties.* Likewise, we wish to express our opposition to the intervention of overseas nongovernmental organizations in the internal disputes of national trade unions. It is entirely unjustifiable that any NAO . . . take on what are practically the functions of a tribunal. [The Mexican NAO] does not believe it should participate in hearings staged by its United States counterpart, since *even its observer status would necessarily jeopardize national sovereignty.* Mex-ico should not permit the United States NAO or any other United States agency to assume the role of a jurisdictional or moral tribunal vis à vis events taking place in Mexico. . . . Public communications were not designed to sub-ject the member nations to proceedings in which persons other than the na-tional authorities may judge the performance of its sovereign power. The Par-ties should therefore not be expected to adapt to or recognize mechanisms which are alien to their traditions and culture. Different groups, persons or organizations frequently resort to the United States NAO with the aim of de-nouncing the supposed violation of Mexican labor legislation. We have noted that these groups often request the intervention of the United States when corresponding legal resources have yet to be exhausted or when the latter are still pending resolution.[5]

Second, investigations were politicized in an ideological sense. The Bush ad-ministration accepted many fewer NAALC cases than the Clinton adminis-tration. Ten cases were accepted for review in the seven years of overlap be-tween the NAALC and the Clinton administration (out of fifteen submissions). As the U.S. NAO investigations increased in the mid-1990s and as the results became more favorable to Mexican labor groups, they devoted more resources to complaints (Nolan 2009). Petitions became more sophisticated legally, and they had greater success because their complaints resonated with the U.S. NAO. Legal, rational vocabulary triumphed where street politics did not.

However, only two cases were accepted in the eight years of the Bush administration (out of four submissions).[6] The former head of Mexico's NAFTA office in Washington, D.C., asserted that claimants believed the Bush administration would be less sympathetic than the Clinton administration to complaints against Mexico (de la Calle interview, 2009). "The Bush Administration has no real stake in NAALC and much less of a political incentive to placate U.S. labor movements" (Graubart 2005: 139). When the United States lost interest and reviewed fewer cases, labor groups turned away. Those most in need of support all but gave up on NAALC because they believed it to be weak and inconsistent. Moreover, there was no permanent institutional standing for NGOs, and so they lost little by abandoning NAALC. Its pressure for change was so limited that workers' organizations turned elsewhere (Alcalde 2006: 175).

By 2004, the Mexican NAO was taking less seriously the requests for information from the U.S. NAO, playing the weaknesses in NAALC to its advantage. According to the AFL-CIO's representative in Mexico City, when there is a complaint, STPS looks to see if there is any real pressure from the U.S. or Canadian side—how serious they are—before it decides how to treat the complaint. Under the Bush administration, there was no real pressure on Mexico, but "basically a nod and a wink" (Davis interview, 2009). Consequently, the Mexican authorities would not bother taking action. They were evasive and passive. In response to written questions by the U.S. NAO, the Mexican side provided partial answers. Moreover, in the Puebla case, although the U.S. NAO requested consultations with its Mexican counterparts, it managed only a brief meeting in Mexico City and was denied access (by the Mexican NAO) to meetings with other government officials.

Politicization has an impact on the commitment of NGOs to bring cases. Even with the assistance of U.S. and Canadian partners, Mexican labor groups found the process to be uncertain and ineffective. "Few tangible benefits" have come about through NAALC, according to one prominent analyst (Polaski 2006: 35).[7] Cooperative mechanisms such as seminars have addressed important issues but have not been followed through, and results have been insufficient. In the eyes of its natural constituents, NAALC has lost legitimacy (Polaski 2006: 50–51). Thus, although NAALC gave standing to civil society groups (because it allowed them to bring complaints), its structure—with ad hoc investigations by national NAOs and the lack of an agenda-setting role—never committed labor unions and NGOs to the process. Its legitimacy was weaker. Even those who understood that the NAALC was about requiring enforcement rather than getting someone's job back found it had no independent resources to assist in capacity building, no process of consulting with NGOs, and no agenda-setting role. Without an independent investigatory agency, the decision on how to treat public communications and conduct hearings was largely in the hands of U.S. agency officials, so that adversarial national antagonisms were always a threat.

The subsequent loss of commitment by Mexican labor groups had considerable consequences because although NAALC strengthened civil society groups when it worked, it worked only on an ad hoc basis. Citing Lance Compa, a former member of the CLC, Nolan states,

> Participation in the NAALC process . . . shifted the political dynamics within Mexico so that independent unions and their supporters gained access to policymakers, and were able to better lobby for reform. Filing a case conferred legitimacy on local Mexican groups, because when they were backed by transnational advocates, they became more important actors within Mexico. (Nolan 2009: 46)

When fewer cases were accepted (and those that were accepted resulted in disappointing outcomes), labor groups stopped making the effort. Mexican labor agencies felt less normative pressure. In comparison, environmental NGOs remain engaged in the trilateral process, and Mexican environmental agencies continue to feel normative pressure. The institutions and resources of NAAEC are part of the domestic environmental policy process in Mexico.[8]

In summary, an independent international organization with fact-finding powers and with permanent standing and access for civil society groups is more likely to facilitate norm transfer. It commits civil society groups to the process of agenda setting, scrutiny, and complaint. It also denationalizes investigations, making them more neutral and more consistent in the sense of not being subject to the political whims of member state governments. In the case of the NAAEC, the member state being investigated must agree to the investigation—it is not imposed—and the agency is staffed in part by Mexicans themselves, mitigating the feeling that sovereignty is being violated. When member states approve the factual records against themselves (or don't reject them), this also commits them to the process. The NAAEC process differs markedly from the NAALC process, in which Mexico may face an investigation whether it likes it or not (or alternatively, for reasons of political sensitivity unrelated to the facts of a given case, the country receiving the complaint may refuse to investigate).

Professionalization and Capacity Building

Professionalization and strengthened technical capacities are also means through which norm socialization is facilitated. As discussed earlier, increased technical proficiency (legal and scientific), professionalization (using understood and recognized procedures), and availability of information lead to better communication between interests and bureaucrats (for a similar argument, see Haas 1992). Social similarities within cultures or organizations facilitate communication and enhance credibility and legitimacy (Meyer and Rowan 1983; Strang and Meyer 1993; Keohane et al. 2000; Farrell 2001). Participants understand problems and issues from the same starting point, and though their interests in the outcome may differ, they agree on definitions, measures, processes and procedures, and validity. Conversely, lack of technical proficiency and professionalization impedes communication and shared understanding. Narrower self-interest is more likely to prevail in making decisions about application of the law. Capacity building *in its own right* increases the likelihood of norm socialization because it changes the abilities, know-how, and attitudes of civil servants and NGOs. They are inducted into a common understanding, and their perspectives become tuned.

On the environmental side, an epistemic community of like-minded bureaucrats was created in SEMARNAT, who then shared common understandings with NGO officials. A new generation of Mexican civil servants appeared, embraced international environmental standards, and no longer shrank from international or domestic scrutiny. The SEMARNAT officials do not necessarily share interests in outcomes with NGO officials (a prerequisite for an epistemic community, as defined by Haas). Environmental NGOs prioritize environmental protection; SEMARNAT conducts impact assessments, issues permits, and participates in enforcement (and thus by following legal procedures, balances the interests of the environment with those of developers). But they do share an interest in the process: greater information and transparency, accountability, rule of law, and participation. On those occasions when decisions are not "green enough" for the environmental groups, they nevertheless continue to work closely and cooperatively with SEMARNAT. They do not take to the streets. Technically proficient NGOs enhance their power and influence within the bureaucracy when they are speaking with technically proficient bureaucrats (Haas 1992: 19).

Technocratic communication, information sharing, and capacity building have increased. Communication through conference calls and e-mails has grown, mostly to deal with NAFTA business. In an official report, SEMARNAT confirmed that since the introduction of NAFTA, it had developed a closer working relationship with its counterparts in the United States and Canada (SEMARNAP 2000: 358). Although communication has not been fully depoliticized, it is much more technical than political. Its Office of International Affairs manages more than a hundred international environmental agreements, but what distinguishes NAFTA is that it is "probably the only international environmental instrument in which technocrats speak directly to their counterparts outside Mexico, and don't go through the filter of the foreign ministry" (Lendo interview, 2008).

But this communication requires agency officials to have sufficient training to understand and make use of transmitted information. Although capacity building is by no means solely the result of the CEC, its working groups do have an impact through technical research and awareness-raising activities, according to SEMARNAT's head of International Affairs, who claimed that most CEC activities result in capacity building in Mexico (Lendo interview, 2008). Examples are the phasing out of DDT and the creation of the PRTR, a tool to raise civil society awareness of emissions (Garver personal communication, 2007).

Reviews of academic and agency publications, firsthand accounts, and interviews with high-ranking policy makers and NGO officials (including the former heads of two environmental agencies, the current number two at SEMARNAT, the head of CEMDA, and the number two at the CEC Secretariat) reveal that NAAEC is the most important causal influence on the wide-ranging institutional and legal reforms in the years 1992–96. There is widespread agreement that NAFTA prompted an upgrading of Mexico's environmental institutional capacity, though progress should not be overstated and there is still a long way to go. The consensus extends to members of NAAEC and border environmental institutions, staff members in Mexico's environmental agencies, NGO participants, and academics. Mexico now sees the benefits of access to technical expertise, according to SEMARNAT's chief advisor to the secretary (Guerrero interview, 2007). Environmental law, institutions, and public participation are stronger, he claims.

Furthermore, the ability of NGOs to be successful in arguing cases depends on their technical abilities. Environmental NGO staff are increasingly professional, gaining law or advanced academic degrees; learning to communicate in a sophisticated ways by compiling data, developing mailing lists, communicating with the press and public, and using the Internet to build international links; and improving their leadership, management, fund-raising, and personnel resources (Puentes interview, 2008). Training among traditional labor leaders remains much lower. They are older, less educated, and less mobile in terms of moving into government agencies. Among labor confederations, the CTM was not represented by a leader with as much as an undergraduate university degree until 2005. The leader of CROM, Ignacio Cuauhtémoc Paleta, likewise has no university education. The third major confederation, CROC, is led by Isaías González Cuevas, a member of the federal Chamber of Deputies for the PRI party. He has a secondary school education.

The most important environmental groups, such as CEMDA and FMCN, are led by individuals with master's degrees, law degrees, or doctorates. Ernesto Enkerlin, who moved to Conanp from an NGO, holds a PhD from Texas A&M. Gustavo Alanís gained a master's in International Law from American University. This makes them candidates to take professional positions not simply in NGOs but in the CEC Secretariat, JPAC, and SEMARNAT. Advanced education facilitates technical communication and makes a common understanding of issues more likely. In combination with their mobility (which I address later), this helps transfer of pro–rule of law norms into SEMARNAT. Environmental groups are no longer reliant on either street protests or a small number of high profile, well-connected individuals—what Alejandra Salazar of Pronatura called "big environmental dudes" (interview, 2008)—but instead are represented by a cadre of trained professionals (Villegas interview, 2008). In short, higher levels of education and training help internalize pro–rule of law norms, dissolving nationalism and clientelism in favor of international norms and standards. An epistemic understanding fosters respect for rule of law.

The capacity of NGOs to contribute to the process of decision making and problem solving is affected by environmental education and training programs. Some of this capacity building is carried out by the environmental

NGOs themselves. Pronatura has trained officials in more than a hundred NGOs, as well as local officials. There are master's degrees on environmental studies at UNAM and Colmex, where many NGO workers study.[9] For example, UNAM has a diploma on the Environmental Dimension in the Design and Execution of Public Policy. Both UNAM and Colmex are in Mexico City, which is where most capacity building occurs, although there are some programs outside the capital, such as at Colegio de la Frontera Norte and Colegio de la Frontera Sur. Mexican higher education institutions have also created new environmental law centers that provide legal advice, train lawyers, and therefore contribute to better understanding and enforcement (Herrera 2008). Likewise, CEMDA's own work on environmental litigation has been part of the process of capacity building, according to Alejandro Villegas (interview, 2008). It has helped other NGOs through alliances, training, and demonstration effects. It trains groups on how to submit cases and structure effective action.

Capacity has also been built through increased linkages with American environmental groups (labor NGOs and independent unions have benefited from similar interaction). Beginning with the announcement in June 1990 that trade negotiations were to begin, Mexican and U.S. environmental groups started to establish contacts and share information. In 1992, the Natural Resources Defense Council met with Mexican environmental groups and found few with the capacity to mobilize opposition to the NAFTA negotiations (Carmona interview, 2008). That realization was a catalyst for U.S. and Canadian groups to promote and support Mexican environmental activists (Torres 2002). In a short period of time, cross-border links between groups had strengthened considerably.

Technical expertise and funding opportunities for Mexican environmental groups increased. A number of Mexican NGOs were created or supported by U.S. foundations (Villegas interview, 2008), which in turn asked for work plans and strategies to be developed, which improved capacity. For example, CEMDA still receives most of its financial support from U.S. organizations, and without NAFTA, it would not have come into existence. Several groups (including Pronatura and the Inter-American Association for the Defense of the Environment) also have links to other Latin American countries. By contrast, cross-border cooperation among labor groups is confined to small, independent unions and labor research NGOs, rather than the large union confederations.

Capacity-building support also comes through the programs of NAAEC's trilateral environmental agency, the CEC (as I pointed out in detail in Chapter 2). It provides Mexico with resources to upgrade its collection and dissemination of data, as the member states work toward compatibility in technical standards, regulations, and environmental data (see Block 2003; Hufbauer et al. 2000). Benefits were felt in the regulatory and permitting processes: as early as 1997, the GAO reported that the CEC "has been an important catalyst for developing a more transparent regulatory process and ensuring a more consistent application of environmental laws in Mexico" (GAO 1997: 22). A further source of capacity building is the power of the Secretariat to create independent reports on nonenforcement issues under Article 13 and the Article 14 and 15 process by which citizens make submissions. These have helped improve environmental impact assessments in Mexico because of greater pressure exerted by NGOs (Gallagher 2004: 77).

A ten-year review of the CEC claimed NAAEC-sponsored achievements in capacity building, citing progress in pesticide control, toxic chemical management, pollution prevention, public participation, habitat protection, government commitment, and environmental awareness (TRAC 2004). The CEC supports the Sustainable Coffee Fund, along with Banamex, the Mexican government, and others, promoting small-scale shade-grown coffee in southern Mexico (Vaughan 2003: 65, 82). It has supported and encouraged developing environmental statutes and norms, as well as benchmarking environmental norms, including harmonization of toxic release data and development of criteria for air emissions (see Vaughan 2003: 66). In addition, NAAEC helped bring about a new registry on emissions in Mexico and worked with NGOs to improve Mexican environmental conditions, according to the director of CEMDA (Alanís interview, 2007). It has induced Mexico to improve its diagnosis of environmental problems, create a list of priorities, and initiate government activities on the environment, all new steps (Blanca Torres, cited in Fox 2004: 267).

Growing information availability and transparency in environmental politics have been part of the capacity-building process. Both the CEC and U.S. NGOs are credited with bringing greater levels of transparency and openness to discussions (Torres 2002; Block 2003: 516). Public expectations have been affected in a positive way. Because of its work with the CEC and civil society groups, SEMARNAT is one of Mexico's most "open and transparent" ministries. A variety of new sources of information have been made available to

Mexican groups and citizens interested in environmental governance and outcomes, such as factual records and the registry on emissions. Along with more general dissemination work through the CEC and SEMARNAT Web sites, these have helped increase the availability and quality of information.

The transparency law and the information agency IFAI, established under the Fox administration (partly the result of NAFTA, according to Torres 2002), made information available on a variety of issues, such as pollution levels, control of permits, environmental impact assessments, and decision processes. Numerous NGOs reported that it is essential for them to have access to this information. Without it, they cannot participate, and accountability standards are poor. Pablo Uribe, from the La Paz office of CEMDA, explained that before IFAI, petitioners for information needed to use Article 103 in the federal law LGEEPA, which gives people the right to obtain documents and access information, but it is complicated because petitioners need to go to a particular office to acquire documents. Now people can make an Internet request and twenty days later get a response with the requested information.

Juan Carlos Carrillo of CEMDA's main Mexico City office said that CEMDA is successful in getting information through IFAI in 90 percent of cases. Uribe explained that IFAI works better at the federal level and that improvements need to be made at state and municipal levels. For example, the state of Baja California Sur has its own transparency law and institution, but they are very new. It does not have the authority to resolve disputes. For that, petitioners need to use the courts, which (at the state level) lack expertise on the environment. Moreover, Baja California Sur does not have an Internet information access system. A person seeking information needs to go to a particular office to present a letter. Officials tend to be resistant to information requests because they require more work. Their files are in disarray, and management is poor, according to Uribe. In other words, they face the same problem SEMARNAT did earlier.

Capacity-building effects have been felt in the border region, too, although the environmental stress there remains extremely serious. In making funding decisions, the Border Environment Cooperation Commission (BECC) requires that environmental impact assessments provide a higher level of reporting than the Mexican government has traditionally required: it asks for analysis of environmental data in addition to reporting of it, thus allowing interested parties to challenge the government's impact assessments (Abel and Sayoc 2006). In addition, NAFTA's border institutions committed both

Mexico and the United States to providing new funding for infrastructure development. The EPA provides grant aid to Mexican communities through the Border Environment Infrastructure Fund. Without NAFTA, these mechanisms would not exist.

Training of officials, both directly by U.S. agencies and through NAFTA border programs (such as the Utilities Management Institute and the Institutional Development Cooperation Program), has improved the abilities of utilities managers and administrators in areas of finance, administration, and other operational areas. Border institutions also provide resources and assistance to communities wishing to apply for funding, so that designs, technical studies, planning, and other tasks are given assistance. Resources from NAFTA have upgraded technical knowledge and problem-solving capabilities. Mandatory public participation is also important because it engenders debate and transparency. Citizen groups participating in consultation exercises build awareness of public policy.

In summary, the NAFTA institutions helped Mexican environmentalists speak a new language, using a vocabulary not of the streets but of the professions. They became scientifically, technically, and legally proficient. Speaking in 2008, CEMDA's director noted that "the law is being used more and more by NGOs in Mexico, and this strengthens NGOs in front of institutions. Technical, scientific and legal arguments are replacing direct action" (Alanís interview, 2008). It is clear from all available evidence that NAAEC and the border institutions played a role in capacity building, though it is by no means responsible for all of it. "Thank God we have NGOs with the technical capacity to discuss issues. Capacity building for Mexican society was very important," asserts a top SEMARNAT official (Guerrero interview, 2007). In his view, NAFTA is the reason. Right-to-know issues are better developed, NGO participation has been promoted, and public participation has been facilitated.

Labor politics has not benefited from such levels of capacity building because it was more institutionally stable, the resources of the CLC did not extend to capacity-building measures (except for occasional reports on labor markets), and the domestic agencies and interests were not receptive. The few initiatives that did occur, such as electronic job banks, were bilateral U.S.-Mexico initiatives. Moreover, there is little sign that traditional co-opted union confederations have made any efforts to increase technical training or professionalization among their own staff. Reviews of cases by the U.S. NAO found that the CABs, especially the state-level ones, were unprofessional and highly politicized, making decisions that favored their own interests at the expense of impartiality. They made procedural errors that delayed resolution of issues and caused confusion. The investigating NAOs often requested that improvements be made to transparency, communication, information, and levels of training and education among local CABs. The problem, as ever, was that they were never followed up.

It would be wrong to suggest that Mexican labor agencies are bereft of trained and skilled individuals. The Mexican NAO (in the labor ministry STPS), for example, has highly capable individuals who are (like their environmental counterparts) in constant communication with officials from other NAFTA member states over technical issues. They know perfectly well what it means to respect the rule of law and engage in good governance. But whatever they may feel as individuals about the propriety of labor politics and the application of labor justice, they steadfastly defend the status quo. They are constrained by a balkanized structure of entrenched interests (at the state level especially and among both labor and employers), most of which have little interest in opening the system to better governance because it would erode their privileges.

Some observers point to changes made to federal policy and practice resulting from NAALC cases as evidence of capacity building. In the Itapsa case, NAALC consultations between the Mexican and American governments resulted in Mexico agreeing to promote secret ballots in CAB votes (*recuentos*) when workers were deciding on the union they wanted to represent them. They also agreed to promulgate public information on collective contracts, so that workers could learn whether they were represented by a union (Nolan 2009). Other changes include the 2003 Federal Prevention and Elimination of Discrimination Act, creation of offices to address discrimination, and agreements between the federal government and a number of state governments to end pregnancy testing (U.S. NAO, 2007). Moreover, independent unions, through their NAALC activities and transnational campaigning, were able to secure better access to federal policy makers and were included in policy discussions. Though these policy adjustments were important, they did not lead to professionalization where it mattered: in the agencies making decisions about how to apply the law. Instead, decisions continued to favor the interests of powerful economic actors, regardless of whether they were legal.

Mobility, Leadership, Permeability: Facilitating
Professionalization
A further set of factors facilitates professionalization (and therefore norm socialization) in domestic agencies. One is movement of personnel. Social psychology and IR literatures lead us to predict that proximity influences persuasion (Cialdini and Trost 1998; Farrell 2001). As personnel move into new
positions, they have an impact on those around them. In addition, leaders of
public agencies can begin to instill changes to agency values by appointing
bureaucrats who are supportive of these values. They can create conditions in
which capacity building is fostered and personnel are encouraged to adopt
attitudes conducive to good governance. The leadership of Julia Carabias (secretary of SEMARNAP under President Zedillo) was an important part of the
normative socialization process in the environmental agencies (Rabasa interview, 2008). Carabias was crucial because she translated broad trends and
pressures into local (institutional) change, including priority for access to information policies and citizen participation (de Buen interview, 2008; Carabias interview, 2010). She encouraged the president to modernize environmental politics. President Fox later contributed to the trend toward openness
by bringing IFAI into being (Block 2003).

Leaders cannot by themselves create a new organizational culture in which
norms of good governance are respected. But they can hire key staff who, if
they share values of good governance and are technically proficient, can begin
to shift the agency in a new direction. This process of shuffling involves officials moving between offices and working with new personnel in new environments. Shuffling occurred in the environmental policy area as Mexican officials moved between jobs in ministerial agencies, the CEC, and NGOs. Gustavo
Alanís, the Director of CEMDA, has twice been a member of JPAC, the citizen
advisory body of the CEC. Victor Lichtinger moved from being head of the
CEC to head of SEMARNAT when the Fox administration took office in 2000.
Javier Cabrera worked in Profepa, the federal environmental enforcement
agency, from 1994 to 1997 and then was head of the BECC from 1997 to 2005.
Ernesto Enkerlin, the head of Conanp (the commission on natural protected
areas), was an official of Pronatura and other NGOs prior to moving to Conanp.
Pronatura and CEMDA act as seedbeds for talented individuals.

Of the twenty-five Mexicans who have worked as professionals in the CEC
since its inception, ten either came from the federal environmental agencies

or moved to them after their time in the CEC. Two individuals moved between STPS and the CLC in fifteen years.[10] A third of professional staff in the
CEC are Mexicans. Communication between NGOs and public officials in
environmental agencies has improved. Much of the interaction is informal—
the individuals involved know each other well and have become friends,
speaking on the phone frequently, part of a fluid, informal network (Guerrero
interview, 2007). Socialization has brought NGO officials and government officials much closer to a meeting of the minds on the environment than existed
prior to NAFTA.

Moreover, a connection between JPAC and Mexico's regional consultative
councils has been established because many personnel serve in both organizations. The CEC invites council representatives to attend its meetings (de
Buen interview, 2008). The experience of the councils strengthened environmental interests not only because they receive a great deal of government
information—and serve as a conduit for this information—but also because
there is a consensus logic at work, with council members from different sectors needing to communicate with each other and work out problems. Understanding among environmental interests is better; they have become sensitive
to the positions of other interests and better informed about the limits of
government capabilities.

Cristina Martin, an official at the Mexico City office of the UN Development Program, worked in SEMARNAP on citizen participation issues in the
1990s. She eventually became president of the central regional consultative
council. She explained that during the 1990s, the environment ministry began
reaching beyond the scientific elite and opening up to civil society (Martin
interview, 2008; Reyes interview, 2008). As NGOs were drawn into the regional councils, they became acquainted with other environmental groups,
and business groups became involved as well. Through meetings and discussions, environmental interests began to change the way they conducted themselves; they were negotiating and presenting alternatives, not simply making
demands. They looked for alliances, and mutual respect grew. Nongovernmental organizations learned to present policy alternatives that actually solved
problems (de Buen interview, 2008; Martin interview, 2008). Contact led to
better understanding.

The epistemic community in environmental politics is not replicated
on the labor side. Labor interests—notably the union confederation CTM
and local CABs—are entrenched and highly biased. Even though there is a

transnational network of trained labor activists that includes Mexicans, they do not interact with a similarly trained set of labor technocrats. Shuffling is virtually nonexistent. Union confederation leaders are old and uneducated, and they stay in position for a very long time. As I pointed out earlier, Fidel Velázquez led the CTM from 1941 until his death in 1997 at the age of ninety-seven.[11] According to a top official in the independent labor organization FAT, not only is there no exchange of personnel with STPS but also the only connection they have is the registration procedure for federally registered unions (Martínez interview, 2010). He believes strongly that a union that criticized the head of STPS would not be allowed to register. Labor politics is politicized rather than professionalized. Dissident civil society voices are ostracized. This undermines the formation of common views and retards the process of normative socialization. It is also why some NAO reports have called for greater training for members of CABs.

The propensity for shuffling depends on the permeability of domestic institutions to outside influence. Path-dependent relationships and practices can hinder inward mobility of actors with new values. On the environmental side, the relative youth of the agencies and their rapid expansion made them more open to normative influence from external ideas imported by new employees. In contrast, long-standing labor agencies with well-established and fixed practices that guaranteed institutionalized privileges for narrow economic interests proved impermeable to outside influence. Moreover, as with other semidemocratic regimes, there can be a marked difference in the attitudes and behavior of state and federal actors. Federal actors in both the environmental and labor agencies have had to answer for the actions of local enforcement officials, who are susceptible to corruption and sometimes poorly trained. Even those with good intentions can find themselves quite vulnerable in the face of strong economic interests. State and municipal governments have been more inclined to promote investment opportunities than safeguard the rule of law in either sector. But when transgressions occurred, federal officials reacted in markedly different ways: environmental officials acknowledged problems and explained how they planned to make improvements. Labor authorities often denied that problems existed, though they also made some ad hoc efforts to rectify injustices.

At the outset of the NAAEC, federal environmental authority was still evolving (from an undersecretariat with few resources in 1990 to a full cabinet agency in 1994), whereas STPS was stable and established. In 1990, environmental policy was part of the ministry SEDESOL, along with social and housing policy, and there were fewer than twenty environmental inspectors for the whole country. Its growth, from roughly a thousand environmental employees in 1990 to 30,000 in 2007, distinguishes it from STPS, which was stable in size.[12] Hiring new personnel to do new jobs created the opportunity for fresh thinking to be inculcated in ministry officials. By contrast, the administration of labor politics, including interaction with the CLC, is centralized in a few hands.[13] Inclusion of outsiders is strongly resisted, and consultation with NGOs and unions (beyond the co-opted unions) is not widespread. A long-standing culture of social control and a network of interests that have benefited from this system proved resistant to inclusion of newcomers (Alcalde 2006; López Guerra interview, 2009).

The most successful pressures on labor practices have come from Mexican court decisions and IFAI. (Both sets of institutions have made reference to NAFTA in their decision making and documentation.) But even these have not brought a new culture of respect for rule of law. An epistemic understanding of the importance of good governance, based on professionalization, technical training, and openness to new personnel, has not taken hold in the labor case because of the presence of co-opted unions with permanent interests opposed to such change. The individuals in these unions are less susceptible to inward or outward movement of technocrats carrying new norms. Thus, institutional permeability is an important contributory factor. Conversely, SEMARNAT was permeable. Shuffling introduced new norms in ways not found in STPS or most of the CABs. Movement of SEMARNAT officials into the CEC (and vice versa), along with exchange of officials between NGOs and SEMARNAT, made a difference: it facilitated spread of the rule of law to the environmental agencies.

In summary, leaders create openings for new professionals to enter public authorities. Shuffling facilitates the spread of norms, provided it increases the representation within the agency of those supportive of the new norms. At the elite and federal level, communication between environmental NGOs and public officials is excellent. On the labor side, the story is less positive. There are fewer formal mechanisms of exchange, and most CABs allow little influence from labor beyond the co-opted corporatist unions. Independent labor interests did gain access to STPS policy-making discussions in the early 2000s as a result of NAALC pressures. They made some impact on reform initiatives, but the reforms eventually perished because of strong opposition from state governors. Independent unions and labor activists have had less success in inserting themselves in CABs.

However, the Mexico City local CAB is an exception. A new leader, Jesus Campos, was appointed in 2001 by the Mexico City government. Edith Ramírez, one of the lawyers hired by Campos when he took office, credits the appointment of Campos to the fact that the new PRD government in the city was democratically inclined and sensitive to the needs of vulnerable groups. Campos had been a labor lawyer for independent unions and made a priority of respect for rule of law. He initially hired eight labor lawyers who had represented independent trade unions and were familiar with (and committed to upholding) trade union rights. This number increased over time. The difference in outcomes is marked. This CAB has by far the best reputation in terms of respect for rule of law.[14]

But is shuffling a mechanism through which agencies are inculcated with new norms and values, carried by agents from outside? Or is it a reflection of the fact that the agencies had *already accepted* these norms and therefore were open to like-minded individuals working there? According to an official in SEMARNAT's Office for Social Participation and Transparency, the answer is the former: interchange of officials has itself built capacity and permitted norms to be transferred among individuals (de Buen interview, 2008). On the labor side, the head of the Mexican NAO stated categorically that the introduction of labor lawyers familiar with labor rights into the Mexico City CAB was the cause of it becoming more open and respectful of rule of law. Shuffling helps spread norms.

It Wasn't Just the Economy, Stupid (It Was the Institutions, Too)

I began this book by relating the famous anecdote of the Clinton campaign in the 1992 presidential race, urging campaign workers to stay focused on the economic recession. In the months preceding the election, the George H. W. Bush administration concluded negotiations on the NAFTA Treaty, prompting a response by candidate Clinton that he would create special environmental and labor institutions to safeguard U.S. interests. Clinton did not disagree with the idea that free trade would lift the economies of North America, but what he overlooked was the effect that new side agreement institutions would have on Mexican governance. Both NAAEC and NAALC apply pressures on

Mexico. Technocratic communication and subtle, depoliticized pressure from other member states have grown. Interagency cross-border communication is encouraged. Both labor and environmental NGOs have strengthened cross-border links. Public complaints in both areas have cast a strong (sometimes harsh) light of scrutiny on Mexico's politics. Greater levels of information, such as reports, public meetings, and studies, and legal enforcement channels have had consequences, too.

But these mechanisms were not enough to guarantee that good governance norms would be internalized at uniform rates across the two ministries. A comparison reveals that important differences in institutional design and domestic capacity facilitated socialization of the norm of rule of law. The first is the design of the side agreement institutions. Where there is relative independence from member state control and civil society groups are given permanent standing, good governance norms are more likely to be fostered. Nongovernmental organizations are more committed; factual reporting is more consistent and less nationalized. The second is professionalization and capacity building. Where bureaucrats and civil society groups upgrade their technical proficiency and professionalism, communication improves, and norms are more likely to be transferred. Capacity-building programs help promote professionalization. So does personnel movement, or shuffling. Where leaders promote norms of good governance and make positions available for key staff who are trained and support these norms, socialization is likely to occur more rapidly. Shuffling is affected by institutional permeability and domestic interests. Where agencies are growing (and assuming they hire staff supportive of new norms), they are more likely to socialize good governance norms. Where agencies have long-standing relationships with special economic interests, socialization of new norms will be more difficult.

Fact-finding is an important mechanism of socialization because it empowers domestic interests who are harmed by noncompliance (Dai 2005; Keck and Sikkink 1998). Fact-finding is triggered by local (Mexican) actors. Simply by describing existing situations, factual reporting can raise the pressure on governments and increase the priority of the issue. But reports are more effective when they come from independent regional investigatory agencies because they are more likely to be neutral of nationalistic concerns and ideological bias. On the labor side, the CLC has no powers of fact-finding and reporting. Instead, any reporting is carried out by the NAO of another member state, making it more likely there will be nationalistic reactions or ideologically based decisions on whether to investigate. Mexican labor interests have been less willing to avail themselves of the complaint mechanisms that do exist. In addition, the CLC lacks a permanent public advisory body similar to the JPAC in the CEC. Labor interests are therefore less committed to the NAALC process, and they gain less credibility and legitimacy from the NAALC than environmental interests do from NAAEC.

Moreover, capacity building in labor has been very limited, and shuffling between NGOs and public agencies is extremely rare. Mexican labor bureaucrats have shown no inclination to allow an epistemic community to develop. On the other hand, SEMARNAT's institutional permeability allowed shuffling of NGO and CEC personnel, which, combined with high levels of education and training, served as a catalyst for absorption of pro–rule of law norms. Some Mexican environmental NGOs trained other NGOs. Legal and technical training (sometimes outside Mexico) resulted in attitudes conducive to internalization of norms of rule of law because personnel were exposed to new ideas stemming from traditions not associated with older prodevelopment and prosovereignty perspectives. Values of nationalism and clientelism were undercut by professionalization. Funding (especially for border communities and civil society) and information resources strengthened human and physical infrastructure. An interesting and unanticipated outcome was that in addition to rule of law norms being internalized in SEMARNAT, a norm of public participation was also internalized through the CEC citizen submissions process, public consultation processes, and the border funding agencies, which mandated inclusion of citizen groups in planning and implementation.

Domestic NGOs play a critical role as capillaries between the trilateral NAFTA institutions and Mexican agencies. They are plugged in at both levels: they argue their cases, get involved in complaints, communicate with each other and with public officials, cajole and persuade, and hold behavior up to the light. Without them, communication between agencies inside and outside Mexico would be sterile. And they sharpen the divide within Mexico between those in favor of rule of law and those in favor of development and sovereignty above rule of law. How environmental and labor officials reacted to this growing gulf tells us much about Mexican politics today. Environmental officials embraced troublesome NGOs and welcomed public participation, even when it was critical. Labor officials sought to keep independent civil society groups at bay.

Thus, socialization in Mexican politics is more complicated than a simple process of external elites pressuring domestic elites. There is also division within domestic agencies between modernizers (believers in the rule of law norm) and traditionalists (believers in sovereignty and development). Socialization is not simply a question of us (on the inside) versus them (on the outside), but rather us (favoring rule of law) versus us (favoring sovereignty and development). The processes and mechanisms of socialization—persuasion, embarrassment, interaction, learning, debate—occurred between elites within the agencies (and courts) and between domestic elites and domestic NGOs. Pressures came from domestic agents (modernizers and NGOs) who were empowered by the new international environment. International pressures sharpened the divide between two sets of domestic elites.

The labor case supports cognitive dissonance theory: nominal acceptance of rule of law, together with the observed failure to respect it in practice, led to efforts to rationalize or justify the apparently contradictory behavior (Fiske 2004; Risse and Sikkink 1999). The most accurate response by STPS to criticism would have been to say that the imperatives of development and job creation outweigh strict observance of labor rights, which many feel are far too heavily weighted in favor of workers and apt to paralyze the economy if observed to the letter. Instead, STPS reduces dissonance by referring to its labor law as progressive, by replacing one norm (respect for rule of law) with another (sovereignty), or by shifting the blame to state governments. The fact that alternative interpretations of Mexican labor politics were available made it possible to deflect pressures for socialization. Mexican bureaucrats distorted the relevance of rule of law norms because of the dissonance between its norm of modernization (in which it implicitly accepts rule of law norms and other norms of good governance) and the practice on the ground, where flagrant violations continue. The difference between federal and state levels of governance is important because being able to blame state governors reduces apparent dissonance and hypocrisy.

Extending the Research Agenda
Some obvious hypotheses emerge from these findings to frame research on other trade agreements. Mechanisms of socialization, as commonly understood in the IR literature, do create strong pressures on governments to adopt new norms. Although I have examined pro–rule of law norms, other norms of good governance (participation, transparency, accountability) are also susceptible to external mechanisms, as are rights norms (human, gender, ethnic) and economic governance norms (fiscal stability and price stability, for ex-

ample). Moreover, although mechanisms of socialization provide transformative pressures, we can hypothesize that their effectiveness will depend on the
contextual factors I have identified in this study: international organizations
with independent fact-finding powers and permanent, institutionalized citizen access; higher levels of technical proficiency and professionalization
among bureaucrats and NGO officials; and opportunities for mobility of
trained personnel. These conditions help to engender, strengthen, support,
justify, and legitimate NGOs in countries with closed political opportunity
structures.

But is there an endogeneity problem here? Was the "newness" and growth
of SEMARNAT determinative of the type of norms it would internalize? And
did the views of civil society groups drive ministerial preferences, such that a
domestic interests explanation is sufficient to tell us all we need to know about
these sectors? The answer is no, but with the caveat that more research is
needed to be certain. Growth of the environmental agencies meant that they
were susceptible to new norms with or without the NAAEC. But this does not
tell us what their views would be or where they came from, simply that they
were receptive. The Mexican government was initially hostile to the NAAEC,
and there was no guarantee that environmental agencies would be favorably
inclined to accept external pressures. Many bureaucrats were deeply suspi-
cious of U.S. intentions, even in the environmental area.

Moreover, prodevelopment interests continue to play a strong role in environmental politics, both in interagency debates at the federal level, where the
Treasury and Economics ministries are extremely powerful, and at the local
level, where authorities are eager to promote development and encourage inward investment. Likewise, although it is true that powerful labor confederations constrained STPS and the CABs from accepting new norms, it is also
true that the environmental ministry did not initially accept the views of environmental interests and, in fact, resisted pressures coming both from Mexican
environmental NGOs and from the CEC, so an interest-driven explanation is
inconsistent between the agencies, as well as inconsistent with SEMARNAT's
later acceptance of the arguments of civil society interests.

Relevant counterfactuals are whether SEMARNAT would have modernized and internalized norms of good governance without NAAEC and
whether STPS would have modernized with a stronger NAALC. The answer
to the former question is that SEMARNAT had begun the process of modernization before NAFTA came into effect, so the answer is probably yes. However,

it would certainly have done so more slowly. The evidence for this is numerous interviews giving credit to NAAEC for the creation of new institutions and citizen participation, along with documentary evidence from SEMARNAT itself praising the effect of NAAEC on environmental governance. Evidence also comes from the fact that, as I pointed out earlier, SEMARNAT initially resisted the CEC Secretariat investigations (and still drags its feet on some votes) but has come to support the CEC and accepts the importance of the rule of law and public participation.

The CABs and STPS would be under greater pressure to conform to international (and Mexico's own) labor standards with a stronger external scrutiny mechanism permitting labor groups to argue their case before an independent trinational body. There *is* public scrutiny on labor through NAALC's public hearings, reports, and seminars, but without an independent body, its impact is likely to remain less significant because labor ministries from other NAFTA member states, who carry out the reviews, are prone to respecting the political sensitivities and modus operandi of ministries that are being investigated. Moreover, without the engagement of major trade union confederations in a strengthened trilateral agency, participation would remain incomplete, and norm transfer would probably be limited.

In conclusion, this study adds detail to the often vague claims that "domestic histories, traditions, and institutions" are responsible for filtering or conditioning the effect of norm socialization arising from pressures external to the state. The notion that depoliticized, technical, noncoercive settings are more conducive to norm transfer is questionable; in the two cases examined here, civil servants engaged in these processes, exchanging information and knowledge about best practices. Likewise, the opposite perspective that shaming may be conducive to norm transfer is also open to question in that publicity and shaming occurred in both cases. Much of the potential variation between the two cases is controlled, making it easier to see what causal factors explain different levels of normative socialization.

Policy Implications

When presidential candidate Barack Obama pledged to "fix NAFTA so that it works for American workers," he joined a long list of legislators, think tankers, activists, academics, and others who believe the side agreements have failed. They have failed, the argument goes, because they have not safeguarded workers or reduced pollution levels. They have neither raised Mexican standards nor protected Americans. Free trade, unmitigated by safeguards and leveraged by an investor-protection provision, has wreaked havoc, especially on Mexico. According to one view, NAFTA is too weak to cause changes to domestic environmental legislation, instead serving as "a device for disseminating information about effective domestic environmental law" (Goldstein et al. 2000: 391). The toughest criticism comes from NGOs and journalists.[15] The Sierra Club, for example, offers a U.S.-Mexico Border Reality Tour that takes a "first-hand look at NAFTA's impact on the environment and communities along the border."

> NAFTA has created a legacy where corporate profits are promoted at the expense of environmental safeguards, health protections, and workers' rights. While NAFTA's impacts have been felt in all three countries, Mexico has been most negatively affected.[16]

Who could argue that Mexico doesn't have a long way to go? Blessed with one of the planet's richest ecosystems and a set of labor laws that provided vanguard rights to its working population in the early twentieth century, it has a poor record in protecting both. Environmental challenges remain daunting. Labor rights are violated every day. Yet condemning the side agreements outright hides important facts, and comparing them sheds light on how they functioned and what their successes were. The Mexican experience allows us to draw conclusions about how to design trade agreements that contain environmental and labor protections. Politicians could benefit from these conclusions, because when the side agreements help Mexico, they also help the United States.

Several important messages emerge. At the regional level, institutions with independence from member state control and with institutionalized access for civil society work better because they increase commitment and legitimacy. Investigations, reports, and other activity by the institution are more effective. Regional institutions (and other broader international organizations for that matter) should incorporate (1) citizen complaint mechanisms; (2) opportunities for factual records to be created by neutral investigating authorities, which are then made public; (3) avenues for civil society groups to influence the agenda and work of the institution; and (4) capacity-building resources for both domestic agencies and civil society groups.

At the domestic level, capacity-building activity aimed at civil servants, NGOs, and others in the developing country is important because it raises their level of technical proficiency in scientific or legal areas and makes it more likely that these individuals will be able to participate as equals, solve problems efficiently, and absorb norms of good governance. Member states should (1) act to foster strong domestic oversight institutions (freedom of information and courts); (2) create opportunities for educating and training both civil servants and NGO officials; (3) encourage personnel movement between NGOs, domestic ministries, and the regional institutions (through secondments, placements, job opportunities, or other means); and (4) depoliticize (and make more secure) the career paths that senior civil servants follow. These actions will help instill values of good governance, promote communication, and increase transparency and accountability.

The environmental side agreement contributed to strengthening institutional and civil society capacity in Mexico. Three main changes occurred, all of them without fanfare and outside the limelight. The first is a growth in the number of Mexican environmental institutions. In 1992, as NAFTA was being negotiated (and *because* it was being negotiated), Mexico created its first-ever environmental enforcement agency, Profepa. Two years later, it created a cabinet-level ministry on the environment. These changes were set in motion by NAAEC. In turn, a striking culture of awareness and enforcement came about that was reinforced by the 2002 Transparency Law, enabling groups to access information on environmental permits and other agency activity.

The second change is at the border. Although the border remains highly polluted and in need of much investment, NAFTA has helped to empower local communities and pumped funds into municipal infrastructure. According to the two NAFTA border agencies, by mid-2008, $2.8 billion worth of water, wastewater, and municipal waste infrastructure projects had been approved and funded, seventy-five of them in the United States and sixty-three in Mexico. Equally important, gaining access to this funding required local authorities in Mexico to create and institutionalize genuine civil society participation.

The third change is that NAFTA created a modern environmental movement in Mexico. Popular opposition to NAFTA tends to focus on cases such as Metalclad and investor rights, but CEMDA and the Cozumel pier project are equally important: CEMDA took advantage of a provision in NAAEC that permits individuals and NGOs to lodge complaints, and it brought the first case in 1996. It claimed that Mexican federal authorities had not gone through the full impact-assessment process when it granted a permit to build a cruise ship pier on the island of Cozumel. The CEC wrote a nonbinding (though damning) report on the issue, and the Mexican government did an about-face. The case made headlines (in Mexico, not the United States), and since then, the number of groups fighting for environmental justice has skyrocketed. Many of them are given legal and other training by CEMDA and also by the CEC Secretariat.

What happened to Mexico's environmental politics was unanticipated (and initially unwelcome). Introducing U.S. and Canadian discipline was not part of Mexico's modernization strategy. Opening the country created a vulnerability: domestic institutions and practices came under pressure in unexpected ways. Mexico faced challenges not simply from its NAFTA partners but also from its own citizens. Many environmental bureaucrats overcame both nationalist suspicions and prodevelopment interests to internalize a norm of respect for domestic law. The NAFTA institutions provided the pressure, but Mexicans themselves drove forward the process of socialization. Javier Cabrera, the former head of the Border Environment Cooperation Commission, explained how it happened:

> NAFTA forced Mexico to understand and participate in environmental issues. We found that it's better to participate, develop, improve. NAFTA has become an element of Mexican foreign policy. Environment policy is used as a tool by the U.S., forcing countries to do certain things. Mexico therefore was forced to change, to prepare itself to deal with the U.S. Now Mexico has a new kind of citizen, more concerned with the environment. These things might have happened anyway, but they happened much more quickly because of NAFTA. We are complying because of external pressure. If we don't have someone pushing us, we don't move. We are a very conservative society. (Interview, 2008)

Nevertheless, NAFTA is not a panacea for the environment. Corruption, lack of adequate resources, and other enforcement problems remain. Pollution erodes the quality of life for people living in urban areas and along the border. Differences persist between the federal government's commitment to the environment and that of state and municipal authorities, most of which remain more enamored of old-fashioned development. But the one-sided criticism of maquiladora pollution and investor rights undermines a wider appreciation of changes to environmental governance. Though Mexico's environmental bureaucrats continue to fight battles with prodevelopment interests, they have succeeded in creating relative gains within the government measured as institutional advances compared to other ministries.

Meanwhile, labor politics remains a dismal story of institutionalized corruption. Neither low-key, behind-the-scenes technical discussions among bureaucrats nor the sunshine of shaming have been effective at changing attitudes within STPS or the federal or local CABs. In 2010, as I waited for an appointment at a local CAB in a northern state, an administrative assistant explained to me how workers are betrayed. (She had worked there for many years but had no operational or policy duties.) They are appointed attorneys to defend them against companies, for example, in injury cases. But what often happens is that the attorney for the firm invites the attorney for the worker to dinner, and they "arrange" a settlement, after which the worker is given a small payment (a fraction of what his attorney received at dinner) and informed that nothing else can be done.

Everyone knows perfectly well what good governance means and why existing practices are bad. Even administrative assistants listening to conversations over the years are conscious of the problems. There is nothing "new" to teach labor bureaucrats. In fact, like this administrative assistant, many officials would like to improve matters. But unless labor agencies build professional capacity, encourage mobility, and welcome external scrutiny, things will remain the same.

In any case, NAFTA was never intended to solve all Mexico's problems and has nowhere near the capacity to do so. Budgets for its trilateral agencies are low, it is weakly institutionalized, and it prioritizes national sovereignty. Moreover, within Mexico, objectives continually evolve. Presidents come to office with new aims. Agency chiefs leave office, and budgets are cut. Nongovernmental organizations chase new funding sources that carry different priorities. But regional trade agreements can be a constant. They can establish mechanisms for institutional development and improvements to governance at the same time they create opportunities for trade and investment-led growth. In contrast to the European Union, where regulatory requirements are much more centralized and the financial burden is heavier, the North American experience shows that a light-touch agreement can be a remarkably good value. Once civil servants and NGO officials have learned how to solve problems by using scientific studies and legal processes, built networks, and improved communication links, they are less vulnerable to shifting priorities. Trust is built. An understanding of how to address conflict and make decisions that are fair and transparent begins to congeal. Decision making becomes less politicized and more technical—and therefore less vulnerable to changes in priority or narrow interests.

New areas (such as technology sectors, competition, services, and investment, in addition to the environment) may be more amenable to socialization because there may be less in the way of fixed, impermeable interests and bureaucracies. Regional trade agreements therefore may have more success in socializing domestic actors in these areas. The legacy of NAFTA is that in the environmental area it encouraged new federal institutions, more professional technocrats, better access to information and decision makers, a more independent and technically proficient civil society, better communication within Mexico and between NAFTA partners, and clear evidence that norms have been socialized within the Mexican federal institutions.

Notes

Chapter 1

1. NAFTA is the result of negotiations between the United States, Canada, and Mexico that began in June 1991 and culminated in August 1992. On the origins, see Hurrell 1995. The record shows that it has brought impressive macroeconomic gains, especially trade and investment flows between Mexico and the United States: U.S. exports to Mexico grew from $46 billion in 1995 to $151 billion in 2008. Imports from Mexico grew from $62 billion in 1995 to $216 billion in 2008 (U.S. Census Bureau, Foreign Trade Division). Total inward foreign direct investment stock in Mexico increased from $41 billion in 1993 to $327 billion in 2010, according to the UN Conference on Trade and Investment. Cited at http://unctadstat.unctad.org/TableViewer/tableView.aspx. For general reviews, see Hufbauer and Schott 2005; Studer and Wise 2007). However, skeptical voices noted problems in Mexico regarding income inequality, unauthorized migration, rural poverty, and environmental, agriculture, and labor issues, along with stagnating incomes (Zepeda et al. 2009; COHA 2007; Polaski 2003; Burfisher et al. 2001; Pastor 2005; McKinney 2005; Weintraub 2005; Middlebrook and Zepeda 2003). A World Bank study on the effects of NAFTA on Mexico criticized the unequal benefits across regions and sectors; insufficient investment in education, innovation, and infrastructure; and the poor quality of institutions, such as accountability, regulatory effectiveness, and control of corruption (World Bank, 2003).

2. According to the World Trade Organization (WTO), 474 regional trade agreements were notified up to July 31, 2010, 283 of which were in force. See www.wto.org/english/tratop_e/region_e/region_e.htm.

3. Regional integration is one of the Inter-American Development Bank's key strategies for development. See http://www.iadb.org/en/about-us/strategies,6185.html.

Regional organizations increasingly incorporate divergent economies in a process intended to promote convergence and development (Hurrell and Fawcett, 1995).

4. Acharya and Johnston (2007: 24–25) enumerate several possible dimensions on which to compare the domestic impacts of regional organizations, including (1) normative and preference change; (2) policy convergence; (3) "extent of institutionalization and legalization" of change; (4) whether adjustment occurs through persuasion, social influence, or material incentives; (5) adjustment of prior policies; (6) achievement of institutional goals; and (7) impact of cooperation in solving broader contextual goals. In a previous article (Aspinwall 2009), I suggested three specific ways in which Europeanization could inform the study of other regions: (1) where does the pressure for adjustment come from? (2) what causes variation in acceptance or resistance to adjustment pressures? and (3) what are the mechanisms of adjustment?

5. Others include independent domestic political decisions, regime change, crises, bilateral negotiations, or change resulting from membership of the GATT, WTO, or other international organizations. See Clarkson (2002) for a discussion of the influence of NAFTA, the WTO, and internal Mexican politics on economic transformation after the mid-1980s.

6. The Europeanization approach refers to the reciprocal influence of European integration and the domestic politics of its member states, especially to domestic transformation under pressure from EU institutional and policy change (Ladrech 1994). That is often cited as an original definition; for a wider set of definitions, see Olsen 2002; Ladrech 2002).

7. See also the UN Development Program's definition of *capacity building,* "the process by which individuals, organizations, and societies develop abilities to perform functions, solve problems, and set and achieve goals" (cited in World Bank 2005: 6). Capacity building in developing countries is an important part of the sustainable development agenda. Both the UN's Agenda 21 and Principle 9 of the Rio Declaration refer to its significance.

8. I use the terms *norm transfer, norm diffusion,* and *norm socialization* to refer to the same process by which norms move into domestic agencies from outside.

9. State governments have been especially eager to promote inward investment, and this is where labor rights violations have been most acute. According to some, labor is also subject to a "social control logic," where labor rights are repressed to maintain order (Diaz interview 2009; López Guerra interview 2009).

10. In addition to NAFTA, the OECD has pushed for legal reform in the labor area, mainly to increase transparency, productivity, and competitiveness. The International Labor Organization (ILO) has argued for protection of workers; it can also review complaints from unions and make recommendations. In the environmental case, the Rio Summit and subsequent agreements have placed pressures on Mexico to improve its environmental record.

11. Strategic responses were evident in the EU too. Case studies of the socialization effect of EU institutions on the central and east European countries (CEECs) show that material rewards—particularly membership—were important in bringing about normative change in CEECs (Schimmelfennig 2005; Kelley 2004).

12. Norms do not "automatically proliferate" to government from the international arena, but activists sometimes need to fight for them (Gurowitz 1999: 432; Schmidt 2002; Olsen 2002).

13. On policy transfer, see Dolowitz and Marsh 2000; Evans and Davies 1999; Stone 2004.

14. However, it *is* possible to find a justification, namely, that the system helped maintain labor peace, avoid the disruptive labor conflicts of some parts of Latin America, and encourage inward investment.

15. The law applies to information that is generated, obtained, acquired by, transformed, or held by these authorities. Limits to accessibility are established for "reserve" and confidentiality purposes. Information is "reserved" if its public availability would harm national interests. Confidentiality refers to private information related, for example, to personal details and private contracts.

16. The environmental legal framework was newer and continued to evolve after NAFTA entered into force, though it had largely been established by 1988. However, the institutional framework went through dramatic changes, as we will see.

Chapter 2

1. See also 2008 *CIA World Factbook;* GAO 1993; Auer 2001; Carter et al. 1996.

2. The two broad criteria for this measure are "(1) reducing environmental stresses on human health, and (2) promoting ecosystem vitality and sound natural resource management." See http://sedac.ciesin.columbia.edu/es/epi/.

3. Middlebrook and Zepeda's study of Mexican transition takes the liberalization of the postdebt crisis as the starting point that led to NAFTA (2003: 24).

4. Several excellent works exist in Spanish on the development of governance capabilities in Mexico, and I make use of them in this chapter. Gil Corrales (2007) is a comprehensive chronology of the legal and institutional development of Mexican environmental politics. See also Azuela 2006; Brañes 2000. The CEC's Web site provides a summary of Mexican environmental law, in English.

5. SEMARNAP was the federal environmental agency from 1994 to 2000. In 2000, its name was changed to SEMARNAT, to reflect a slightly different set of responsibilities.

6. The problem, as before, was a lack of commitment: the level of funding provided was only $4.3 million in 1989. Through the 1980s, Mexico's "attention to environmental quality remained largely symbolic" (Husted and Logsdon 1997: 29). In 1996, the OECD commended the creation of LGEEPA, but it was critical of the way powers were splintered between separate agencies and urged more to be done to improve public access to information (OECD 1996).

7. "Deconcentrated" agencies have administrative independence from the main federal environmental agency (now SEMARNAT), but their budgets come from SEMARNAT and they have no independent legal identity. These agencies include the present-day INE, Profepa, Conagua, and Conanp. "Decentralized" agencies have

autonomy in their budgets, as well as administration and legal autonomy. They include the present-day IMTA and Conafor.

8. Note that the quality of SEMARNAT's reporting has been criticized. In some cases, the agency has replicated information from year to year in their reports. Also, SEMARNAT has an office on human rights and the environment but little knowledge in practice (Puentes interview, 2008).

9. Data are from SEMARNAT (2003) and the Hacienda Web site: www.shcp.gob .mx/EGRESOS/PEF/pef/pef_08/index.html.

10. Some of this compliance was coming from the EPA's pressure on U.S. businesses with plants in Mexico.

11. Cited at www.cec.org/Page.asp?PageID=1324&SiteNodeID=581&BL_Expand ID=.

12. Gallagher (2004) singled out the Fund for Pollution Prevention Projects in Mexican Small and Medium-Sized Enterprises (FIPREV), which, at the time he wrote, had more than $2 million in resources and twenty-five loans worth $610,000 outstanding.

13. *New York Times*, August 1, 1995. Cited at www.nytimes.com/1995/08/01/science /treaty-partners-study-fate-of-birds-at-polluted-mexican-lake.html?sec=&spon=& pagewanted=all.

14. Mexican citizens have other access points under Mexican law. They include the *denuncia popular* from LGEEPA, in which complaints can be made to Profepa; the right to information on the environment, which was included in the LGEEPA reforms of 1996 and strengthened by the 2002 transparency law; the public consultation process, also part of the 1996 LGEEPA reform, along with public information meetings; the regional councils created in the mid-1990s; the National Commission on Human Rights; and the Congress.

15. See Dorn 2007 for a brief review of this and five other citizen submissions against Mexico.

16. *Ejidos* are communal land units, often the homes of indigenous communities.

17. See the SEMARNAT Web site, http://app1.semarnat.gob.mx/retc/tema /anteced.html. Translation mine. Antonio Azuela, former head of Profepa, explained in an interview that officials of the Mexican government discussed whether to include a PRTR within the LGEEPA 1996 reforms but decided against a mandatory reporting program. "It would have been fifteen minutes' work and no one would have objected. We simply forgot to put it into law" (Azuela interview, 2008).

18. The CEC provides assistance to other states as well, depending on need and receptiveness. Its strategy is to finance pilot projects and later let them operate independently. For example, in its work on greening the supply chain, the CEC engaged directly with the government of the state of Querétaro, as well as SEMARNAT and foreign investors. In 2008, the Secretariat was doing a full evaluation of the project to determine its effectiveness (it was managed by the CEC office in Mexico). The assessment is that the project would not have happened without the CEC (Fernández interview, 2008). Meanwhile, the government of Querétaro has taken over responsibility, including funding and personnel.

19. A Green Party was formed in the 1980s by a splinter faction of the Mexican Ecology Movement (MEM), itself affiliated to the PRI party. However, the party has never been successful.

20. For example, when the La Paz office was created, there were just three lawyers working on environmental protection in the entire northwestern region of five states.

21. Improvements were made in subsequent years, and by the end of 2000, the figures had improved in all categories, to 93, 75, and 75 percent, respectively. See www .epa.gov/usmexicoborder/issues.html.

22. Some feel that political pressure from citizen groups and activists in southwestern U.S. states resulted in the border having disproportionate resources devoted to it and that Mexican regions of old heavy industry, such as the oil-processing areas of the southern Gulf coast, as well as biodiversity and environmental justice, should have been higher priorities for Mexico (Azuela interview, 2008).

23. BECC & NADB 2008: 3; see also GAO 2000 for a more complete description of BECC activities.

24. www.epa.gov/usmexicoborder/framework/background.html.

25. The city of Ciudad Juarez, for example, which borders El Paso, Texas, was due to get its first sewage treatment plant in 2000.

26. Public input into BECC and NADB activities also takes place through the mandatory meetings of the councils of these two organizations.

Chapter 3

1. Figures on levels of unionization are very imprecise. According to the transparency agency IFAI, there are 4 million union members in Mexico (Giménez Cacho 2007: 25). De la Garza (2006: 308) claims that the decline of unionism between 1992 and 2002 was nearly 50 percent, from 22 percent of the workforce to 11.6 percent. Citing Michael Boyle, writing in 2002 in the magazine *Business Mexico,* Nolan (2009) indicates that almost 90 percent of the unionized labor force was represented by unions affiliated with the CTM.

2. According to Fidel Velázquez, leader of the CTM for several decades, the origins of the term *charro* date back to the 1940s. The leader of the railway workers union at that time, Luis Gómez Zepeda, liked to dress as a *charro*—a cowboy from the western states—although according to Velázquez, Gómez Zepeda never once rode a horse. The president, Miguel Alemán, began referring to Gómez Zepeda as a *charro,* and the Communists took to calling the CTM's brand of unionism *charrismo* because of their supposed friendliness with business interests and the government (Krauze 2000: 99).

3. Fidel Velázquez, Mexico's most influential twentieth-century labor leader, led the CTM from 1941 until his death in 1997 at the age of ninety-seven.

4. These descriptions were made off the record by officials in various respectable, orthodox organizations, including noncompeting labor unions.

5. Exclusion clauses permitted employers to exclude from their employment any-one not belonging to a collective contract at that company, the so-called closed shop. They were codified in Article 395 of the 1931 federal labor law (Bensusán 1999: 196).

6. In other words, public authorities—not simply businesses or co-opted unions—permitted this to occur.

7. Translation by the author.

8. In one of the initial cases, for example, the complainants asked NAALC to force their employer to change the route of the company bus.

9. They are freedom of association and protection of the right to organize, the right to bargain collectively, the right to strike, prohibition of forced labor, labor pro-tections for children and young persons, minimum employment standards, elimina-tion of employment discrimination, equal pay for women and men, prevention of oc-cupational injuries and illnesses, compensation in cases of occupational injuries and illnesses, and protection of migrant workers.

10. I interviewed several individuals in the Commission for Labor Cooperation and Lewis Karesh in the Office for Trade Agreement Implementation, U.S. Depart-ment of Labor, and have made use of their views here.

11. This is also obvious from the CLC Web site. In late 2011, the seminar proceed-ings page contained only two seminars, from 1998 and 2000. Briefs, notes, and past events pages contained information as recent as 2004. The most recent press release was from 2003 (www.naalc.org). A report on migrant workers' rights from 2011 was the only publication after the year 2007.

12. A GAO report identified several challenges facing the operation of the labor secretariat in its early years, including recruitment, staff turnover and morale, lower than expected funding, and politicization of its role (GAO 1997).

13. Data were taken from the NAALC Web site and the U.S. Department of Labor Web site on November 8, 2011. See http://new.naalc.org/index.cfm?page=229, www.dol.gov/ILAB/programs/nao/status.htm#iia1, and AFL-CIO (2008). See also Vargas 2006.

14. All reports on U.S. cases are at www.dol.gov/ilab/media/reports/nao/public-reports-of-review.htm.

15. Paid maternity leave of twelve weeks is mandatory under Mexican law. How-ever, pregnancy testing was not banned at the time, though Mexico had already en-tered into international commitments to forbid it (under ILO conventions and others).

16. The Canadian report on this case is at http://new.naalc.org/index.cfm?page=227.

17. The Canadian report on this case is at www.hrsdc.gc.ca/eng/lp/spila/ialc/pcnaalc/pdf/report.pdf.

18. There is no consensus on whether IFAI or NAALC is responsible for the cre-ation of a union registration Web page. Alfonso Bouzas (an academic) and a top offi-cial in STPS credit IFAI. Graciela Bensusán (another academic) credits NAALC.

19. Compa was director of labor law and economic research, 1995–97 at the CLC Secretariat.

20. The U.S. NAO pointed out this weakness in NAO 9703 (U.S. NAO 1998c). Legally, unions were not required to share the contents of a collective bargaining agreement with their own members.

21. Information on RMALC came from numerous of its affiliated organizations in interviews in 2005 and 2007: Alejandro Villamar, 2005; Juan Sandoval, 2007; Alberto Arroyo, 2007; Norma Castañeda, 2007; Hector de la Cueva, 2005.

22. These points were confirmed in interviews with the executive director of the AFL-CIO's Industrial Council (Bob Baugh), as well as the head of the organization's Mexico City office (Baugh interview, 2005; Davis interview, 2009).

23. Campos was a founding member of ANAD and its president from 1993 to 1995.

24. Campos believes this is very tentative and much remains to be done (interview, 2010).

25. Exclusion clauses (or closed shops) required workers to belong to the workplace union or risk losing their jobs.

26. Labor authorities—at both federal and local levels—and union leaderships continue to resist giving access to information regarding collective contracts and union registration. In many cases, the authorities deny requests on the grounds that proceedings have not concluded and therefore the information should not be made public.

27. In the 2001–2 reform discussions, the secretary of STPS was prepared to accept secret votes for union leaders and a public registry of unions but was opposed by state governors.

Chapter 4

1. Numerous other high-ranking officials share this view, and there is no real counterargument except to say that certain other international processes, such as the Rio and Kyoto agreements, as well as pollution problems inside Mexico, contributed to pressures to strengthen environmental institutions.

2. The four groups were CEMDA, Environmental Education and Communication, Mexican Citizen Presence, and Ecology Culture. See World Resources Institute, www.wri.org/project/principle-10.

3. See www.semarnat.gob.mx/temas/ordenamientoecologico/Documents/docu mentos_taller_revision_tr/guadalajara/1_consulta_publica.pdf.

4. Cited at www.naalc.org/english/review_annex2.shtml.

5. Cited at www.naalc.org/english/review_annex2.shtml. Emphasis added.

6. Data from the NAALC Web site, http://new.naalc.org/index.cfm?page=229.

7. Polaski became deputy undersecretary of the U.S. Department of Labor in April 2009, heading up the International Labor Affairs Bureau, which has responsibility for NAALC investigations, and where the U.S. NAO is housed. Prior to that, she worked at the Carnegie Endowment for International Peace.

8. It is worth pointing out, however, that environmental NGO participation in the CEC declined after the 2003 closure of NAFEC, the NAAEC-sponsored fund

mobilizing NGOs (Fernández interview, 2008). The NGOs remain engaged but participate in fewer meetings.

9. Many believe there is a pressing need to expand education programs.

10. Both sets of data come from personal communication with officials in STPS and CEC.

11. The leader of the confederation CROM, Ignacio Cuauhtémoc Paleta, retired in 2010 at the age of eighty-eight, after twenty-five years in charge. The legendary and controversial leader of CROC, Alberto Juárez Blancas, led the organization from 1980 to 2004.

12. Hochstetler and Keck (2007) make a similar point about Brazil, where officials working on environmental policy increased dramatically, from a very low number during the military regime to many thousands at present, and that the civil society sector matured considerably.

13. I was able to interview only one person in the labor ministry, though he did agree to meet several times. All requests for interviews with other officials were declined.

14. The reputation is confirmed by several labor activists and lawyers, such as Arturo Alcalde and Benedicto Martínez, who are most likely to be skeptical about the actions of local CABs.

15. A research NGO specializing in the Americas, COHA, referred to NAFTA's investor protection provision, in which investors can sue governments for local legislation that undermines their operation, as "an affront to the workings of democratic institutions." See www.coha.org/2007/06/fast-track-to-trade-failure-the-political-economic-and-environmental-consequences-of-executive-trade-negotiations/. For other negative views, see www.naomiklein.org/articles/2001/03/time-fight-free-trade-laws-benefit-multinationals. The U.S. NGO Public Citizen called NAFTA a "failed model." See www.citizen.org/trade/nafta.

16. See www.sierraclub.org/trade/downloads/nafta-and-mexico.pdf. When the media present a positive image of Mexico's environmental record, as COHA did in mid-2009, it is not the result of incentives provided by NAFTA, but rather policies on transport and energy use by President Felipe Calderón's government that are aimed at reducing the country's carbon footprint (see COHA 2009).

References

Personal Interviews

Alanís, Gustavo (2005, 2007, 2008, 2010) President, CEMDA

Alcalde, Arturo (2010) National Association of Democratic Lawyers, Mexico

Arroyo, Alberto (2007) RMALC

Azuela, Antonio (2008) Institute for Social Research, UNAM, former head of Profepa

Baugh, Bob (2005) Executive Director of the AFL-CIO's Industrial Council, Washington, D.C., office

Bensusán, Graciela (2010) Professor, FLACSO

Bouzas, Alfonso (2010) Professor, UNAM

Cabrera, Javier (2008) Former General Manager of Border Environment Cooperation Commission

Callejo, Oscar (2008) Deputy Director General for Research, SEMARNAT

Campos, Jesús (2010) Former Director of the Mexico City CAB

Carabias, Julia (2010) Former Secretary of SEMARNAP

Carmona, Carmen (2008) Profepa

Carrillo, Juan Carlos (2008) CEMDA

Carrillo, Oscar (2005) EPA, Washington, D.C.

Castañeda, Norma (2007) RMALC

Castillo, Mateo (2008) Director, Social Participation and Transparency Unit, SEMARNAT

Cruikshank, Susana (2008) Oxfam

Dannenmeier, Eric (2008) Professor, University of Indiana

Davis, Ben (2009) AFL-CIO, Head of the Mexico City office

de Buen, Bertha Helena (2008) Deputy Director General of Social, Gender and Ethnic Participation, SEMARNAT de Buen, Carlos (2009) Independent labor lawyer

de la Calle, Luis (2009) Former head of Mexico's NAFTA office in Washington, D.C.

de la Cueva, Hector (2005) Centro de Investigaciones Laborales

Díaz, Luis Miguel (2009) President, Inter-Disciplinary Center for Conflict Management. Former diplomat involved in labor side agreement negotiations

Fernández, Jose Carlos (2008) Program Manager, Environment and Trade, Commission on Environmental Cooperation

Gambrill, Monica (2009) Professor, UNAM, CISAM

García, Héctor (2008) Mexico City representative, Commission on Environmental Cooperation

Garver, Geoffrey (2007) Director of SEM Unit, Commission on Environmental Cooperation

Guadarrama, Luis (2008) WWF

Guerra, Luis Manuel (2008) President, INAINE

Guerrero, Hernando (2007) Chief Advisor to the Secretary, SEMARNAT, Mexico City

Hansen-Kuhn, Karen (2007) Action Aid (formerly of Alliance for Responsible Trade)

Heredia, Marco Antonio (2008) Project Manager for Law Enforcement, Commission on Environmental Cooperation

Hernández, Lourdes (2008) Director General of Environmental Crimes and Litigation, Profepa

Juan, Patricia (2010) National Association of Democratic Lawyers, Mexico

Karesh, Lewis (2005) U.S. Department of Labor, NAO

Lejarza, Mateo (2010) Retired official of the telephone workers' union

Lendo, Enrique (2008) Director of International Affairs Unit, SEMARNAT

Lloyd, Evan (2008) Director of Programs, Commission on Environmental Cooperation

Lópex Guerra, Patricia (2009) Executive Director, International Resource Center for Civil Organizations

López Morales, Germán (2009) Director, International Labor Organization, Mexico City office

Martin, Cristina (2008) UNDP Mexico

Martinez, Benedicto (2010) President of the Miner's Union and board member of the Authentic Workers' Front, Mexico City

McGraw, Dan (2005) Center for International Environmental Law, Washington, D.C.

Medina, Salvador (2009) Undersecretary, Mexican Worker's Federation

Mejía, Rocio (2008) SEMARNAT

NAO office (2007, 2009, 2010) STPS, Mexico

Navarro, Ernesto (2008) Commission on Environmental Cooperation Mexico City representative

Puentes, Astrid (2008) Co-Director, Interamerican Association for the Defense of the Environment

Rabasa, Alejandra (2008) Legal Advisor, Conanp

Ramírez, Edith (2010) Mexico City Conciliation and Arbitration Board

Reyes, Sergio (2008) Former Director of National Ecology Institute

Richardson, Kevin (2009) Labor Attaché, U.S. Embassy, Mexico City
Rubio, Luis (2009) President, CIDAC
Salazar, Alejandra (2008) Pronatura
Sandoval, Juan (2007) RMALC
Serrato, Gerardo (2008) Head of SEMARNAT Querétaro office
Solano, Paolo (2008) Legal Officer, Commission on Environmental Cooperation
STPS (2007, 2009, 2010) Anonymous official
Tudela, Fernando (2008) Undersecretary of Planning and Environmental Policy,
    SEMARNAT
Uribe, Pablo (2008) Director, CEMDA La Paz office
Villamar, Alejandro (2005) RMALC
Villareal, Jorge (2008) Boell Foundation
Villegas, Alejandro (2008) Hewlett Foundation

Other Sources

Abel, Andrea (2003) "NAFTA's North American Agreement for Environmental Co-
    operation: A Civil Society Perspective," America's Program, Interhemispheric Re-
    source Center, March, cited at www.cipamericas.org/archives/1081.
Abel, Andrea, and Marico Sayoc (2006) "North American Development Bank: An
    Institution Worth Saving," Center for International Policy, June 6. Cited at http://
    www.cipamericas.org/archives/895.
Acharya, Amitav (2004) "How Ideas Spread: Whose Norms Matter? Norm Localiza-
    tion and Institutional Change in Asian Regionalism," *International Organization*,
    vol. 58, Spring, 239–75.
Acharya, Amitav, and Alastair Iain Johnston (eds.) (2007) *Crafting Cooperation: Re-
    gional International Institutions in Comparative Perspective* (Cambridge: Cam-
    bridge University Press).
AFL-CIO (2008) *Justice for All: A Guide to Workers' Rights in the Global Economy*, 3rd
    ed. (Washington, DC: Solidarity Center).
Aiken, Olga (2010) "Socializing International Human Rights Norms into Mexico's
    Domestic Policy Practices: The Femicide Agenda During Fox's Administration,"
    paper delivered at the 2010 conference of the International Studies Association,
    New Orleans.
Alcalde, Arturo (2006) "El sindicalismo, la democracia, y la libertad sindical," in José
    González and Antonio Gutiérrez (eds.), *El Sindicalismo en México: Historia, Crisis
    y Perspectivas* (Mexico City: Plaza y Valdés), 161–76.
Americas Society and Council of the Americas (2007) *Rule of Law, Economic Growth,
    and Prosperity,* Report of the Rule of Law Working Group, New York and Wash-
    ington. July. Cited at www.as-coa.org/files/PDF/pub_562_363.pdf.
Arias García, Sergio (2008) "La Legislación Forestal en México: A Cinco Años de la
    Ley General de Desarrollo Forestal Sustentable," *Derecho Ambiental y Ecología*,
    vol. 5, no. 27, October–November, 53–57.

Aspinwall, Mark (2009) "NAFTA-ization: Regionalization and domestic political adjustment in the North American economic area," *Journal of Common Market Studies*, vol. 47, no. 1, 1–24.

—— (undated) "Side Effects: Institutional Design Capacity-Building and Socialization in NAFTA's Labor and Environmental Accords," working paper, University of Edinburgh.

Auer, Matthew (2001) "Energy and Environmental Politics in Post-Corporatist Mexico," *Policy Studies Journal*, vol. 29, no. 3, 437–55.

Azuela, Antonio (2006) *Visionarios y Pragmáticos: Una Aproximación Sociológico al Derecho Ambiental* (Mexico City: Instituto de investigaciones sociales, UNAM).

Balarezo, Tomás, and Alberto Ramírez (2008) *Crecimiento en el suministro de servicios urbanos ambientales a comunidades fronterizas del Norte de México* (1995–2005) (Ciudad Juárez: BECC).

BECC & NADB (2008) *Joint Status Report*, June 30, Ciudad Juarez and San Antonio.

Bensusán, Graciela (1999) "Integración regional y cambio institucional: la reforma laboral en el norte del continente," in Graciela Bensusán (ed.), *Estandares Laborales después del TLCAN* (Mexico City: Plaza y Valdés Editores), 177–209.

—— (2006a) "Relación Estado-sindicatos: oportunidades para la renovación durante el primer gobierno de alternancia," in José González and Antonio Gutiérrez (eds.), *El Sindicalismo en México: Historia, Crisis y Perspectivas* (Mexico City: Plaza y Valdés) 253–79.

—— (2006b) "Diseño legal y desempeño real: México," in Graciela Bensusán (ed.), *Diseño legal y desempeño real: instituciones laborales en América Latina* (Mexico City: Miguel Angel Porrúa), 313–409.

—— (2007) "Los determinantes institucionales de los contratos de protección," in Alfonso Bouzas (ed.), *Contratación Colectiva de Protección en México* (Mexico City: ORIT), 11–48.

Block, Greg (2003) "Trade and Environment in the Western Hemisphere: Expanding the North American Agreement on Environmental Cooperation into the Americas," *Environmental Law*, vol. 33, 501–46.

Booz, Allen & Hamilton (1991) Reestructuración Estratégica y Organizacional para la Subsecretaria de Ecología, Mexico City, December 16.

Börzel, Tanja A., and Thomas Risse (2003) "Conceptualizing the Domestic Impact of Europe," in Kevin Featherstone and Claudio M. Radaelli (eds.), *The Politics of Europeanization* (Oxford: Oxford University Press), 57–80.

Bourget, Ann (2004a) "Ten Years of the North American Commission for Environmental Cooperation's Joint Public Advisory Committee" (Montreal: Commission for Environmental Cooperation).

—— (2004b) "Globalization and Public Participation Building Linkages" (Montreal: Commission for Environmental Cooperation).

Bouzas, José (2006) "Los contratos de protección y el sindicalismo mexicano," in José González and Antonio Gutiérrez (eds.), *El Sindicalismo en México: Historia, Crisis y Perspectivas* (Mexico City: Plaza y Valdés), 115–30.

Brañes, Raul (2000) *Manual de Derecho Ambiental Mexicano*, 2nd ed. (Mexico City: Fondo de Cultura Economica).

Bravo, Gonzalo (2008) "Comisión de Cooperación Ecológica Fronteriza: La COCEF y la Participación Comunitaria," *Derecho Ambiental y Ecología*, vol. 5, no. 27, October–November, 41–45.

Brooks, David, and Jonathan Fox (eds.) (2002) *Cross-Border Dialogues: US-Mexico Social Movement Networking* (La Jolla, CA: Center for US-Mexican Studies).

Bruszt, Laszlo, and Gerald McDermott (forthcoming) "Integrating Rule Takers: Transnational Integration Regimes Shaping Institutional Change in Emerging Market Democracies," *Review of International Political Economy*.

Burfisher, Mary, Sherman Robinson, and Karen Thierfelder (2001) "The Impact of NAFTA on the United States," *Journal of Economic Perspectives*, vol. 15, no. 1, Winter, 125–44.

Camp, Roderic Ai (2002) *Mexico's Mandarins: Crafting a Power Elite for the 21st Century* (Berkeley, CA: University of California Press).

Campos, Jesús (2009) *Historia Oral de una Vida en Defensa de los Trabajadores* (Mexico City: Eduardo Solís Impresores).

Canadian NAO (1999) "Review of Public Communication CAN 98-1," Parts I & II, Ottawa.

——— (2005) "Review of Public Communication CAN 2003-1," Gatineau, Quebec.

Carlsen, L., and T. Nauman (2004) "10 Years of NAFTA's Commission on Environmental Cooperation in Mexico: Resolving Environmental Problems and Fostering Citizen Participation," cited at http://www.cipamericas.org/archives /1316.

Carter, Dean E., Carlos Pena, Robert Varady, and William A. Suk (1996) "Environmental Health and Hazardous Waste Issues Related to the U.S.-Mexico Border," *Environmental Health Perspectives*, vol. 104, no. 6, 590–94.

Centeno, Miguel Angel (1997) *Democracy Within Reason: Technocratic Revolution in Mexico*, 2nd ed. (University Park: Pennsylvania State University Press).

Centeno, Miguel Angel, and Sylvia Maxfield (1992) "The Marriage of Finance and Order: Changes in the Mexican Political Elite," *Journal of Latin American Studies*, vol. 24, no. 1, 57–85.

Chamber of Deputies (1996) Crónica Parlamentaria, Mexico City. Cited at http:// cronica.diputados.gob.mx/Iniciativas/56/161.html.

Checkel, Jeffrey (2001) "Why Comply? Social Learning and European Identity Change," *International Organization*, vol. 55, no. 3, 553–88.

——— (2005) "International Institutions and Socialization in Europe: Introduction and Framework," *International Organization*, vol. 59, Fall, 801–26.

CIA World Factbook (2008). Cited at https://www.cia.gov/library/publications /the-world-factbook/.

Cialdini, Robert, and Melanie Trost (1998) "Social Influence: Social Norms, Conformity, and Compliance," in D. T. Gilbert, S. T. Fiske, and G. Lindzey (eds.), *The Handbook of Social Psychology*, 4th ed. (New York: McGraw-Hill), 2:151–92.

Clarkson, Stephen (2002) "NAFTA and the WTO in the Transformation of Mexico's Economic System," in Joseph S. Tulchin and Andrew D. Selee (eds.), *Mexico's Politics and Society in Transition* (Boulder, CO: Lynne Rienner), 215–53.

COHA (2007) "Fast Track to Trade Failure? The Political, Economic and Environmental Consequences of Executive Trade Negotiations," July 29, cited at www.coha.org/2007/06/fast-track-to-trade-failure-the-political-economic-and-environmental-consequences-of-executive-trade-negotiations/.

—— (2009) "Mexico: A Model for Developing Countries?" August 12, cited at www.coha.org/2009/08/mexico-a-model-for-developing-countries/.

Commission for Environmental Cooperation (undated) "Capacity Building: Report on Mexico's Activities to Assess Needs in Environmental Enforcement and Sustainable Development," Montreal.

—— (1996) Recommendation of the Secretariat to Council for the Development of a Factual Record in Accordance with Articles 14 and 15 of the North American Agreement on Environmental Cooperation, A14/SEM/96-001/07/ADV, Montreal.

—— (1997) Final Factual Record of the Cruise Ship Pier Project in Cozumel, Quintana Roo, SEM 96-001, Montreal.

—— (2001) Mesa Redonda sobre Oportunidades y Desafíos del Registro de Emisiones y Transferencias de Contaminantes de México, Mexico City, March 5.

—— (2002a) "Bringing the Facts to Light" (Montreal). Cited at www.cec.org/files/pdf/SEM/BringingFacts-Jun02_en.pdf.

—— (2002b) Resumen del Taller sobre Análisis de Datos de los Registros de Emisiones y Transferencias de Contaminantes en América del Norte: Experiencias y Oportunidades Futuras en la Comunidad Académica. Montreal.

—— (2002c) Factual Record. Metales y Derivados Submission, SEM-98-007, Montreal.

—— (2003a) Factual Record. Río Magdalena Submission, SEM-97-002, Montreal.

—— (2003b) Factual Record. Aquanova Submission, SEM-98-006, Montreal.

—— (2004) Factual Record. Molymex II Submission, SEM-00-005, Montreal.

—— (2005) Factual Record. Tarahumara Submission, SEM-00-006, Montreal.

—— (2007) Factual Record. ALCA-Iztapalapa II Submission, SEM-03-004, Montreal.

—— (2011) "Crossing the Border: Opportunities to Improve Sound Management of Transboundary Hazardous Waste Shipments in North America," cited at www.cec.org/Storage/128/15337_crossing_the_border_en8(web).pdf.

Compa, Lance (1999) "El ACLAN: un recuento de tres años," in Graciela Bensusán (ed.), *Estandares Laborales después del TLCAN* (Mexico City: Plaza y Valdés Editores), 73–96.

—— (2001) "NAFTA's Labor Side Agreement and International Labor Solidarity," *Antipode*, vol. 33, no. 3, 451–67.

Cornelius, Wayne, and David Shirk (2007) *Reforming the Administration of Justice in Mexico* (Notre Dame: University of Notre Dame Press).

Cortell, Andrew P., and James W. Davis Jr. (2005) "When Norms Clash: International Norms, Domestic Practices, and Japan's Internalisation of the GATT/WTO," *Review of International Studies*, vol. 31, 3–25.

Dai, Xinyuan (2005) "Why Comply? The Domestic Constituency Mechanism," *International Organization*, vol. 59, Spring, 363–98.

Dannenmaier, E. (2005) "The JPAC at Ten: A Ten-Year Review of the Joint Public Advisory Commission of the North American Free Trade Agreement," NAFTA Commission on Environmental Cooperation, Montreal.

de Buen Unna, Carlos (1999) "Mexican Unionism and the NAALC," unpublished paper, Mexico City.

—— (2002) "Mexican Trade Unionism in a Time of Transition," in Joanne Conaghan, Richard Michael Fischl, and Karl Klare (eds.), *Labour Law in an Era of Globalization* (Oxford: Oxford University Press), 401–16.

De Groot, Judith, and Linda Steg (2009) "Morality and Prosocial Behavior: The Role of Awareness, Responsibility, and Norms in the Norm Activation Model," *The Journal of Social Psychology*, vol. 149, no. 4, 425–49.

de la Garza, Enrique (2006) "El sindicalismo y el cambio en las relaciones de trabajo," in José González and Antonio Gutiérrez (eds.), *El Sindicalismo en México: Historia, Crisis y Perspectivas* (Mexico City: Plaza y Valdés), 305–30.

Deere, Carolyn, and Daniel Esty (2002) "Trade and the Environment in the Americas: Overview of Key Issues," in Carolyn Deere and Daniel Esty (eds.), *Greening the Americas: NAFTA's Lessons for Hemispheric Trade* (Cambridge, MA: MIT Press), 1–26.

Delgado, Javier, Aron Jazcilevich, Silke Cram, Christina Siebe, Naxhelli Ruiz, Gabriella Angeles-Serrano, and Marcos Hernández (2006) "The Environment: Or How Social Issues Affect the Commitment of Environmental Tasks," in Laura Randall (ed.), *Changing Structure of Mexico: Political, Social and Economic Prospects*, 2nd ed. (Armonk, NY: M. E. Sharpe), 297–329.

Díaz, Luis Miguel (2004) "Propuesta para Enmendar la Ley Laboral Mexicana," *University of Detroit Mercy Law Review*, vol. 81, no. 4, Summer, 555–69.

Dolowitz, David, and David Marsh (2000) "Learning from Abroad: The Role of Policy Transfer in Contemporary Policy-Making," *Governance*, vol. 13, no. 1, 5–24.

Domínguez, Jorge I. (1996) *Technopols: Freeing Politics and Markets in Latin America in the 1990s* (University Park: Pennsylvania State University Press).

—— (2004) "The Scholarly Study of Mexican Politics," *Mexican Studies*, vol. 20, no. 2, Summer, 377–410.

Dorn, Jonathan (2007) "NAAEC Citizen Submissions Against Mexico," *Georgetown International Environmental Law Review*, vol. 20, no. 1, 129–60.

Duina, Francesco (2006) *The Social Construction of Free Trade* (Princeton, NJ: Princeton University Press).

Evans, Mark, and Jonathan Davies (1999) "Understanding Policy Transfer: A Multi-Level, Multi-Disciplinary Perspective," *Public Administration*, vol. 77, no. 2, 361–85.

Evans, Peter, and James Rauch (1999) "Bureaucracy and Growth: A Cross-National Analysis of the Effects of 'Weberian' State Structures on Economic Growth," *American Sociological Review,* vol. 64, no. 5, 748–65.

Farrell, Theo (2001) "Transnational Norms and Military Development: Constructing Ireland's Professional Army," *European Journal of International Relations,* vol. 7, no. 1, 63–102.

Finn, John E. (2004) "The Rule of Law and Judicial Independence in Newly Democratic Regimes," *The Good Society,* vol. 13, no. 3, 12–16.

Finnemore, Martha, and Kathryn Sikkink (1998) "International Norm Dynamics and Political Change," *International Organization,* vol. 52, no. 4, 887–917.

Fisher, Richard (2002) "Trade and Environment in the FTAA: Learning from the NAFTA," in Carolyn Deere and Daniel Esty (eds.), *Greening the Americas: NAFTA's Lessons for Hemispheric Trade* (Cambridge, MA: MIT Press), 183–220.

Fiske, Susan T. (2004) *Social Beings: A Core Motives Approach to Social Psychology* (Hoboken, NJ: John Wiley & Sons).

Fondo Mexicano para la Conservación de la Naturaleza, *Directorio Mexicano de Conservación* (Mexico City: Fondo para la Comunicación y Educación Ambiental), various editions.

Fox, Jonathan (2004) "The Politics of North American Economic Integration," *Latin American Research Review,* vol. 39, no. 1, 254–72.

Galindo, Luis Miguel (2000) "Elementos para un Análisis de las Perspectivas Ambientales," in Carlos Muñoz Villarreal and Ana Citlalic González Martínez (eds.), *Economía, sociedad y medio ambiente: Reflexiones y avances hacia un desarrollo sustentable en México* (Mexico City: SEMARNAT), 181–94.

Gallagher, Kevin (2004) *Free Trade and the Environment: Mexico, NAFTA and Beyond* (Stanford, CA: Stanford University Press).

Gallagher, Kevin, and Timothy Wise (2009) "Reforming North American Trade Policy: Lessons from NAFTA. The Americas Program," cited at http://ase.tufts.edu/gdae/Pubs/rp/AmerProgNAFTADec09.pdf.

GAO (1993) *North American Free Trade Agreement: Assessment of Major Issues,* vol. 1 (Washington, DC: Author).

—— (1997) *North American Free Trade Agreement: Impacts and Implementation* (Washington, DC: Author).

—— (2000) *U.S.-Mexico Border: Despite Some Progress, Environmental Infrastructure Challenges Remain,* GAO-00-26 (Washington, DC: Author).

—— (2001) *North American Free Trade Agreement: U.S. Experience with Environment, Labor, and Investment Dispute Settlement Cases,* GAO-01-933 (Washington, DC: Author).

Garver, Geoff (2001) "Factual Record helped in Cozumel Pier case, says petitioner," cited at http://www.cec.org/Page.asp?PageID=122&ContentID=2451&SiteNodeID=462&BL_ExpandID=.

Gibson, Edward L. (2005) "Boundary Control: Subnational Authoritarianism in Democratic Countries," *World Politics,* vol. 58, no. 1, 101–32.

Gil Corrales, Miguel Ángel (2007) *Crónica Ambiental: Gestión Pública de Políticas ambientales en México* (México, DF: Instituto Nacional de Ecología).

Gilbreath, John (2003) *Environment and Development in Mexico* (Washington, DC: CSIS).

Giménez Cacho, Luis Emilio (2007) *Transparencia y Derechos Laborales* (Mexico City: IFAI).

Goldrich, Daniel, and David V. Carruthers (1992) "Sustainable Development in Mexico? The International Politics of Crisis or Opportunity," *Latin American Perspectives*, vol. 19, no. 1, 97–122.

Goldsmith, Arthur (1999) "Africa's Overgrown State Reconsidered: Bureaucracy and Economic Growth," *World Politics*, vol. 51, no. 4, 520–46.

Goldstein, Judith, Miles Kahler, Robert O. Keohane, and Anne-Marie Slaughter (2000) "Introduction: Legalization and World Politics," *International Organization*, vol. 54, no. 3, 385–99.

Graubart, Jonathan (2005) " 'Politicizing' a New Breed of 'Legalized' Transnational Political Opportunity Structures: Labor Activists Uses of NAFTA's Citizen-Petition Mechanism," *Berkeley Journal of Employment & Labor Law*, vol. 26, no. 1, 97–142.

––––– (2008) *Legalizing Transnational Activism: The Struggle to Gain Social Change from NAFTA's Citizen Petitions* (Philadelphia: University of Pennsylvania Press).

Green Cowles, Maria, James Caporaso, and Thomas Risse (eds.) (2001) *Transforming Europe: Europeanization and Domestic Change* (Ithaca: Cornell University Press).

Grindle, Merilee S. (1977) "Power, Expertise and the 'Tecnico': Suggestions from a Mexican Case Study," *The Journal of Politics*, vol. 39, no. 2, 399–426.

––––– (2010) "Constructing, Deconstructing, and Reconstructing Career Civil Service Systems in Latin America," Harvard University working paper, RWP 10-025.

Gurowitz, Amy (1999) "Mobilizing International Norms: Domestic Actors, Immigrants, and the Japanese State," *World Politics*, vol. 51, no. 3, 413–45.

Gutiérrez, Antonio (2006) "Breve recorrido histórico del sindicalismo mexicano," in José González and Antonio Gutiérrez (eds.), *El Sindicalismo en México: Historia, Crisis y Perspectivas* (Mexico City: Plaza y Valdés), 17–42.

Gutiérrez, Daniel (2003) *Democracia Sindical en Aguascalientes* (Mexico City: Plaza y Valdés).

Haas, Peter M. (1992) "Introduction: Epistemic Communities and International Policy Coordination," *International Organization*, vol. 46, no. 1, 1–35.

Haber, Stephen, Herbert Klein, Noel Maurer, and Kevin Middlebrook (2008) *Mexico Since 1980* (Cambridge: Cambridge University Press).

Hall, Peter A. (1993) "Policy Paradigms, Social Learning, and the State: The Case of Economic Policymaking in Britain," *Comparative Politics*, vol. 25, no. 3, 275–96.

Hernandez-Coss, Raul (2005) "A Proposed Framework to Analyze Informal Funds Transfer Systems," in Samuel Munzele Maimbo and Dilip Ratha (eds.), *Remittances: Development Impact and Future Prospects* (Washington, DC: World Bank), 244–74.

Herrera, Juan (2008) "Law Clinics in the Context of the Citizen Submission Mechanism," unpublished paper, Autonomous University of Tamaulipas.

Hertel, Shareen (2006) "New Moves in Transnational Advocacy: Getting Labor and Economic Rights on the Agenda in Unexpected Ways," *Global Governance*, vol. 12, 263–81.

Herzenberg, Stephen (1996) "Calling Maggie's Bluff: The NAFTA Labor Agreement and the Development of an Alternative to Neoliberalism," *Canadian-American Public Policy*, September. Paper provided by author.

Hinojosa-Ojeda, Raúl (2002) "Integration Policy from the Grassroots Up: Transnational Implications of Latino, Labor and Environmental NGO Strategies," in David Brooks and Jonathan Fox (eds.), *Cross-Border Dialogues: US-Mexico Social Movement Networking* (La Jolla, CA: Center for US-Mexican Studies).

Hochstetler, Kathryn, and Margaret E. Keck (2007) *Greening Brazil: Environmental Activism in State and Society* (Durham, NC: Duke University Press).

Hogenboom, Barbara (1996) "Cooperation and Polarisation Beyond Borders: The Transnationalisation of Mexican Environmental Issues during the NAFTA Negotiations," *Third World Quarterly*, vol. 17, no. 5, 989–1005.

Hooghe, Liesbet (2005) "Many Roads Lead to International Norms, But Few via International Socialization. A Case Study of the European Commission," *International Organization*, vol. 59, no. 4, 861–98.

Hufbauer, Gary, Daniel Esty, Diana Orejas, Luis Rubio, and Jeffrey Schott (2000) *NAFTA and the Environment: Seven Years Later* (Washington, DC: Institute for International Economics).

Hufbauer, Gary, and Jeffrey Schott (2005) *NAFTA Revisited* (Washington, DC: Institute for International Economics).

Hurrell, Andrew (1995) "Regionalism in the Americas," in Andrew Hurrell and Louise Fawcett (eds.), *Regionalism in World Politics* (Oxford: Oxford University Press), 250–82.

Hurrell, Andrew, and Louise Fawcett (1995) *Regionalism in World Politics* (Oxford: Oxford University Press).

Husted, B. W., and Logsdon, J. M. (1997) "The Impact of NAFTA on Mexico's Environmental Policy," *Growth and Change*, vol. 28, Winter, 24–48.

INE (2000) *La evaluación del impacto ambiental: logros y retos par a el desarrollo sustentable, 1995–2000* (Mexico City: Instituto Nacional de Ecología).

Johnston, Alastair Iain (2001) "Treating International Institutions as Social Environments," *International Studies Quarterly*, vol. 45, 487–515.

—— (2005) "Conclusions and Extensions: Toward Mid-Range Theorizing and Beyond Europe," *International Organization*, vol. 59, Fall, 1013–44.

JPAC (2008) *Advice to Council No 08-01* (Montreal).

Kaufmann, Daniel, Aart Kraay, and Massimo Mastruzzi (2009) "Governance Matters VIII: Aggregate and Individual Governance Indicators, 1996–2008." Policy Research Working Paper 4978 (Washington, DC: World Bank).

Kay, Tamara (2005) "Labor Transnationalism and Global Governance: The Impact of NAFTA on Transnational Labor Relationships in North America," *American Journal of Sociology*, vol. 111, no. 3, 715–56.

—— (2011) *NAFTA and the Politics of Labor Transnationalism* (Cambridge: Cambridge University Press).

Keck, Margaret, and Kathryn Sikkink (1998) *Activists Beyond Borders: Advocacy Networks in International Politics* (Ithaca, NY: Cornell University Press).

Kelley, Judith (2004) "International Actors on the Domestic Scene: Membership Conditionality and Socialization by International Institutions," *International Organization*, vol. 58, Summer, 425–57.

Kelly, Mary (2002) "Cross-Border Work on the Environment: Evolution, Successes, Problems and Future Outlook," in David Brooks and Jonathan Fox (eds.), *Cross-Border Dialogues: US-Mexico Social Movement Networking* (La Jolla, CA: Center for US-Mexican Studies), 133–43.

Keohane, Robert O., Andrew Moravcsik, and Anne-Marie Slaughter (2000) "Legalized Dispute Resolution: Interstate and Transnational," *International Organization*, vol. 54, no. 3, 457–88.

Knill, Christoph (2001) *The Europeanisation of National Administrations: Patterns of Institutional Persistence and Change* (Cambridge: Cambridge University Press).

Krauze, Enrique (2000) *Fidel Velázquez: Los Trabajos y los Días* (Mexico City: Clío).

Ladrech, Robert (1994) "Europeanization of Domestic Politics and Institutions: The Case of France," *Journal of Common Market Studies*, vol. 32, no. 1, 69–88.

—— (2002) "Europeanization and Political Parties," *Party Politics*, vol. 8, no. 4, 389–403.

Legro, Jeffrey W. (1997) "Which Norms Matter? Revisiting the 'Failure' of Internationalism," *International Organization*, vol. 51, no. 1, 31–63.

Lehman, John (2001) *US-Mexico Border Five-Year Outlook* (San Antonio, TX: North American Development Bank).

Levitsky, Steven, and Lucan Way (2010) *Competitive Authoritarianism: Hybrid Regimes After the Cold War* (Cambridge: Cambridge University Press).

Liverman, Diana (2002) "Seguridad y Medio Ambiente en México," in Sergio Aguayo Quezada and Bruce Michael Bagley (eds.), *En Busca de la Seguridad Perdida: Aproximaciones a la Seguridad Nacional Mexicana*, 2nd ed. (Mexico City: Siglo Veintiuno Editores), 233–63.

Lustig, Nora (2001) "Life Is Not Easy: Mexico's Quest for Stability and Growth," *Journal of Economic Perspectives*, vol. 15, no. 1, 85–106.

McFadyen, Jacqueline (1998) "NAFTA Supplemental Agreements: Four Year Review," working paper 98-4, Peterson Institute for International Economics, cited at www.piie.com/publications/wp/wp.cfm?ResearchID=145.

McKinney, Joseph (2005) "NAFTA's Effects on North American Economic Development: A United States Perspective," paper presented at the conference on NAFTA and the Future of North America: Trilateral Perspectives on Governance, Economic Development and Labour, University of Toronto, February 7.

McRae, Donald (2000) "Inclusion in a Factual Record of Information Developed by Independent Experts and the Autonomy of the Secretariat of the CEC in the Article 14 and 15 Process," paper prepared for the Secretariat of the CEC, University of Ottawa, February 7.

Meyer, John, and Brian Rowan (1983) "Institutionalized Organizations: Formal Structure as Myth and Ceremony," in John Meyer and W. Richard Scott (eds.), *Organizational Environments: Ritual and Rationality* (Beverly Hills, CA: Sage), 21–44.

Middlebrook, Kevin, and Eduardo Zepeda (2003) "On the Political Economy of Mexican Development Policy," in Kevin Middlebrook and Eduardo Zepeda (eds.), *Confronting Development: Assessing Mexico's Economic and Social Policy Challenges* (Stanford, CA: Stanford University Press), 3–52.

Mumme, Stephen P. (1992) "System Maintenance and Environmental Reform in Mexico: Salinas's Preemptive Strategy," *Latin American Perspectives,* vol. 19, no. 1, 123–43.

Nolan Garcia, Kimberly A. (2009) "Transnational Advocacy and Labor Rights Conditionality in the International Trading Order." Unpublished PhD Dissertation, Department of Political Science, University of New Mexico.

Nuccio, Richard, Angelina Ornelas, and Ivá Restrepo (2002) "El Medio Ambiente en México: Seguridad Para el Futuro," in Sergio Aguayo Quezada and Bruce Michael Bagley (eds.), *En Busca de la Seguridad Perdida: Aproximaciones a la Seguridad Nacional Mexicana,* 2nd ed. (Mexico City: Siglo Veintiuno Editores), 264–92.

OECD (1996) *The Environmental Information System of Mexico* (Paris, OCDE/GD), (96)172.

—— (2006) *Water Management Policy Brief for the Mexican Project* (Paris: Author).

Olsen, Johan P. (2002) "The Many Faces of Europeanization," *Journal of Common Market Studies,* vol. 40, no. 5, 921–52.

Pastor, Robert (2005) "A Proposal for a North American Investment Fund: Adopting Europe's Model and Avoiding its Mistakes," in Robert Pastor (ed.), *The Paramount Challenge for North America: Closing the Development Gap* (Washington, DC: North American Development Bank), 1–4.

Pevehouse, Jon (2002) "Democracy from the Outside-In? International Organizations and Democratization," *International Organization,* vol. 56, no. 3, 515–49.

Polaksi, Sandra (2003) "Jobs, Wages, and Household Income," in John Audley, Demetrios Papademetriou, Sandra Polaksi, and Scott Vaughan (eds.), *NAFTA's Promise and Reality: Lessons from Mexico for the Hemisphere* (Washington, DC: Carnegie Endowment for International Peace).

—— (2006) "Perspectivas sobre el futuro del TLCAN: La mano de obra mexicana en la integración de América del Norte," in Monica Gambrill (ed.), *Diez Años del TLCAN en México* (Mexico City: UNAM), 35–56.

Presidencia (1989) *Presupuesto de Egresos de la Federación para el Ejercicio Fiscal de 1990* (Mexico City: Author).

—— (2008) *Presupuesto de Egresos de la Federación* (Mexico City: Author).

Profepa (1996) *Discrepancia, consenso social y unanimidad legislativa: crónica de la reforma a la ley general del equilibrio ecológico y la protección al ambiente, 1995–1996* (Mexico City: Profepa).

Pronatura (2006) *25 años conservando el color de nuestra naturaleza* (Mexico City: Author).

—— (2007) *Informe Annual 2007* (Mexico City: Author).

Quintana Romero, Luis (2004) "NAFTA's Institutions: An Evaluation 10 Years On," *Voices of Mexico*, UNAM, no. 69, October–December, 58–64.

Randall, Laura (2006) *Changing Structure of Mexico: Political, Social and Economic Prospects*, 2nd ed. (Armonk, NY: M. E. Sharpe).

Randall, Stephan, and Herman Konrad (1995) *NAFTA in Transition* (Alberta: University of Calgary Press).

Reimann, Kim D. (2006) "A View from the Top: International Politics, Norms and the Worldwide Growth of NGOs," *International Studies Quarterly*, vol. 50, 45–67.

Risse, Thomas (2000) "Let's Argue! Communicative Action in World Politics," *International Organization*, vol. 54, no. 1, 1–39.

Risse, Thomas, and Kathryn Sikkink (1999) "The Socialization of International Human Rights Norms into Domestic Practices: Introduction," in Thomas Risse, Stephen Ropp, and Kathryn Sikkink (eds.), *The Power of Human Rights: International Norms and Domestic Change* (Cambridge: Cambridge University Press), 1–38.

Robles, Jorge, Patricia Juan Pineda, Bertha Luján, and Eduardo Díaz (eds.) (2009) *La Libertad Sindical* (Mexico City: Friedrich Ebert Stiftung).

Schimmelfennig, Frank (2005) "Strategic Calculation and International Socialization: Membership Incentives, Party Constellations, and Sustained Compliance in Central and Eastern Europe," *International Organization*, vol. 59, Fall, 827–60.

Schmidt, Vivien A. (2002) "Europeanization and the Mechanics of Economic Policy Adjustment," *Journal of European Public Policy*, vol. 9, no. 6, 894–912.

SEMARNAP (2000) *La Gestión Ambiental en México*, Mexico City.

SEMARNAT (2001) *Programa Nacional de Medio Ambiente y Recursos Naturales, 2001–2006*, Mexico City.

—— (2003) *Unidad de Enlace por parte de la Dirección General de Programación, Organización y Presupuesto de la Oficialía Mayor*, Mexico City.

—— (2004) *Guía Ciudadana para el Acceso a la Información Ambiental*, Mexico City.

—— (2006) *Capacidades y Sinergias: El Desafío Ambiental en México*, Mexico City.

—— (2007) *Programa Sectorial de Medio Ambiente y Recursos Naturales, 2007–2012*, Mexico City.

—— (2008) *Estrategia Nacional para la Participación Ciudadana en el Sector Ambiental*, Mexico City.

Silvan, Laura (2005) "Resolving Environmental Problems and Fostering Citizen Participation," www.cipamericas.org/archives/1316.

State Department (2005) *Security and Prosperity Partnership: Report to Leaders* (Washington, DC: Author).

Steinberg, Paul (2001) *Environmental Leadership in Developing Countries: Transnational Relations and Biodiversity Policy in Costa Rica and Bolivia* (Cambridge, MA: MIT Press).

Stone, Diane (2004) "Transfer Agents and Global Networks in the 'Transnationalization' of Policy," *Journal of European Public Policy*, vol. 11, no. 3, 545–66.

Strang, David, and John W. Meyer (1993) "Institutional Conditions for Diffusion," *Theory and Society*, vol. 22, 487–511.

Stromseth, Jane (2008) "Post-Conflict Rule of Law Building: The Need for a Multi-Layered, Synergistic Approach," *William & Mary Law Review*, vol. 49, 1443–71.

—— (2009) "Strengthening Demand for the Rule of Law in Post-Conflict Societies," *Minnesota Journal of International Law*, 18, 415–24.

Studer, Isabel, and Carol Wise (eds.) (2007) *Requiem or Revival? The Promise of North American Integration* (Washington, DC: Brookings Institution Press).

Suprema Corte (2008) "Contradicción de Tesis 74/2008-SS, Mexico City." Suprema Corte de la Justicia de la Nación.

Teague, Paul (2002) "Standard-Setting for Labour in Regional Trading Blocs: The EU and NAFTA Compared," *Journal of Public Policy*, vol. 22, no. 3, 325–48.

Thelen, Kathleen, and Sven Steinmo (1992) "Historical Institutionalism in Comparative Politics," in Sven Steinmo, Kathleen Thelen, and Frank Longstreth (eds.), *Structuring Politics: Historical Institutionalism in Comparative Analysis* (Cambridge: Cambridge University Press), 1–32.

Torres, Blanca (2002) "The North American Agreement on Environmental Cooperation: Rowing Upstream," in Carolyn Deere and Daniel Esty (eds.), *Greening the Americas: NAFTA's Lessons for Hemispheric Trade* (Cambridge, MA: MIT Press), 201–20.

TRAC (2004) *Ten Years of North American Environmental Cooperation: Report of the Ten-Year Review and Assessment Committee* (Montreal: Commission for Environmental Cooperation).

United States Institute of Peace (2011) *Peace Brief 90*, 20 (Washington, DC: Author).

U.S. NAO (1994) "NAALC Submission 940001 and 940002," Bureau of International Labor Affairs, U.S. Department of Labor, Washington DC.

—— (1995) "NAALC Public Report of Review of NAO Submission No. 940003," Bureau of International Labor Affairs, U.S. Department of Labor, Washington, DC.

—— (1996) "Follow-up Report of NAO Submission No. 940003," Bureau of International Labor Affairs, U.S. Department of Labor, Washington, DC.

—— (1997) "NAO Submission No. 96-01. Public Report of Review," Bureau of International Labor Affairs, U.S. Department of Labor, Washington, DC.

—— (1998a) "Public Report of Review of NAO Submission No. 9701," International Labor Affairs Bureau, Department of Labor, Washington, DC.

—— (1998b) "Public Report of Review of NAO Submission No. 9702," International Labor Affairs Bureau, Department of Labor, Washington, DC.

—— (1998c) "Public Report of Review of NAO Submission No. 9703," International Labor Affairs Bureau, Department of Labor, Washington, DC.

——— (2000) "Public Report of Review of NAO Submission No. 9901," International Labor Affairs Bureau, Department of Labor, Washington, DC.

——— (2001) "Public Report of Review of NAO Submission No. 2000-01," International Labor Affairs Bureau, Department of Labor, Washington, DC.

——— (2004) "Public Report of Review of NAO Submission No. 2003-01," International Labor Affairs Bureau, Department of Labor, Washington, DC.

——— (2007) "Public Report of Review of NAO Submission No. 2005-03," International Labor Affairs Bureau, Department of Labor, Washington, DC.

Vargas, Clementina (2006) "Resolución de conflictos en el marco legal del Acuerdo de Cooperación Laboral de América del Norte," in Monica Gambrill (ed.), *Diez Años del TLCAN en México* (Mexico City: UNAM), 441–50.

Vaughan, Scott (2003) "The Greenest Trade Agreement Ever? Measuring the Environmental Impacts of Agricultural Liberalization," in John Audley, Demetrios Papademetriou, Sandra Polaksi, and Scott Vaughan (eds.), *NAFTA's Promise and Reality: Lessons from Mexico for the Hemisphere* (Washington, DC: Carnegie Endowment for International Peace), 61–87.

Vernon, Raymond (1964) *Public Policy and Private Enterprise in Mexico* (Cambridge: Cambridge University Press).

Weingast, Barry (2009) "Why Developing Countries Prove So Resistant to the Rule of Law," in James J. Heckman, Robert L. Nelson, and Lee Cabatingan (eds.), *Global Perspectives on the Rule of Law* (New York: Routledge), 28–52.

Weintraub, Sidney (2005) "A North American 'Community': Pros and Cons," *Issues in International Political Economy*, CSIS, no. 61, January, 2 pp.

Winfield, Mark (2003) "North American Pollutant Release and Transfer Registries: A Case Study in Environmental Policy Convergence," in David Markell and John Know (eds.), *Greening NAFTA: The North American Commission for Environmental Cooperation* (Stanford, CA: Stanford University Press), 38–56.

World Bank (2003) *Lessons from NAFTA for Latin American and Caribbean (LAC) Countries: A Summary of Research Findings* (Washington, DC: Author).

——— (2005) *Capacity-Building in Africa: An OED Evaluation of World Bank Support* (Washington, DC: Author).

World Justice Project (2011) *Rule of Law Index 2011* (Washington DC: Author).

Zepeda, Eduardo, Timothy Wise, and Kevin Gallagher (2009) *Rethinking Trade Policy for Development: Lessons from Mexico Under NAFTA* (Washington, DC: Carnegie Endowment).

Zimbardo, Philip, and Ebbe Ebbesen (1969) *Influencing Attitudes and Changing Behavior* (Reading, MA: Addison-Wesley).

Index

access, to RIs, 14–15
accountability, 87
acid rain, 56
acquis communautaire, 6, 8
actors. *See* domestic actors
AFL-CIO, 124–27
air emissions, 58, 65; enforcement of, 56
Alanís, Gustavo, 70, 142, 147, 153, 159
Alliance for Responsible Trade (ART), 124
arbitrary confiscation, 5
Article 13 public reports, 44
Article 14/15 citizen submissions, 44–45, 47; process of, 46. *See also* factual records
attitude change, 9; in environmental agencies, 12, 136; in labor agencies, 12, 136; to rule of law, 10–12, 136
Authentic Labor Front (FAT), United Electrical Workers and, 125
Authentic Workers' Front (FAT), 103
authoritarianism, to democracy, 5
authority, abuse of, 2

best practices exchanges, 121
biodiversity, of Mexico, 26

border: capacity building at, 76–79, 156–57; development, 72; growth, 75; NAFTA treaty at, 72–79, 157, 170; problems, 74; technical assistance, 77
Border Environmental Cooperation Commission (BECC), 73, 79, 142, 171; requirements of, 156; scope of, 75
Border Environment Infrastructure Fund (BEIF), 73; NADB and, 76; restrictions by, 74–75
Border Industrialization Plan, 72
border institutions, reliance on, 76
Border XXI program, 74, 76
boundary control, 20
Bradshaw, Claudette, 118

Cabrera, Javier, 78–79
Canada: environmental standards in, 1; labor standards in, 1
capacity building, 9, 60, 176n7; at border, 76–79, 156–57; by CEC, 66, 138, 152; by CEMDA, 70; contributing factors of, 19–21; of domestic elites, 12; importance of, 4, 80, 169–70; in

161; craft union, 111; failures of, 87,
167; leaders of, 161; participation in,
92, 179*n*1; registration of, 88, 119, 123;
representation by, 106, 145. *See also*
charro unions; ghost unions;
independent unions; Mexican
Workers Confederation; paper
unions
United Electrical Workers, FAT and, 125
United States (U.S.): counterpart to
RMALC, 124; criticism of Mexico,
37–38; Mexico's cooperation with,
61–62, 124
U.S. NAO, 101–2

Value Lending Program, 75
voting intimidation, 116, 130, 132

wages, free trade and, 7
wastewater treatment, 52–53
water, governance of, 29
welfare region, 6
wildlife inspection training program,
60–61
wildlife laws, 60
Wildlife Without Borders program, 62
workers: control over, 116; exposure of,
122–23; legal rights of, 130; legal
standards for, 92
workplace intimidation, 109–10, 132

Yale Center for Environmental Law and
Policy, 28

Zapatista movement, 123

Printed and bound by CPI Group (UK) Ltd, Croydon, CR0 4YY

23/04/2025

14660937-0004